# MAKING
# A DIFFERENCE

# Research on Teaching Monograph Series

### PUBLISHED TITLES

JERE E. BROPHY AND CAROLYN M. EVERTSON, *Student Characteristics and Teaching*

SUSAN URMSTON PHILIPS, *The Invisible Culture: Communication in Classroom and Community on the Warm Springs Indian Reservation*

HARRIS M. COOPER AND THOMAS L. GOOD, *Pygmalion Grows Up: Studies in the Expectation Communication Process*

THOMAS L. GOOD, DOUGLAS GROUWS, AND HOWARD EBMEIER, *Active Mathematics Teaching*

ROBERT E. SLAVIN, *Cooperative Learning*

LEONARD S. CAHEN, NIKOLA FILBY, GAIL McCUTHEON, AND DIANE W. KYLE, *Class Size and Instruction*

PHILIP A. CUSICK, *The Egalitarian Ideal and the American High School*

LARRY CUBAN, *How Teachers Taught: Constancy and Change in American Classrooms: 1890–1980*

GARY NATRIELLO AND SANFORD M. DORNBUSCH, *Teacher Evaluative Standards and Student Efforts*

CHARLES W. FISHER AND DAVID C. BERLINER, *Perspectives on Instructional Time*

BARBARA LARRIVEE, *Effective Teaching for Successful Mainstreaming*

GRETA MORINE-DERSHIMER, *Speaking, Listening, and Learning in Elementary Classrooms*

DEE ANN SPENCER, *Contemporary Women Teachers: Balancing School and Home*

PATRICIA T. ASHTON AND RODMAN B. WEBB, *Making a Difference: Teachers' Sense of Efficacy and Student Achievement*

# MAKING
# A DIFFERENCE

## TEACHERS' SENSE OF EFFICACY AND STUDENT ACHIEVEMENT

**Patricia T. Ashton**
**Rodman B. Webb**
UNIVERSITY OF FLORIDA

Longman
New York & London

Dedicated to the memory of
Ralph Edward Teague
and
To Nancy and Jean Webb
with love and gratitude from
"a previous collaboration"

Executive Editor: Raymond O'Connell
Text Art: Brenda Booth
Compositor: Graphicraft Typesetters Ltd.

**Making a Difference:** *Teachers' Sense of Efficacy and Student Achievement*

Longman Inc.
95 Church Street
White Plains, N.Y. 10601

Associated companies:
Longman Group Ltd., London
Longman Cheshire Pty., Melbourne
Longman Paul Pty., Auckland
Copp Clark Pitman, Toronto
Pitman Publishing Inc., Boston

**Library of Congress Cataloging in Publication Data**

Ashton, Patricia T.
  Making a difference.

  (Research on teaching monograph series)
  Bibliography: p.
  Includes index.
  1. Teachers—Attitudes.  2. Teachers—Psychology.
3. Academic achievement.  4. Motivation in education.
I. Webb, Rodman B., 1941–      II. Title.
III. Series.
LB2840.A75   1986        371.1'001'9          85-9643
ISBN 0-582-28480-5

    87  88  89  9  8  7  6  5  4  3  2

# Contents

# Preface

This book and the research it reports represent an experiment in collaboration among its authors, a team of researchers, and the many teachers who allowed us to enter their classrooms and their professional lives. The work also involved a collaboration of methodologies. Qualitative techniques were used to generate hunches, ideas, and hypotheses that could be tested quantitatively. Quantitative studies, in turn, were augmented by qualitative investigations to insure that the meanings of teachers' acts and beliefs would not get lost in a flood of numbers or artificially organized in statistical tables. We were in search of findings that could be corroborated by both methodologies.

Ashton took primary responsibility for the quantitative portion of the research, and Webb oversaw the qualitative studies. However, it was our intention from the start to keep these two portions of the research in close alliance. Each new phase of the project was jointly planned. Members of the research team met frequently to discuss strategies, experiences in the field, methodological issues, and data analysis. Preliminary findings were discussed with teachers, and their comments and suggestions were noted.

The research also entailed a collaboration of disciplines. Ashton, a psychologist, brought psychological questions to the issues under study. Webb applied a sociologist's angle of vision. Here again, however, our effort was not simply to run concurrent studies but to combine our perspectives to achieve a fuller picture of what teachers believe and achieve. This book is the final product of this multifaceted collaboration.

All researchers come to their work with sets of assumptions and biases. They have an obligation to see that these biases do not intrude too deeply into their research and to make their biases public so that others may judge if their findings are expressions of the reality of the subjects' lives or simply projections of the researchers' own beliefs. Thus, a word about our beliefs and assumptions is appropriate.

We came to a study of teacher motivation because we wanted to know the degree to which teachers' beliefs about teaching and children affected their classroom performance and accomplishments. Both of us have long been interested in issues of equal opportunity and are concerned that children from poverty families frequently receive an inadequate education. In our view, the democratic mandate to provide all children with an equal opportunity to learn is not discharged simply by requiring that students stay in school until they are 16 years old. Equality of educational opportunity will be achieved only when students from varying backgrounds receive the same quality of instruction and course material and enjoy the same school-wide expectation that all students can and must learn. If this means that certain pupils need more instruction or smaller classes in order to make up for academic deficits, so be it. There is little in the compensatory model of schooling that would offend us, as long as the ultimate goal and accomplished aim of remedial programs are to provide compensatory students with a quality education. Insofar as remedial programs provide an alternative to quality by substituting "functional literacy" for literacy itself, "life management skills" for the skill of critical thinking, or "minimum competencies" for real academic accomplishments, then remediation only serves to segregate and warehouse low-achieving students. Such programs are undemocratic and unacceptable. They do nothing to advance the aim of equalizing educational opportunity.

We came to this study with an interest in the education of poverty's children and we left with our biases intact. However, in the course of the study, and as a direct result of what we were finding, our interests were broadened to include the problems facing teachers—especially the problems of teachers who work with large numbers of low-achieving students. We learned that teachers are working in an imperiled profession and that calls for reform that suggest only that teachers change their attitudes or improve their performance are just cries in the wind. Such proposals do not take into account the conditions that influence what teachers think and do and, thus, are unlikely to improve the quality of education offered in our schools.

In our research, we tried to gain a perspective that was not so firmly based in our respective disciplines that we were blinded to the reality before us or so identified with the views of teachers that we could not see beyond their construction of reality. Teachers' perspectives were taken into account and we borrowed methodologies and research findings from the social sciences, but we relied most heavily on the ethnographic and systematic observation data we gathered in schools. Data were drawn from classroom observations, interviews with teachers and principals, question-naires, teacher workshops, formal and informal faculty meetings, lesson plans, student comments and behaviors, and achievement test results. Our challenge was to find order in the data we gathered. This book is a summary of that effort. Interested readers can find a more detailed description of the methodologies and analytical procedures we used in the research in the final report to the National Institute of Education (Ashton, Webb, & Doda, 1983).

"Science," wrote Bronowski (1956), "is nothing else than the search to discover unity in the wild variety of nature—or more exactly, in the variety of our experience" (p. 16). Unfortunately, the order that exists in social environments (especially an environment as complex as a school) is not easily discovered. "If it can be said to be there at all," Bronowski warned, "it is not there for the mere looking. There is no way of pointing a finger or camera at it; order must be discovered and, in a deep sense created" (p.

14). Ultimately, of course, the order that researchers construct must square with and make sense of the reality under investigation. The goal, as Bronowski made clear, "is to take parts of the universe that have not been connected hitherto and ... show ... them to be connected" (p. 110). It is through connection and order that predictability and intelligibility are discovered. In our research, we set out to find if there were connections between specific teacher attitudes (their beliefs regarding their ability to teach and their students' ability to learn) and student achievement.

We hoped to accomplish something else as well. We tried to interpret the professional lives of teachers in a way that would make their accomplishments and troubles more intelligible to policy makers, the polity, and teachers themselves. The interpretation of what people are and do is probably the greatest contribution of social science, for it is only when others become intelligible to us that we can empathize with their situations and enlarge and enlighten our sense of community and common purpose. These elements (a warranted interpretation of the lives of teachers and students, a sense of community and a commonality of purpose) are sadly lacking in education today. Their absence constitutes a significant impediment to school improvement.

The research reported in this volume was performed pursuant to Contract No. 400–79–0075 of the National Institute of Education. It does not, however, necessarily reflect the views of that agency. We want to express our appreciation to NIE for its financial support. We especially thank Virginia Koehler, our Project Officer, for her encouragement. Michael Cohen and Joseph Vaughn gave us helpful insights into the ecology of teaching.

Richard deCharms sparked the obsession with the notion of personal efficacy that culminated in our research, and he provided us with an invaluable model for judging our research efficacy. Dan Lortie and Ray Rist offered important guidance in the initial conception of the research.

Nancy Doda shared her enthusiasm for ethnographic research with us and added important dimensions to our understanding of teachers' sense of efficacy. Data for the microethnographic portion of Chapter 4 were gathered, analyzed, and reported by Nancy. We gratefully acknowledge her contribution, though due to our additions and changes, we accept responsibility for whatever shortcomings may exist in the chapter.

Mel Lucas and Gayle McLaurin graciously provided assistance in gathering student achievement data, and Linda Crocker, Stephen Olejnik, Marilyn McAuliffe, and Dianne Buhr furnished technical expertise in data analysis and offered ideas for measuring teachers' sense of efficacy.

We are indebted to Robert and Ruth Soar for their inestimable contribution to the study through their patient training of our observers and their meticulous analysis of the process-product data. Our observers, Patricia Birkett, Tess Bennett, Marty Peters, and Barbara Rubin, persisted in learning a complicated system of interaction analysis and met a rigorous observation schedule.

Robert Sherman, our department chairman during the term of the project, gave us the support without which our work would have been impossible.

Our student assistants, Zulal Balpinar, Linda DerHaag, and Wendy Elliott, transcribed endless audiotapes, typed myriad letters, notes, memos, and manuscripts, and courageously endured the trauma of mastering the computer. Elsie Voss's contribution to our work on this and other projects was enormous and deeply appreciated.

We wish to acknowledge the special contributions of our children, Heather, Lindsey, and Laurie, for their love and support, their patient endurance of their parents' preoccupations with a project that seemed never-ending and for the daily reminders that teachers make a difference in the lives of children.

Heartfelt appreciation goes to Louise and L.V. Teague for their support and encouragement. They contributed in countless ways to the completion of this work.

Elise Webb helped code and interpret ethnographic data and took over many tasks, academic and domestic, that freed others to concentrate on this research. This acknowledgement is no recompense but stands as an IOU drawn in public.

We are indebted to the constructive comments of many scholars who read early drafts of our book or responded to papers we have written on this research. David Berliner's encouragement and suggestions were especially helpful. Jim Giarelli's philosophical and political perspectives were useful and appreciated. The insights of Ference Marton and Claus Goren of the Goteborgs University were original and constructive. Tom Good, our academic editor, read the entire manuscript and made numerous comments and suggestions that considerably improved the final product. We appreciate the care with which he worked, the encouragement he supplied, the quality of his insights, and the rigor of his criticisms and suggestions. The shortcomings that remain in this book belong solely to its authors; its merits are communal property. We have benefited from the patience and advice of our editor, Naomi Silverman, and appreciate her encouragement and commitment to this project.

We gratefully acknowledge Academic Press for the permission to reproduce portions of a chapter entitled "Motivation and the Teachers' Sense of Efficacy," from *Research on Motivation in Education: The Classroom Milieu*, edited by Carole and Russell Ames. Permission was also granted by the *Journal of Thought* to reproduce portions of "Teacher Status Panic: Moving Up the Down Escalator" (1983, *18*, 39–48).

Finally, we wish to thank the principals, teachers, and students who welcomed our intrusions into their busy lives and gave generously of their time and ideas to help us better understand the frustrations and rewards of teaching.

# Introduction

Americans are good-hearted. When fire is discovered or a flood is imminent, nearly everyone responds. Fire, police, ambulance, and hospital crews go into action. Sophisticated communication and transportation systems are called upon to help alleviate the problem. Community volunteers turn out to minister to the homeless and the injured. Shelters are found. Food and clothing drives are organized. Scores of charitable acts are recorded. The government provides low-interest loans. Banks delay mortgage payments. The best in the American people often comes out when disaster is sudden and highly visible.

This book is a fire alarm. It sounds for anyone who pays attention. This book provides documentation of a disaster partway through its occurrence. The damage from this disaster is not as easily noticed as that caused by fire and flood, but to any discerning eye the debris is already mounting up. The disaster discussed in this book is the change in the profession of teaching and its impact on teachers and students. Using sociological lenses, the authors let us see how status panic—reductions in purchasing power and in the regard of society—has resulted in profound questions by teachers about their worth to society. In this book we learn about the physical and psychological isolation of teachers from other professionals. We come to understand how status panic and isolation influence a teacher's thinking and motivation to teach. Through the observations, interviews, and questionnaires of Ashton and Webb, we experience the feelings of powerlessness that envelop some teachers. We are forced to think about what happens to some people who entered the profession in order to live out and communicate the American dream—and who lost the ability to do either. These people entered teaching feeling competent and high-minded, committed to public service, possessing feelings of integrity, with an expectation that they could maintain their own feelings of self-worth and could communicate those feelings to others regardless of social, racial, or ethnic background. What we hear, later in their careers, are the voices of severely troubled people.

We find in this book teachers who entered the field to serve their students but who now make an implicit contract with their students—''don't cause me any trouble and I'll not bother you much either.'' That contract of least effort is renewed annually, with each new class. We recognize the magnitude of our disaster when we meet people who once entranced us with their enthusiasm but who now find teaching unrewarding, unrelenting, and uninteresting. I imagine that toll collecting at a bridge is unrewarding, unrelenting, and uninteresting— inherently so. But teaching? How can an inherently interesting job like teaching become transformed into one perceived to be so uninteresting? What social organizations, leadership styles, and demands of the workplace could produce such a transformation among good-intentioned, intelligent people?

We are fortunate to have Ashton and Webb document our disaster while we are in it because they do more than just describe teachers and students who are severely undermotivated and disheartened. They document, as well, the lives of teachers high in feelings of personal power and self-efficacy. They have found in the midst of the educational enterprise teachers who are highly motivated and whose self-worth has been maintained. These people may be individual teachers, working alone, but more often than not they work together with others like themselves in some particular organizational setting. In such settings they are apparently innoculated against the disasters that befall others. It is as though, in their community, fire and flood are not allowed to occur. From lemons they make lemonade. They try, day after day, to make silk purses from sows' ears. They feel good about their lives as professionals, and they do believe they make an impact on their students. The organizational climate that fosters people with a high sense of efficacy is very special. Ashton and Webb help us to gain insight into the nature of workplaces that keep people highly motivated about their work. We learn from them that we have to change the social relations among teachers, administrators, and students. An insight also gleaned from this book is that the best way to change the norms of the workplace is to provide teachers with the opportunity to do it themselves. Self-efficacy begins by making people feel that they have the power to change their own world. The kind of leadership needed in the teaching profession today is leadership that hands over power to teachers to solve their own problems. Unlike the cases of fire and flood, we need not call out the police or fire department. This turns out to be one disaster that can best be overcome by giving the people in the middle of it some power to solve their own problems. That is the charity needed from the American people.

Ultimately, we learn that anytime we want to we can turn off the fire alarm. That is the importance of this book. If we want our American public educational system to be the force it once was in our society, we must read and reflect on research such as this.

*David C. Berliner*
Professor, University of Arizona
President, American Educational Research Association

# MAKING
# A DIFFERENCE

# 1

## The Conceptual Framework and Design of the Study

### INTRODUCTION

Criticizing education has long been a minor industry in the United States, but it has been thriving of late. Commission reports (Boyer, 1983; The National Commission on Excellence in Education, 1983) manifestos (Adler, 1982), and research studies (Goodlad, 1984) all have "taken the pulse of the public school and found it faint" (Boyer, 1983, p. 1). All agree that the need for reform is great and the time for reform is now. All suggest their own programs and strategies for improvement. Some wish to standardize the school curriculum and increase the requirements for graduation. Others suggest that we lengthen the school day and the school year. Most mention the need to attract talented and qualified people into the teaching profession and a few call for the improvement of teacher education programs. Many mention but none analyze what we take to be the single greatest impediment to school improvement, namely, the crisis in teacher motivation. Boyer (1982), a former United States Commissioner of Education, described the crisis in these terms:

> The teaching profession is caught in a vicious cycle, spiraling downward. Rewards are few, morale is low, the best teachers are bailing out, and the supply of good recruits is drying up. Simply stated, the profession of teaching in this nation is imperiled. (Cited in Denemark & Nutter, 1984, p. 204)

Unless something is done to overcome the demoralization of teachers, it is unlikely that any reforms will improve significantly the quality of education in the United States. There are no teacher-proof reforms. Ultimately, the success of all improvement efforts depends on the quality and determination of the classroom teacher. However, teaching is an imperiled profession precisely because it deprives so many good teachers of their motivation and sense of professional self-esteem. Increasing the length of the school day or school year or tightening the requirements for high school graduation, two recommendations made by the National Commission on Excellence in Education (1983), would mean little if such large numbers of teachers remain demoralized by the compromises they are forced to make and the conditions under which they are forced to work.

Unfortunately, there is little research to help us understand the decline in teachers' motivation. In the past, it was generally assumed that teachers were motivated people who wanted to teach. Only recently have researchers begun to examine the conditions that make teaching a frustrating and stressful profession for too many of its members. The purpose of this monograph is to (1) describe a program of research that examined the motivation problems that jeopardize the teaching profession and (2) suggest an approach to educational reform that addresses the motivation problems teachers face.

A number of factors have contributed to the decline in teacher morale, including the failure of teacher salaries to keep pace with inflation, the lack of a career ladder that rewards competence, the loss of public confidence in teachers, and the disrespect and hostility of many students (Boyer, 1983; Gallup, 1985). Even educational research has given teachers reason to question their effectiveness. Some researchers, most notably Coleman et al. (1966) and Jencks et al. (1972), have examined the relationship between family socioeconomic background and student achievement and have concluded that schools can do little to narrow the achievement gap between children who live in comfort and stability and those who live in poverty, discomfort, and instability.

Two studies by the Rand Corporation (Armor et al., 1976; Berman, McLaughlin, Bass, Pauly, & Zellman, 1977) offer a heartening challenge to the conclusions drawn by Coleman and Jencks and their colleagues. In their evaluation of a reading program used in Los Angeles schools, Armor et al. reported that teachers' sense of efficacy was "strongly and significantly related to increases in reading [achievement]" (p. 24). In the second Rand study, an evaluation of teachers' uses of innovations, Berman et al. found a "strong positive relationship" between teachers' sense of efficacy and all of the evaluation's dependent variables—the percent of project goals achieved, the extent of teacher change, improved student performance, and teachers' maintenance of the innovations (p. 137). The researchers concluded that "teachers' attitudes about their own professional competence, in short, appear to have major effects on what happens to projects and how effective they are" (p. 137). The sense-of-efficacy construct referred to in the Rand studies is discussed in the next section. Suffice it to say here that *sense of efficacy* refers to teachers' beliefs regarding the ability of poverty-level students to learn in school and the teacher's confidence that he or she can teach such students effectively.

In the past, research efforts to correlate specific teacher attitudes with student achievement have been discouraging (Dunkin & Biddle, 1974; Getzels & Jackson, 1963). Thus, the two Rand Corporation evaluation studies were a breakthrough because they suggest that teachers' sense of efficacy is a component of teacher motivation associated with student achievement.

The decline in teacher motivation signals an urgent need to increase our understanding of teacher motivation in general and most specifically the impact of teacher motivation on student achievement. The findings of the Rand Corporation studies suggest that research on teachers' sense of efficacy can advance our understanding of teacher motivation. In this volume we describe a program of research designed to investigate (1) the nature of teachers' sense of efficacy, (2) the conditions that foster and inhibit its development, (3) the teacher and student behaviors that are related to teachers' sense of efficacy, and (4) the relationship of teachers' sense of efficacy to student achievement.

## DEFINITIONS

*Teachers' Sense of Efficacy.* The construct of teachers' sense of efficacy refers to teachers' situation-specific expectation that they can help students learn. That expectation rests on assumptions of how much students are capable of learning what schools have to teach. Teachers' efficacy expectations influence their thoughts and feelings, their choice of activities, the amount of effort they expend, and the extent of their persistence in the face of obstacles (Bandura, 1981). For example, teachers with a low sense of efficacy doubt their ability to influence student learning; consequently, they tend to avoid activities they believe to be beyond their capabilities. They reduce their efforts or give up entirely when confronted with difficulties. They are preoccupied with thoughts of their own inadequacies and believe their difficulties are more serious than they actually are. Their preoccupation with their own limitations raises their level of stress and reduces their teaching effectiveness by diverting their attention from the demands of instruction to worries about their personal competence. In contrast, teachers with a strong sense of efficacy believe that they are capable of having a positive effect on student performance. They choose challenging activities and are motivated to try harder when obstacles confront them. They become engrossed in the teaching situation itself, are not easily diverted, and experience pride in their accomplishments when the work is done.

Teachers' sense of efficacy consists of two independent dimensions: sense of teaching efficacy and sense of personal teaching efficacy. Teachers integrate their expectations from these two dimensions into a course of action.

***Sense of Teaching Efficacy.*** This dimension of teachers' sense of efficacy refers to teachers' expectations that teaching can influence student learning. Teachers differ in the extent to which they believe that teaching can have an effect on student performance, despite external obstacles such as family background and student ability. Teachers with a low sense of efficacy have come to believe that some students cannot or will not learn in school and that there is nothing any teacher can do to alter this unhappy reality. For example, teachers persuaded by the research of Coleman et al. (1966) that most of the variation in student achievement is due to home background may feel there is not much they can do to improve students' achievement. On the other hand, teachers with a high sense of teaching efficacy believe all their students are capable of learning. For example, they are likely to agree with Bloom (1981) that "what any person in the world can learn, almost all persons can learn if provided with appropriate prior and current conditions of learning" (p. 132).

***Sense of Personal Teaching Efficacy.*** This dimension of teacher efficacy refers to individuals' assessment of their own teaching competence. Teachers' perceptions of their own teaching abilities influence their choice of classroom management and instructional strategies. Teachers generally will avoid situations in which they doubt their ability to perform successfully. For example, if they feel threatened by confrontations with students' parents, they will avoid situations that might provoke such a confrontation. Teachers who doubt their ability to manage the behaviors of certain students may allow those students to ignore classroom rules. If they doubt their ability to motivate certain students, they may permit those students to remain off-task during instruction and may refrain from pushing those students to meet standards of performance expected of other pupils in the class. Teachers who doubt their sense of effectiveness experience debilitating stress. They are unable to perform as well as they might in the classroom, because they are distracted by the worry that they are not as competent as they should be.

## A Model of Teachers' Sense of Efficacy

Our conception of the hierarchically organized relationships that comprise teachers' sense of efficacy is presented in Figure 1.1. At the top of the model are generalized beliefs about response-outcome contingencies. These beliefs refer to the extent to which the teacher believes that actions can produce desired outcomes. Teachers' sense of teaching efficacy is derived, at least in part, from their more general beliefs about response-outcome contingencies and, consequently, is represented below the more general category of response-outcome beliefs. Similarly, teachers' general

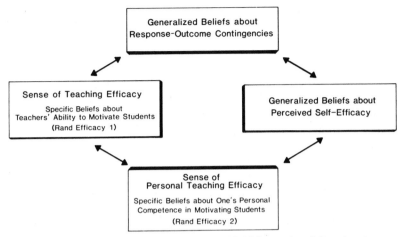

**Figure 1.1**   Teachers' Sense of Efficacy: The Multidimensional Construct

sense of effectiveness as a person is dependent on response-outcome beliefs and is also represented as influenced by those beliefs. Finally, teachers' beliefs about teaching-response outcomes and perceived self-efficacy are integrated to form a dimension that directly influences behavior in specific teaching situations—their personal teaching efficacy. Experiences that directly affect the most specific level of the hierarchy, personal teaching efficacy, will be most powerful in influencing teachers' motivation and future behavior, but other levels of the hierarchy also can influence teachers' sense of efficacy. When teachers have had no previous experience in a situation, generalized expectations of response-outcome and personal efficacy will be important determinants of their behavior.

We assume that reciprocal relationships exist among the various levels of the efficacy hierarchy. For example, if teachers are successful in getting across a difficult concept to students they believed could not learn it, they may modify both their personal assessment of their ability to teach such students (sense of personal teaching efficacy) and also their belief that such students cannot be taught (sense of teaching efficacy). The experience might also increase their generalized belief regarding the relationship between action and outcome and their sense of self-efficacy. On the other hand, if their sense of teaching efficacy is low and resistant to change, they may attribute the students' success to something other than their own teaching ability, and the various dimensions of their perceived efficacy may remain unchanged.

## Distinguishing between Teachers' Sense of Teaching Efficacy and Personal Teaching Efficacy

The distinction between teaching efficacy and personal teaching efficacy is important, because appropriate interventions depend on which dimension of teachers' sense of efficacy is low. If teachers' sense of efficacy is low because they believe their students cannot learn, changing their expectations requires evidence that, in fact, they can positively affect the performance of their low-achieving students. On the other hand, if teachers' low sense of efficacy is based on the belief that they lack skills needed to teach low-achieving students, their sense of efficacy will be altered only if they learn teaching skills that they can see from experience make a difference in student learning.

Research on learned helplessness (Abramson, Seligman, & Teasdale, 1978) suggests a further distinction between a low sense of teaching efficacy and a low sense of personal teaching efficacy. Teachers with a low sense of teaching efficacy are likely to experience what Abramson et al. call *universal helplessness*. Such teachers do not expect that they, or any other teacher, will have much effect on the achievement of their poorest students, and it is difficult for them to learn that such students can be helped. Teachers who experience universal helplessness give up on low-achieving students quickly and are unlikely to extend an extra effort in their behalf. Further, they are unlikely to experience high levels of stress or guilt or suffer a loss in their professional self-esteem when their poorest students perform poorly. That, after all, is just what the teachers expected these students to do.

Teachers with a low sense of personal teaching efficacy are likely to experience *personal helplessness*. Like those who doubt the efficacy of teaching, they are unsure of their ability to teach low-achieving students. However, instead of placing the responsibility for low achievement solely on the shoulders of the students themselves, they share the blame for student failure. They are quite sure that low-achieving students could learn if only they were better teachers and more knowledgeable, talented, and dedicated. Thus, when teachers with a sense of personal helplessness are asked to teach low-achieving students, they are likely to feel guilty, experience a high degree of stress, and suffer a loss of professional self-esteem. The cognitive, motivational, and affective outcomes of a low sense of teaching efficacy and a low sense of personal efficacy are illustrated in Figure 1.2.

The difference in motivation reflected in a low sense of teaching efficacy versus a low sense of personal teaching efficacy is evident in the following quotes from teachers we interviewed during our study. The first teacher maintained her sense of professional self-esteem in spite of a low teaching efficacy expectation. Her comments suggest that she is untroubled by her inability to reach her low-achieving students when her students do not learn material from the standard sixth-grade curriculum:

> I don't want to teach grammar, and I told the principal that. In fact, I told him not to assign me to a language arts class again. We argued about it. I said I'm not interested in teaching grammar to illiterates. He said that's because I don't

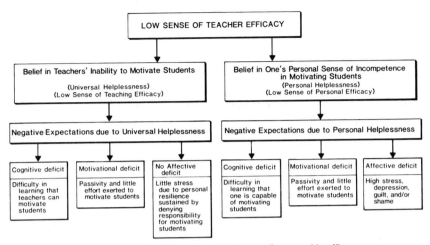

**Figure 1.2** Comparison of Universal and Personal Sense of Inefficacy

like teaching grammar. But I said, wrong. I love grammar. I'm a whiz at grammar. It's the easiest thing in the world to teach. But these students can't get it, and I don't agree with teaching it to them.

In contrast, a teacher with a low sense of personal teaching efficacy said she felt depressed and inadequate when her students failed to learn:

For a while I thought I'd quit teaching. I just felt kind of useless because I was going through long periods of time thinking that I wasn't doing any good for anybody.

Teachers' sense of teaching efficacy is an expectancy construct. It refers to the learning outcomes teachers expect will result from teaching. Therefore, the research on teacher expectations is relevant to our understanding of how teachers' sense of efficacy affects student achievement. The teachers' specific outcome expectations regarding the efficacy of teaching are filtered through their judgments of how able they are to influence student achievement. Thus, teachers' sense of personal teaching efficacy is an integrating construct that mediates the relationship between teachers' expectations about the efficacy of teaching specific students and teachers' classroom interactions with those students. For example, if teachers have a low expectation regarding the ability of girls to learn mathematics, this expectation will influence their expectation of effectiveness in teaching specific mathematical concepts to the girls in their class. The low expectation of personal teaching efficacy will then be translated into the kind of nonteaching behaviors that have been observed in many teacher-expectations studies. The teachers may pay less attention to female students, call on them less often to answer questions, wait less time for them to answer questions, give them less assistance in failure situations, criticize them more frequently for incorrect responses, praise them less frequently for correct responses, praise them more frequently for inadequate responses, demand less work and effort from them, and interrupt their performance more frequently (Cooper & Good, 1983).

## The Evolution of Our Concept of Teachers' Sense of Efficacy

In the two Rand studies (Armor et al., 1976; Berman et al., 1977), teachers' sense of efficacy is defined as "the extent to which the teacher believed he or she had the capacity to affect student performance" (p. 137). In both Rand studies, sense of efficacy was measured by the total score obtained from two Likert-scale items:

1. When it comes right down to it, a teacher really can't do much because most of a student's motivation and performance depends on his or her home environment.
2. If I really try hard, I can get through to even the most difficult or unmotivated students. (Berman et al., 1977, pp. 136–137)

Early in our research, we found that teachers' scores on the two Rand items were not significantly correlated (Ashton, Olejnik, Crocker, & McAuliffe, 1982). Consideration of the differences in the two items suggested the conceptual distinction between teaching efficacy and personal teaching efficacy discussed in the preceding section. The first Rand item corresponds to an outcome expectation of the efficacy of teaching, and the second item refers to the teachers' specific assessment of personal competence. Since the discovery that teachers' scores on the two items were not correlated, we have treated teachers' scores on the two items as separate dimensions.

Although the Rand Corporation researchers cited Rotter's social learning theory as the basis for the development of the teacher efficacy measure, we turned to Bandura's (1977, 1978, 1981, 1982) conception of the cognitive social learning theory of self-efficacy as a more adequate conceptual framework for our study. According to Bandura, *self-efficacy* is a cognitive mechanism that regulates behavior. A sense of self-efficacy develops as an individual acquires a conviction of personal competence; that is, when the individual believes he or she has mastered the behaviors necessary to achieve a desired outcome. The strength of an individual's sense of self-efficacy determines whether he or she will initiate and sustain a behavior in the face of difficulties. Thus, the individual's expectations of personal efficacy influence future learning and motivation. Contrary to strict behavioristic assumptions, Bandura contended that behavior is controlled by the individual's personal efficacy beliefs rather than by the presence of reinforcing consequences. Studies of learning in children support Bandura's contention that successful performance alone does not guarantee behavior change (Schunk, 1984). For example, Dweck (1976) found that giving success experiences to children who had a history of failure did not improve their motivation. Only after children underwent training in which they were taught to take responsibility for their failure and attribute it to insufficient effort were they able to improve their performance.

Bandura emphasized that perceived self-efficacy is a situation-specific determinant of behavior, not a global personality trait, and he pointed out that the study of self-efficacy must be based on a microanalysis of the situational determinants of self-efficacy. Therefore, in our study we sought to identify the contextual influences that affect teachers' sense of efficacy. In the next section, we describe the ecological framework that guided our search for situational determinants of teachers' sense of efficacy.

## THE NEED FOR AN ECOLOGICAL ANALYSIS

Bronfenbrenner (1976) insisted that if the scientific study of education is to progress, educational researchers must seek to discover the dynamic environmental processes that promote development. Encouraged by Bronfenbrenner's description of the power of an ecological analysis of educative processes to improve education and human development, we adopted his ecological model as the basic framework guiding our research.

Four basic assumptions characterize an ecological analysis: (1) behavior is a function of the subjective perceptions of the individual; to understand an individual's behavior, we must understand the individual's definition of the situation; (2) behavior is a function of the interaction between individuals and the various settings in which they live; in other words, behavior is strongly influenced by the environment; (3) behavior is influenced not only by direct effects between two individuals in a face-to-face setting but also by the indirect influences of others who may not be present in the immediate setting; (4) behavior in social settings is reciprocal; A affects B, and B in turn affects A. In the next four sections, we examine the importance each of these assumptions has to our study of teachers' sense of efficacy.

### Phenomenological Analysis of Teachers' Subjective Perceptions

Traditionally, studies of teacher effectiveness have not examined teachers' goals or their perceptions of their teaching situation (Medley, 1978). Consistent with the behavioristic perspective, researchers have attempted to identify relationships between behavior and its outcomes without regard for the purposes that motivated the teachers' behavior. A serious problem with this approach is that teachers are evaluated in terms of criteria of effectiveness that may not correspond to their own criteria. Teachers generally do not define their effectiveness in terms of their students' scores on achievement tests (Jackson, 1968), but most studies define teacher effectiveness solely in terms of students' achievement test scores. A second problem associated with the failure of researchers to examine teachers' intentions is the various meanings that a specific behavior can convey. Brophy (1981) discussed this problem in his effort to clarify the confusing research results on the relationship of teacher praise to student achievement. Brophy and Evertson (1981) also noted that teacher behaviors do not always mean what one might expect them to mean. As an example, they described teachers who used physical displays of affection to modify the behavior of immature or low-achieving students rather than as an expression of genuinely positive feelings toward their students. Teachers may exhibit the same behavior for quite different reasons, and students may interpret that behavior in a variety of ways. Consequently, to treat behavior as though it has the same meaning for all the actors involved may lead to invalid conclusions.

Fenstermacher (1979) pointed out another problem arising from the failure of traditional teacher-effectiveness researchers to examine teachers' subjective perceptions. Teachers behave as they do because of subjectively held beliefs that their behaviors are appropriate. They will maintain those behaviors unless evidence is presented that challenges their subjectively reasonable beliefs. If researchers wish to change those behaviors, Fenstermacher argued, they must first understand the intentions and beliefs underlying teachers' behavior. Citing Shulman and Lanier, Fenstermacher emphasized the importance of recognizing that teachers' actions must be understood in light of the meanings they attach to those actions:

> How teachers behave and what they do is directed in no small way by what they think. It is the relationship between thought and action that becomes the critical issue in research on teaching. (Shulman & Lanier, 1977, p. 44)

Once we understand teachers' motivation, we can identify strategies for changing the beliefs that maintain their ineffective behaviors.

The need for phenomenological analysis of teachers' beliefs was especially crucial in our study, because teachers' sense of efficacy refers to a subjectively reasonable belief. Therefore, it was vital for us to abandon the traditional research focus on teacher behavior and explore at length the subjective perceptions of teachers regarding their sense of effectiveness.

## Situational Effects on Teachers' Sense of Efficacy

A variety of studies provide insight into the situational features that influence teachers' behavior, including the size of the class (Glass & Smith, 1979), characteristics of students (Brophy & Evertson, 1981; Good & Grouws, 1979), the subject matter (McDonald & Elias, 1976) and the activity structure of the lessons (Bossert, 1979). Similarly, teachers' sense of efficacy is likely to be influenced significantly as a result of the context in which the teacher works.

A study by Cooper, Burger, and Seymour (1979) provided a number of insights into the situationally specific nature of teachers' sense of efficacy and its susceptibility to subtle classroom variables. This study identified three major factors as having causal influences on the teacher's classroom-control perceptions and success expectancies for a specific instructional interaction: (1) the initiator of the interaction (teacher or pupil), (2) the interaction setting (public or private), and (3) the performance expectations for the student (high or low). Three kinds of teacher control were considered: (1) control over timing, (2) control over content, and (3) control over duration. Results indicated the following: teachers perceived high-ability students to be more controllable than low-ability students; the teachers believed that they had more control when they initiated reactions than when students initiated them, and the teachers perceived that they had more control over private interactions than public interactions; teachers expected interactions with high-ability students to lead to successful outcomes more often than interactions with low-ability students.

Another study, conducted by Metz (1978), also suggests that the specific teaching situation affects teachers' sense of efficacy. In comparing two junior high schools, Metz found that teachers who taught in a school where disruptive student behavior was a visible problem were less likely to attribute their classroom management problems to their own personal inadequacies than were teachers who taught in a school with no visible student behavior problems. When other teachers' classrooms were perceived as orderly, teachers were more likely to blame themselves for their students' disorderly conduct and were less likely to admit difficulties and seek help than were their counterparts who taught in schools with visible student disruption. Metz concluded that the differences among schools in observable disorder promoted different teacher attitudes in dealing with disorder in their classrooms. Teachers in schools with visible order problems tended to seek solutions in major school changes through reevaluation of school goals and relationships. In contrast, teachers who perceived themselves as individually responsible for their classroom management difficulties sought solutions in pragmatic methods designed to deal with specific student behavior or motivation problems. In support of the impact of contextual effects, Metz observed that teachers in the school with visible order problems responded to their difficulties by evolving a more articulated awareness of their philosophical attitudes toward teaching and students. Teachers at the school without such problems remained unable to articulate their philosophical approach to teaching, their goals, or student-teacher relationships.

The studies by Cooper et al. (1979) and by Metz (1978) demonstrate that the classroom context plays an important role in teachers' perceptions of their effectiveness. *Context* can refer to specific classroom interaction, for example, public versus private teacher–student conversations, as in the Cooper et al. research, or it can refer to the total school climate, as in the Metz study.

### Indirect Effects on Teachers' Sense of Efficacy

The view of the teacher as the independent determinant of students' classroom behavior and learning has dominated classroom research (Carew & Lightfoot, 1979). This perspective oversimplifies the reality of life in classrooms. The indirect effects of the home, community, and culture assume an important role in life in classrooms, affecting both the teacher and students in subtle and complex ways. To obtain an adequate understanding of the influences on teacher efficacy, these indirect influences must be considered.

### Reciprocal Effects on Teachers' Sense of Efficacy

Bronfenbrenner (1976) applauded the general acceptance of the premise that behavior in social settings is reciprocal, but he noted that few research studies have actually examined the reciprocal influences of behavior. Traditional research in teaching has focused on the teacher as the central, controlling figure in classroom interaction and has utilized a simple linear causal model for analyzing the effect of teacher attitudes and behavior on student achievement (Carew & Lightfoot, 1979). Cohen (1972) emphasized the importance of conceptualizing teacher–student interaction in the classroom in terms of a reciprocal model:

> The relationship between teacher activities and student learning will depend on the state of the social system in the classroom. It is most unwise to use a simple unidirectional causal model to characterize the classroom.... Studies of the classroom as a complex social system suggest that cause and effect can run in several directions. Students have effects on the teacher, who in turn affects the learning of the student.... The informal social structure produces differential treatment of students by the teacher. Furthermore, the effects which students have on the teacher and on other students tend to build up over time. This kind of a characterization of learning in the classroom calls for theories capable of handling feedback effects and processes which change over time. (p. 444)

In his description of reciprocal determinism as a basic analytic principle for analyzing psychosocial processes, Bandura (1978) emphasized the reciprocal relationship between perceived self-efficacy and behavior. Sense of self-efficacy influences behavior, and the consequences of that behavior alter perceived self-efficacy through a continual bidirectional determinism. Similarly, we hypothesize that the relationship between teachers' sense of efficacy and student achievement is reciprocal.

From our theoretical framework we predict that teachers with a high sense of efficacy have higher expectations for student achievement and, as a result, work harder with their students, than do teachers with a low sense of efficacy; consequently, the students of teachers with a high sense of efficacy perform better on achievement tests. The students' success then has a positive effect on their teachers' sense of efficacy, and the process of reciprocal determinism continues in a mutually reinforcing cycle. In a similar fashion, teachers with a low sense of efficacy have low expectations of success for low-achieving students and do not work as hard to motivate and teach them. As a consequence, these students perform poorly on examinations, and their failure reinforces their teachers' low sense of efficacy. In sum, our model assumes that the relationship between teachers' sense of efficacy and student achievement is reciprocal. We postulate that teachers' perceived efficacy influences and, in turn, is influenced by student achievement.

In summary, our ecological framework for the study of teachers' sense of efficacy was based on four assumptions:

1. The study of teachers' sense of efficacy requires an exploration of the subjective perceptions of teachers.
2. Teachers' sense of efficacy is context-specific. It varies with specific characteristics of the teaching situation.
3. Teachers' sense of efficacy is affected by direct and indirect influences; direct influences include the students in the classroom and the principal. Indirect influences include the students' families, the school organization, the community, and the culture.
4. Teachers' sense of efficacy is reciprocally determined; it affects teachers' behavior and is, in turn, influenced by the teachers' perceptions of the consequences of that behavior.

## THE ECOLOGICAL FRAMEWORK

Bronfenbrenner's (1976) description of the ecological structure of the educational environment provides a useful framework for identifying the many variables that may affect teachers' sense of efficacy. Bronfenbrenner used terminology adapted from Brim (1975) to describe the nested arrangement of structures that comprise the educational environment:

1. The *microsystem* consists of the teachers' immediate setting, typically the classroom.
2. The *mesosystem* is comprised of the interrelations among the teachers' major settings.
3. The *exosystem* refers to the formal and informal social structures that influence the teachers' immediate setting, including the socioeconomic level of the community; the nature of the school district; the mass media; the state and national legislative agencies.

4. The *macrosystem* consists of the predominant cultural beliefs and ideologies that have an impact on teacher thought and behavior or on the various other systems impinging on teachers.

We searched the educational research literature for studies suggesting variables that might be related to teachers' sense of efficacy. We discuss the results of our review in terms of the four ecological structures described by Bronfenbrenner.

## The Microsystem

In Bronfenbrenner's ecological system, the classroom is designated as the microsystem. In the following sections, we describe a number of microsystem characteristics that are likely to influence teachers' sense of efficacy.

*Student characteristics.* Numerous studies have shown that students' personal characteristics are related to teacher expectations and teacher behaviors (Persell, 1977). From a meta-analysis of 77 studies of teacher expectancies, Dusek and Joseph (1983) concluded that socioeconomic class, race, attractiveness, and classroom conduct of students affect teachers' expectations for student performance.

Teachers' expectations about students' ability appear to be the single most influential student characteristic affecting their behavior. If teachers have low expectations of their students' ability to learn, these low expectations will contribute to a low sense of teacher efficacy and lessened effort in teaching the students they believe to have low ability. In her comparative study of two junior high schools, Metz (1978) reported that teachers with differing philosophical orientations toward teaching responded to differences in the ability level of their students in similar ways, despite their philosophical differences. When teachers were assigned low-achieving student groups, they assigned more written and individual work. Metz speculated that teachers resorted to highly structured routine written work with low-ability groups partly to protect themselves from the threats that these students posed to their sense of efficacy.

Brophy and Evertson's (1981) Student Attribute Study suggested that teachers' sense of efficacy mediates the effect of student characteristics on teacher behavior. Brophy and Evertson found that teachers avoided and criticized uncooperative students. These researchers speculated that teachers abandon their roles as adult facilitators with uncooperative students because they are uncertain about their ability to control such students. The low sense of efficacy that teachers experience in dealing with uncooperative students then leads them to "concentrate on controlling their behavior and neutralizing the trouble they cause rather than on teaching and socializing them in a more positive sense" (Brophy & Evertson, 1981, p. 169). In addition to the negative pattern of interactions with uncooperative students, Brophy and Evertson found that teachers tended to reject students who were openly hostile and disruptive. With these students, teachers were "locked into a pattern in which each was continually frustrating the other and producing reactions of negative affect and hostility" (p. 172). Brophy and Evertson concluded that the teachers' behavior was the result of the teachers' attributions of the causes of the students' behavior. Teachers attributed students' uncooperative behavior to deliberate acts of will that teachers feel powerless to change. The low sense of efficacy that this sense of powerlessness produces leads to continuing negative interactions with these students.

Brophy and Evertson's (1981) analysis suggests that teachers' attributions lead to teacher expectations that affect their sense of efficacy, which subsequently influences their behavior and student performance. Research has indicated that certain student characteristics are likely to lead to attributions that affect expectations, sense of efficacy, and ultimately, student performance: These characteristics include student ability, race, socioeconomic class, and sex (Persell, 1977).

*Teacher characteristics.* The sex of the teacher may be an important determinant of teachers' sense of efficacy. Maccoby and Jacklin (1974), in their extensive review of research on sex differences, reported that in a number of studies comparing college men and women, women were less confident than men about their ability to perform on tasks they were asked to complete. Because college women also tended to score lower than college males on measures of internal control, Maccoby and Jacklin suggested that the cultural shaping that women experience contributes to a lowered "sense of personal potency" and fewer significant achievements than males (p. 163). Frieze, Fisher, Hanusa, McHugh, and Valle (1979) reached a similar conclusion in their review of the research showing that females are more likely than males to attribute their failure to lack of ability. Dweck, Davidson, Nelson, and Enna (1978) provided support for the cultural conditioning hypothesis. In a study of fourth and fifth graders, they found that girls were more likely than boys to attribute their failure to lack of ability and to show impaired performance under failure conditions. Classroom observations revealed that teachers tended to attribute the failure of girls to lack of ability, whereas they attributed the failure of boys to lack of motivation, thus contributing to the girls' greater tendency to succumb to learned helplessness. The tendency of females to attribute their failure to lack of ability may lead female teachers to develop a lower sense of efficacy than male teachers when they are faced with difficult teaching conditions.

One study of teachers, however, challenges the socialization theory that suggests that female teachers are more likely than male teachers to succumb to a low sense of teacher efficacy. Garrett (1977) compared the perceptions of 373 male and female teachers. He found that female teachers were more likely than male teachers to attribute teaching success to teacher-controlled activity. Male teachers were more likely than female teachers to attribute teaching success to the socioeconomic level of the students' families. Male teachers also placed a higher priority on teaching students who are more academically able. Garrett concluded that female teachers had greater confidence in their ability to control their professional destiny. The contrast between socialization theory and Garrett's results indicates the need to examine the relationship of sex-role identity and teachers' perceptions of their effectiveness.

*Teacher ideology.* Ethnographic study of education has shown that teachers' beliefs influence their interactions with students, colleagues, administrators, and parents. Bernier (1981) recommended *ideological mapping* to identify teachers' beliefs that affect their relationships and behavior. In support of Bernier's recommendation, Mosenthal (1984) compared the writing of students in a classroom with an academically oriented teacher with the writing of students in a classroom with a cognitive–developmental teacher. Mosenthal concluded that students' stories differed as a function of the teachers' ideological orientation. Lightfoot (1973) compared the educational philosophy and practices of two black teachers who differed in their political and social ideologies. She concluded that the differences in the beliefs and values of the two teachers had a "profound impact" on their students' development (p. 197). Such ideological differences are likely to influence teachers' classroom behavior through the mediating process of teachers' sense of efficacy.

*Role definitions.* The isolation of teachers from collegial interaction contributes to the variation in the ways that teachers conceptualize their role (Dreeben, 1973). When left on their own to identify their strengths and weaknesses and to select their own goals, teachers differ in their perceptions of what constitutes effective teaching.

Two studies lend support to our belief that teachers' role behavior is related to teachers' sense of efficacy. A 5-year longitudinal study of 11 beginning high school teachers (Gehrke, 1981) showed that teachers chose to focus on one of three orientations—student, peer, or authority—and that their choice depended on their sense of competence and self-esteem as a teacher. The teachers selected the reference group that provided them with the most security. In her study of two junior high schools, Metz (1978) identified four teacher-role orientations that were distinguished on the basis of two dimensions: (1) whether or not teachers and students share goals, and (2) whether or not students should participate in defining classroom goals and activities. The majority of teachers observed by Metz agreed on the sharing of goals with students but differed regarding student participation in the selection of goals and activities. *Incorporative teachers*, as Metz called them, focused on the transmission of knowledge, whereas *developmental teachers* were more concerned with stimulating students' interests. Two smaller groups of teachers believed that their students did not share their educational goals and should not participate in choice of activities. The first group used an approach Metz called *proto-authority*; they believed that students must be forced to work and, therefore, maintained strict, militaristic discipline. The other group of teachers used a pattern of teaching Metz called *non-directive guidance*. This latter group believed that students should define their own goals and encouraged students' personal growth by maintaining a therapeutic role with their pupils. We believe that such differences in role definition are likely to influence teachers' sense of efficacy. Teachers who define their role in terms of socialization aims may not be troubled by students' small academic gains on standardized achievement tests, whereas similar test scores might give academically oriented teachers serious doubts about their effectiveness.

*Class size.* Teachers have traditionally insisted that class size affects their ability to be effective instructors. A meta-analysis conducted by Glass and Smith (1979) gave empirical support to teachers' long-held assumption that class size is related to student achievement. Glass and Smith obtained a "clear and strong" relationship between class size and achievement (p. 15). The relationship was somewhat stronger for the high school data than for the elementary grades and was unaffected by demographic variables, such as school subject and pupil IQ. Glass and Smith concluded that "the difference in achievement resulting from instruction in groups of 20 pupils and groups of 10 can be larger than 10 percentile ranks in the central regions of the distribution" (p. 15).

To examine the changes that occur in the classroom when the number of students decreases, Cahen, Filby, McCutcheon, and Kyle (1983) designed a field study of four classes whose size was reduced at midyear. They found an improvement in student attention, but they concluded that this improvement was larger in teachers' minds than in the students' observable classroom behavior. Consequently, the improvement may have resulted more from teachers' sense of efficacy—their belief that they can be more effective with smaller classes—than from the actual reduction in the number of students.

*Activity structure.* Teachers' sense of efficacy is likely to vary with the activity or task. For example, some teachers perceive themselves to be more effective in small group than large group instruction. Such personal assessments will influence the teacher's choice of future activities, and, as the growing research literature indicates, choice of activity structure has important implications for student achievement and social development (Bossert, 1979; Carew & Lightfoot, 1979; Cohen, 1979; Johnson & Johnson, 1974; McDermott, 1977; Rosenholtz & Wilson, 1980). The cycle of reciprocal determinism is likely to reinforce a teacher's preference for specific activity structures.

## The Mesosystem

Research on effective schools by Brookover, Beady, Flood, Schweitzer, & Wisenbaker, 1979, and by Rutter, Maughan, Mortimore, Ouston, and Smith (1979) indicated that no single variable accounts for school effectiveness. Rather, schools are more likely to have higher student achievement when the overall school climate reflects a strong commitment to student achievement. These findings suggest that a variety of meso-system variables may influence school effectiveness; our model of teachers' sense of efficacy suggests that many of the mesosystem variables are likely to affect student achievement through the mediating influence of teachers' sense of efficacy. Important mesosystem variables we expect to influence teachers' sense of efficacy include the size and demographic characteristics of the school, school norms, collegial relationships, principal–teacher relationships, school decision-making structures, and teachers' relationships with their students' families.

*School size and demographic characteristics.* In a study of 10 junior high schools in a large eastern metropolitan school district, Anderson (1968) reported that as school size increased, teachers' impersonal treatment of students and their resistance to innovations increased. Research by Berman et al. (1977) showing a strong relationship between teachers' sense of efficacy and implementation of innovations suggests that teachers' perceived efficacy may moderate the relationship between school size, treatment of students, and resistance to innovations. If the factors related to size of the school affect teachers' perceptions of their effectiveness, then teachers' relationships with students are likely to suffer, and they will be reluctant to try new approaches.

Anderson also reported that in schools with a large number of students from low socioeconomic status homes, more authority conflicts occurred between the school administration and the teachers. Administrators in these schools tended to perceive their teachers as lacking in motivation and instituted a large number of rules and procedures governing curriculum, grading, and testing procedures. If teachers perceive such rules to mean that their administrators question their motives and ability, their sense of efficacy may be affected.

Larkin (1973) provided further evidence that the demographic characteristics of schools significantly affect teachers' attitudes. On the basis of a study of 75 classrooms in southern California, he concluded that in schools with a large minority student population, teachers tended to be more authoritarian than teachers in schools with a majority of middle-class students. Teachers' sense of efficacy is likely to mediate the relationship between a large minority student population and teachers' authoritarian behavior. If teachers doubt their ability to control their students' behavior, they may become more authoritarian as a self-protective stance (Leacock, 1969).

*School norms.* Within a single school, prevailing attitudes of teachers toward students tend to coalesce into organizational norms. In her comparative study of four schools of varying socioeconomic and racial composition, Leacock (1969) described the development of a school culture, comprised of collectively accepted expectations for the students and styles of relating to them. Leacock concluded that, when teachers agree that certain groups of students are uneducable, a low sense of efficacy can become a school pattern with organizational sanction. In such schools, new teachers are pressured to accept the norm (Hargreaves, 1972; McPherson, 1972). If the socialization process succeeds and teachers become convinced that significant academic achievement is an impossible aim with the students they teach, maintaining order may become the teachers' primary goal (Cohen, 1972). Thus, school norms are expected to be an important influence on teachers' sense of efficacy.

*Collegial relations.* Teachers in traditionally organized schools often feel isolated from their colleagues. Lortie (1975) poignantly described the loneliness that many teachers experience because of their isolation from other adults during the school day. Teachers tend to have strong social needs (Holland, 1973; Super, 1970), and their isolation in individual classrooms may contribute to many teachers' dissatisfaction with their profession. School structures that enhance teachers' opportunities for collegial interaction have a positive effect on teacher attitudes and student performance (Ellett & Masters, 1977; Meyer & Cohen, 1971). For example, in a comparison of four relatively successful schools with two that were relatively unsuccessful, Little (1982) found that norms of collegiality prevailed in the successful schools. Strong collegial support may bolster and sustain teachers' sense of efficacy, enabling teachers to be more effective with their students.

*Principal–teacher relations.* The influence of the principal on teacher motivation and student achievement has been suggested in a number of studies of school effectiveness (Brookover & Lezotte, 1977; Ellett & Walberg, 1979; Wellisch, MacQueen, Carriere, & Duck, 1978). These studies indicate that an effective principal is a strong instructional leader (Cohen, 1981); however, they provide little information on the specific processes and behaviors that enable the principal to be an effective school leader. One aspect of the principal's role that is likely to be related to teachers' sense of efficacy is the principal's recognition and support of teachers. Chapman and Lowther (1982) reported that the recognition and approval that teachers felt they had received from their administrators was positively related to their job satisfaction.

In an extensive review of the research on the role of the elementary school principal in program effectiveness, Leithwood and Montgomery (1982) identified several dimensions of principal behavior related to school effectiveness. In terms of goals, the first priority of effective principals was the achievement and happiness of their students. In their relationships with teachers, effective principals assumed a task orientation focused on improving the school program rather than a "human relations" orientation. The effective principals communicated high expectations for their teachers as well as for themselves and their pupils and concentrated on a number of school and classroom factors in their efforts to increase school effectiveness. Assignment of students to teachers and the provision of personnel and other resources to support program development were among their most important concerns. Effective principals consulted teachers on decisions that affected program design and implementation, and they fostered cooperative working relations among their staff and community. We anticipate that these dimensions of principal effectiveness, especially high expectations for teachers and participation in program decision making, affect school effectiveness through the moderating influence of teachers' sense of efficacy.

*Decision-making structures.* Research on job satisfaction has consistently shown that workers' satisfaction is positively associated with the extent to which they participate in decision making. In a study of 325 primary school teachers, Hornstein, Callahan, Fisch, and Benedict (1968) found that, like workers in other organizations, teachers reported the greatest job satisfaction when they perceived themselves as sharing in the decision-making process. Although Hornstein et al. suggested that student performance is likely to increase if teachers are allowed a significant role in school decision making, Sarason (1982) and Goodlad (1975) have cautioned that teachers have become so accustomed to a subordinate role that involving teachers in school decision making may not be without serious difficulties. Duke, Showers, and Imber (1980) conducted interviews with 50 California teachers and found that although teachers reported increased feelings of self-efficacy from participating in school decisions, they were reluctant to become involved in decision making. They were afraid it would take time from valued classroom tasks and might result in losing some of their autonomy. They also doubted that their participation would make a real difference. Research is needed to identify means of involving teachers in decision making that enhance teachers' sense of efficacy and student achievement.

*Home–school relations.* Positive relationships between the school and the home are important for student achievement. Reanalysis of the Coleman et al. (1966) research revealed that the common contribution of the school and the family to student achievement exceeded their unique contributions, indicating that the interactive relationship between school and home is more important than either the home or school effect alone (Mayeske et al., 1972).

A serious potential for teacher–parent conflict exists. Sieber and Wilder (1967) compared the preferences of 1334 mothers for four typical teaching styles with the professional role definitions selected by 271 of their children's teachers; they found that 69% of the children had a teacher whose role-definition was in conflict with the mother's preference.

In a review of parent and school teaching practices, Laosa (1982) concluded that one factor contributing to school failure is discontinuity between the teaching and learning strategies developed in the home and those practiced in the school. Laosa proposed a socioculturally relativistic developmental paradigm to explain the learning difficulties of children whose parents have had relatively little schooling. These parents use modeling as their predominant instructional mode and are less likely than more highly schooled parents to use the problem-solving, information-processing interactional patterns common to teacher–student interactions in classrooms. As a consequence, their children are at a disadvantage in accomplishing school tasks.

Cultural discontinuities arising from racial and socioeconomic differences between teachers and parents may culminate in teachers' developing a low sense of efficacy in dealing with students and parents from backgrounds different from their own. Lightfoot (1978) identified the problem as one of misperceptions between parents and teachers rather than one of conflicting values:

> The literature shows overwhelmingly that blacks (regardless of social status) universally view education as the most promising means for attaining higher socioeconomic status. The dissonance between black parents and teachers, therefore, does not lie in the conflicting values attached to education but in the *misperceptions* they have of one another.
>
> Despite the passionate and often unrealistic dreams of black parents, teachers continue to view them as uncaring, unsympathetic, and ignorant of the value of education for their children and unconcerned about their children's academic success in school. Often they perceive the parents' lack of involvement in ritualistic school events and parent conferences as apathy and disinterest and rarely interpret it as the inability to negotiate the bureaucratic maze of schools or as a response to a long history of exclusion and rejection at the school door. Their lack of success in effectively participating in the relatively superficial and peripheral roles allowed ghetto parents is perceived by teachers as a lack of interest and concern in their children's education. The irony, of course, is that they care too much—a kind of caring that limits their view of alternative strategies for moving forward; a blinding preoccupation that makes black parents and children more vulnerable to the modes of subtle and explicit exclusion they face in relation to schools. (p. 166)

When teachers are unable to cope with these cultural discontinuities, they feel less effective with these students and their parents. To protect themselves from this threat to their sense of efficacy, teachers may limit their contacts with these families, thereby increasing the likelihood of further discontinuity and, ultimately, alienation of these families from the school. Ineffective relationships with parents pose a serious threat to teachers' sense of efficacy. Investigation of ways of promoting positive home–school relationships is an important issue in the study of teachers' sense of efficacy.

## The Exosystem

Many formal and informal social structures external to the school environment are potential influences on teachers' sense of efficacy. For example, the mass media, through their coverage of the decline in public confidence in teachers and the drop in students' test scores, have been identified as a major contributor to the decline in teachers' professional self-esteem (Chapman & Hutcheson, 1982; NEA, 1982). It is likely that two of the most powerful influences on teachers' sense of efficacy are the specific characteristics of the school district and legislative and judicial mandates.

*The nature of the school district.*   The community's location, size, socioeconomic and ethnic composition, the role of the teacher organizations in the district, management–labor relations between teachers and administrators, and parental involvement in school district decisions are among the many school district characteristics that can influence teachers' sense of efficacy (Bidwell & Kasarda, 1975). For example, Gross and Herriott's (1965) research demonstrated the important influence of the school district on the attitudes of teachers and the achievement of students. They found that the support of higher administrative levels was related to principals' effectiveness, which, in turn, was related to teachers' morale, their professional performance, and student achievement. School district decisions can have a major impact on teacher stress. Teachers reported serious tension because of a school district policy that subjected them to involuntary transfers (Cichon & Koff, 1978). Teaching in a school district during a strike can lead to negative attitudes and high levels of stress (Kalis, 1980). Such stress—an example of the emotional arousal cited by Bandura (1982) as a major source of efficacy information—is likely to have an impact on teachers' sense of efficacy and classroom interaction.

*Legislative and judicial mandates.*   The courts have been the most potent force for educational change in recent years (Sarason, 1982). Responding to the role of legislation in education at both the federal and state levels, Wise (1979) warned that the increase in legally mandated educational policy will increase the "bureaucratization" of the classroom. Wise's analysis of the dangers of bureaucracy suggests that the loss of teacher autonomy that accompanies an expanding bureaucracy is a serious threat to teachers' sense of efficacy.

## The Macrosystem

A number of our basic cultural beliefs have important implications for teachers' sense of efficacy. One of these beliefs is our conception of the nature of the learner and the role of the teacher. Another important influence is our cultural expectation regarding the role of education in society.

*Conceptions of the learner.* Research on the attributions that individuals make to explain behavior (Weiner, 1980) has helped us understand the thoughts and feelings that underlie teacher and student achievement behavior. When failure is attributed to lack of ability, motivation tends to decline; when failure is attributed to effort, motivation is less likely to suffer (Dweck, 1976). However, little attention has been focused on the question of why students and teachers make the attributions that they do. Developmental theorists (Ruble, 1980) have suggested that students' cognitive development influences their attributions, but Rosenholtz and Simpson (1984) rejected the developmental explanation as inadequate and argued that "our culture makes developmental explanations seem obvious because we reify intelligence as an inevitable quality of individuals" (p. 32). Our cultural belief in intelligence as a stable trait varying widely among individuals contributes to the tendency to attribute school success and failure to ability. Psychological conceptions of ability and intelligence support and strengthen our cultural belief in ability as a stable trait (Bloom, 1978; Brookover & Erickson, 1969; Sarason, 1982). Thus, when teachers confront low-achieving children, they are supported by their cultural beliefs and by psychological theory in attributing the students' problems to the students' lack of ability. This attribution is then translated into a low expectation for the students' academic success and a low-efficacy belief—*I can't teach these children*—that affects the teachers' future interactions with the students and their students' subsequent achievement behavior.

Teachers are further encouraged to attribute failure to inadequacies in their students by the deeply ingrained tendency in our culture to blame individuals for their own failure (Ryan, 1976). According to Lewis (1978), individuals are socialized to believe that their self-worth depends on their ability to surpass the achievements of others; thus, in our culture, an individual's ability to excel where others have failed is taken as evidence of competence or strength of character, whereas failure is indicative of incompetence or weakness of character. Lewis's account of the cultural beliefs that support our attributions helps us understand the thinking and behavior of teachers in their classrooms. Teachers can relieve themselves of the burden of responsibility for students' failure and protect their professional self-esteem if they attribute failure to their students' lack of ability or motivation. By blaming their students, they can maintain their sense of efficacy and avoid debilitating stress and self-doubt.

Effort can become a "double-edged sword" for low-achieving students; if they try and fail, they must face further evidence of their inability. As long as they do not try, they do not have to accept a low self-concept of their ability (Covington & Omelich, 1981). Students who believe that they are doomed to a limited future by poverty, race, or other inescapable constraints may see no advantage in trying and may resist teachers' efforts, because by trying they risk not only academic failure but also loss of social status among their peers. In failing, students may also be engaged in protecting their self-esteem. Thus, teachers and students may become entrapped in a vicious cycle as they work to protect their sense of efficacy. Teachers blame students because they believe their pupils lack the necessary ability or motivation, and students refuse to try for fear of revealing their inadequacies. Ultimately, both teachers' and students' sense of efficacy will suffer.

In recent years, educational research, most notably the Coleman Report (Coleman et al., 1966), has contributed to the societal belief that home environment, not schooling, is the critical factor in determining achievement. Thus, when new teachers emerging from educational institutions determined to reach every student meet resistance in the classroom, they can use cultural values and psychological theory to support their contention that they should not be held responsible for student failure. As Rist (1978) concluded in his book, *The Invisible Children*, the tragedy of this ready defense is that it frees teachers, and teacher educators, from having to face the fact that they do not possess the knowledge and skills needed to motivate some students. Without an admission of this inadequacy, no effort is made to discover more effective strategies, and thousands of teachers simply learn to live with a low sense of efficacy and complacently accept student failure.

***Conceptions of the role of education.*** The basic assumption underlying the educational system in the United States is that education offers success and advancement for all individuals with the ability and motivation to take advantage of the opportunities it provides. Given this assumption, when individuals fail, the unavoidable conclusion is that they lack either ability or motivation or both. This widely held view of education places responsibility for failure with the individual student. Thus, freed from the responsibility for student failure by the cultural belief in individual freedom of choice, teachers in the United States are unlikely to engage in an analysis that might raise doubts about their efficacy as teachers or challenge their beliefs about the equity of the educational system (Jackson, 1968). Analyses

(Bowles & Gintis, 1976) of schooling in the United States, however, have indicated that the educational system tends to maintain the economic and social status quo. In this system, the need of teachers to protect their fragile sense of efficacy may result in their becoming unknowing accomplices in perpetuating the social and economic inequities in the society.

## THE DESIGN OF THE STUDY

Guided by the ecological framework described in the preceding pages, a two-phase study was designed to further develop the theoretical framework and to identify directions for future research. Our specific objectives were to investigate (1) the nature of teachers' efficacy attitudes, (2) factors that facilitate and inhibit development of a sense of efficacy, (3) teacher behaviors associated with teachers' sense of efficacy, and (4) the relationship between teachers' sense of efficacy and student achievement. Having only Bandura's theoretical framework and the Rand Corporation's two-item scale of teachers' sense of efficacy to guide us in our conceptualization of the efficacy construct, we decided that we needed to take a developmental approach to the research.

The first phase of data collection took place during March, April, and May of 1980. This phase consisted of an exploratory study designed to examine the nature of teachers' sense of efficacy and some of the factors that promote its development. The design of the second stage of data

TABLE 1.1.   Multiple Data Sources for the Study of Teachers' Sense of Efficacy

1. Methods
    1.1 Questionnaires
    1.2 Projective measures
    1.3 Observation
    1.4 Informal interviews
    1.5 Documents
2. Persons
    2.1 Students
    2.2 Cooperating teachers
    2.3 Principals
    2.4 Other teachers
3. Situations
    3.1 Students
    3.2 Classroom teaching
    3.3 Multiple schools
    3.4 Curriculum planning meetings
    3.5 Faculty meetings
4. Variables
    4.1 Individual: traits, attitudes, perceptions, motives, behaviors
    4.2 Group: interaction, activity
    4.3 Organizational: schools

collection emerged from our analysis of data gathered during the first phase, and consisted of a systematic observation study designed to verify quantitatively the relationships we observed during the first phase. Many methodologists (e.g., Campbell & Fiske, 1959; Smith, 1979) have noted that multiple data sources should be consulted in building a comprehensive conceptual framework. Table 1.1 outlines the multiple data sources we included in the two phases of this study.

## PHASE 1: THE SEARCH FOR A GROUNDED THEORY

Because we wanted to ground our understanding of teachers' sense of efficacy in the experiences and perceptions of teachers, we chose Spradley's (1980) ethnographic approach as the method for the first phase of our research. The samples selected for study were maximally differentiated on a number of variables believed to have theoretical relevance to the construct of interest. We selected two schools that differed on three organizational dimensions expected to influence teachers' sense of efficacy: (1) interdisciplinary team versus department organization, (2) multi-age versus single-age grouping, and (3) an adviser–advisee program versus homeroom program.

The two middle schools selected for study consisted of grades six through eight and were similar in size (approximately 1,000 students), in urban location, and in racial and socioeconomic composition (predominantly minority and low socioeconomic level students). One school, hereafter referred to as the middle school, had a modern middle school orientation—that is, team teaching, multi-age grouping, and an adviser program. Approximately 160 students were assigned to a team of five teachers who shared responsibility for the curriculum. These students remained in the same group with the same teachers for 3 years. The other school, hereafter referred to as the junior high, was organized in a traditional junior high format, with students assigned to different teachers for different subject matter. We expected that the two school organizations would differ in their effect on teachers' sense of efficacy, because Meyer and Cohen (1971) found that teachers in open-space schools developed a higher sense of autonomy than teachers in traditional schools. They attributed the greater autonomy among teachers in the open-space schools to the increase in interaction among teachers that is offered by team teaching and to an increase in the teachers' perceived sense of schoolwide influence and participation in decision making.

Half of the teachers at each of the two schools responded to our request to complete a questionnaire (see Appendix A for a copy of the questionnaire). Twenty-nine Middle School teachers and 20 Junior High teachers completed the questionnaire. From the teachers' scores on the two-item Rand measure, we selected two teachers with a high efficacy score and two teachers with a low efficacy score from each of the schools. To reduce the confounding effect of context, we chose teachers of similar subject matter—social studies, language arts, and reading. Observers visited two classes of each teacher at least four times over a 6-week period in April and May of 1980 and completed ethnographic descriptions of the classroom interaction. After completing the classroom observations, the observers had an hour-long interview with the teachers they observed (see Appendix B).

The following year, a microethnographic study was conducted to explore in greater depth the processes through which school organization variables influence teachers' sense of efficacy. Two teachers from each school were observed over the course of a year as they taught their classes and interacted with their colleagues, administrators, and parents.

## PHASE II: THE SYSTEMATIC OBSERVATION STUDY

The year after the middle school research study, we designed a presage-process-product study (Dunkin & Biddle, 1974) of 48 basic-skills communication and mathematics teachers from four high schools. Basic skills classes were selected for study because we believed that these classes, comprised primarily of low-socioeconomic status black students who had experienced repeated failures, were likely to make teachers' sense of efficacy especially salient.

The teachers completed a questionnaire (see Appendix C) designed to measure their sense of efficacy and other attitudes expected to be associated with their sense of efficacy, including their level of stress, the amount of responsibility they assumed for student learning, and questions about their instructional practices. Observers were trained in the use of three systematic observation instruments: The Climate and Control Schedule (Medley, Coker, & Soar, 1984; Soar & Soar, 1981) (see Appendix E), Teacher Practices Observation Record (Brown, 1968), and a student engagement rate form—an observational schedule adapted from Stallings and Kaskowitz (1974) by Research for Better Schools (Huitt, Traver, & Caldwell, 1981; Squires, Huitt, & Segars, 1983). Following training, observers visited the teachers' classrooms from two to six times during a 4-month period and completed a series of observations using the three instruments during each of their visits. The majority of participating teachers also completed an hour-long interview with one of the observers (see Appendix D).

## OVERVIEW OF THE BOOK

Bronfenbrenner's (1976) ecological perspective provides the structure for the report of our research on teachers' sense of efficacy. In Chapter 2 we describe the macro- and exosystem characteristics that contribute to the social–psychological milieu in which teachers must struggle to maintain a strong sense of efficacy. Chapter 3 presents an ethnographic theory generated from teachers' subjective perceptions of the experience of teaching. In Chapter 4, we examine the influence of one important aspect of the mesosystem—the school organization. In Chapter 5, we describe our study of the microsystem—the relationships among teacher attitudes and behavior and student behavior and achievement. We consider the implications of our research for refining the conceptual framework for studying teachers' sense of efficacy in Chapter 6. In Chapter 7, we describe an ecological approach to research and reform, using teachers' sense of efficacy as the organizing construct.

# 2

# The Social-Psychological Context of Teaching

## INTRODUCTION

An analysis of the social-psychological milieu in which teachers work is essential to an understanding of how efficacy attitudes develop in teachers. A comparison of the efficacy attitudes of 61 preservice teachers with those of 38 basic skills high school teachers revealed that teachers-in-training had significantly higher efficacy scores than the experienced teachers (Ashton, Webb, & Doda, 1983), suggesting that the social-psychological milieu in which teachers work adversely influences their efficacy attitudes. The purpose of this chapter is to identify those aspects of the school environment that appear to influence how teachers define and evaluate their work.

## SOCIAL-CLASS ASPIRATIONS OF TEACHERS

Lortie (1975) pointed out that teaching in the United States "is clearly white collar, middle-class work, and as such offers upward mobility for people in blue collar or lower-class families" (p. 35). According to National Education Association data, 58% of male teachers and 52% of female teachers had fathers who were farmers, unskilled, or semiskilled workers (NEA, 1982, p. 184).

The oft-stated observation that teachers are carriers of middle-class values is undoubtedly true. The life experiences of most teachers demonstrate their allegiance to the ethic of vertical mobility, self-improvement, hard work, deferred gratification, self-discipline, and personal achievement. These individualistic values rest on the assumption that the social system (the nation's economic organization and its component institutional systems) generally works well, is essentially fair, and moves society slowly but inevitably toward progress (Webb, Damico, & Bell-Nathaniel, 1978).

The middle-class system of values puts the individual at the center (Lewis, 1978). If individuals develop their talents, work hard, and persevere in the face of adversity, it is assumed that they will eventually "get ahead" in life. Conversely, those who lack talent and/or ambition will eventually and justifiably fail. Winners in the American competition will have ample opportunity to display their success through the consumption of goods, the utilization of leisure time, and the exhibition of power and status. Those who fail suffer the just deserts of their own incompetence and/or indolence (Feagin, 1975).

Teachers feel themselves to be respectable members of the white-collar middle class. Lerner (1967) has described this stratum of American society as a

> loose collection of [occupations], probably more anxiety-ridden than the rest of the culture, dominated by the drive to distinguish themselves from the working class, incohesive, held together by no common bond except the fact that they are caught in a kind of purgatory between the hell of the poor and the weak and the heaven of the rich and the powerful. (p. 188)

White-collar workers are achievement oriented, remembering, as they often do, their family roots in the working class. Most take pride in their social and economic ascent and see potential for future status advancement for themselves and/or their children. However, white-collar employees generally, and teachers in particular, are made anxious when they discover that (1) their salaries are lower than most workers with comparable training and responsibility and that their profession provides limited opportunities for continued economic and status achievement; (2) their salary increases have fallen behind the rate of inflation; (3) blue-collar wages in some areas meet or significantly exceed their own yearly earnings; (4) a stereotypical image of teachers' work and worth, promulgated by the press and widely held by the public, has lowered the status of the teaching profession, or at least teachers worry that this is so; and (5) teachers feel their achievements go unrecognized by the public and by school administrators. Any one of these five conditions can throw teachers into what Mills (1951) called *status panic*. That panic becomes particularly acute when all of these conditions are perceived to be at work simultaneously, as is presently the case in education. Each of these conditions will be discussed in this chapter.

A rich literature details how middle-class teachers tend to favor students who affirm middle-class values and to disfavor those whose demeanor and behavior contradict that value system (Brophy & Good, 1974; Webb, 1981, pp. 371–389). However, little attention has been paid to how that same value system affects teachers themselves. By better understanding the aspirations of school teachers and the white-collar, bureaucratic world in which they work, we will better understand the hopes and complex anxieties that grip so many teachers today, and we will be better able to grasp the connections that may exist between teachers' efficacy attitudes and the social realities of the teaching profession. This chapter details how the conditions of teaching promote status panic among classroom teachers, isolate them from their colleagues and, too often, alienate them from their work and their students, especially low-achieving students.

## METHODOLOGY

During the first year of research, ethnographic interviews were conducted with four middle and junior high school teachers who had high Rand efficacy scores and four teachers with low scores. The classrooms of these teachers also were studied using ethnographic techniques of participant observation. (See Chapter 4 for a description of the middle and junior high schools.) During the second year of the study, 48 teachers in four high schools participated in a systematic observation study. (Findings relating to teacher efficacy attitudes and student achievement are detailed in Chapter 5.) Teachers at three schools were asked to be interviewed and 23 agreed. By prior agreement with the principal at one school, teachers were observed but were not asked to be interviewed.

Some basic skills teachers taught a full load of six compensatory classes a day, whereas others taught one to five compensatory classes and spent the remainder of their time teaching classes of regular or advanced students. Basic skills classes were offered in arithmetic and communications skills and were required of all students who failed one or more portions of the 10th grade Florida Basic Skills Examination. High school freshmen whose Metropolitan Achievement Test scores were one standard deviation or more below the mean for 9th grade students in Florida were also required to take basic skills classes.

Ten hours of ethnographic observations were made in the classrooms of four middle school teachers and four junior high school teachers during the spring of 1980. Toward the end of the observation period, each teacher was interviewed. Open-ended questions centered on the teachers' educational objectives; definitions of the teacher role; classroom difficulties; their perceptions of low-achieving, low-socioeconomic-status students; the rewards of teaching; their relationships with students, peers, and administrators. Each teacher was asked questions regarding specific classroom occurrences (see Appendix B).

The following year, basic skills teachers in four high schools were observed three times over the course of 2 months. Classroom observers used systematic observation instruments to record the behavior of teachers and students. Findings relating to teachers' behavior, teachers' efficacy attitudes, students' behaviors, and student achievement are detailed in Chapter 5. A total of 48 basic skills teachers were observed. Teachers at three of the four schools were asked if they would agree to be interviewed. Interviews were completed with 23 teachers, or 48% of the basic skills teachers at the three schools. Classroom observation and demographic data from questionnaires teachers completed earlier in the year suggested that the interviewed teachers were generally representative of the teacher population at the three schools. One group appeared to be underrepresented, however. Three highly anxious, experienced teachers, with apparent academic deficiencies of their own, were assigned to teach a full complement of basic skills classes. All three declined our interview requests. High school basic skills teachers were asked a battery of questions that was similar to that asked of middle and junior high teachers the year before (see Appendix D).

Teacher interviews were conducted in private, during free periods of the school day, and each lasted from 30 minutes to 2 hours. The average interview took about 50 minutes and was completed in one sitting. Scheduling difficulties made it necessary to conduct three interviews in two sessions of 30 minutes each. Two other teachers agreed to be interviewed together.

Interviews were generally tape recorded. In one instance, when a teacher preferred that her interview not be taped, and in two cases, when the tape recorder malfunctioned, extensive notes were taken in longhand. Small tape recorders and long-playing tapes were utilized to reduce whatever distraction taping the interviews might have caused for teachers. Interviews were conducted in the teacher's classroom or other school locations that offered privacy. Interviews were transcribed from tapes and notes. All teachers were assured that care would be taken to protect their anonymity and the anonymity of their schools. Throughout this book, names have been omitted or changed and, occasionally, where it would not affect the meaning or significance of findings, references to gender, subject matter, and grade level have been altered as well.

We made a conscious attempt to minimize formality and to make the discussions with teachers as comfortable and conversational as possible. Though interviewers worked from a common set of questions, an open-ended format was followed. The order in which questions were asked changed from teacher to teacher. Interviewers followed leads provided by teachers, probed for further information, tested ideas, and checked to see if views expressed by some teachers were shared by their colleagues.

Interviewers tried not to take it for granted that they understood the meaning of familiar words that appeared to carry special significance for a teacher. For example, if a teacher referred to students in her class as "illiterates," the interviewer encouraged the teacher to explain the term. When another teacher said that her basic skills students "would do okay in life," the interviewer asked her to describe the life she envisioned for those pupils. On two occasions, such probing appeared to annoy a teacher and to disrupt the equilibrium of the interview. In these cases the interviewer changed the topic and came back to the issue again only after the conversational rapport had been reestablished.

Five researchers—an educational psychologist, an anthropologist of education, a sociologist of education, a social psychologist, and a graduate student with experience as a middle school teacher and training in anthropology—observed in the middle and junior high school classrooms and interviewed teachers. The research team met together periodically to discuss observational strategies, to read one another's fieldnotes and interview transcripts, and to discuss methods of data analysis. Only two researchers interviewed the high school basic skills teachers and had primary responsibility for analyzing qualitative interview data. Spradley's (1980) method of domain analysis was employed to organize and interpret teacher interview data.

## THE COMPONENTS OF TEACHER STATUS PANIC

### Great Expectations and Limited Opportunities

Historically, teaching has provided an honorable and easily accessible route to the white-collar world of the middle class (Lortie, 1975). From the vantage point of many young adults from blue-collar families—those nonrebellious, generally attentive students who have experienced at least modest success at school—the job of the classroom teacher appears secure, socially desirable, relatively prestigious and inviting. These students discover that colleges of education are numerous and often do not have rigorous admission or graduation requirements. Over a period of time the cost of education proves high enough and the course requirements difficult enough to convince teacher candidates that they have made significant sacrifices to achieve their upwardly mobile, white-collar status.

Once on the job, however, neophyte educators begin to feel the social and economic impact of their career choice. The starting salaries of beginning teachers are lower than those of college graduates entering most other fields. As shown in Figure 2.1, starting teachers' salaries have fallen significantly in recent years while they have risen substantially in other professions (Sykes, 1984).

Starting off at a salary disadvantage, beginning teachers look ahead to the earning potential of their chosen profession. They soon realize that their pay is determined by district salary schedules that limit the salaries of the most experienced teachers at about 2 to 2.5 times the earnings of beginning teachers. The vertical mobility aspirations that brought blue-collar college students into teaching are thus thwarted by a system in which

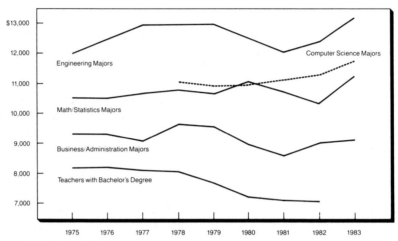

**Figure 2.1**  Starting Salaries for College Graduates in 1975 Dollars

there is scant economic reward for years of service, and no advancement opportunities for teachers who wish to remain in the classroom. As Boyer (1983) has noted,

> Two of the most troublesome aspects of the teaching profession are the lack of a career ladder and the leveling off of salaries. The irony is that to "get ahead" in teaching you must leave it. The notion seems to be that, if you are good, you will move out of the classroom and become a school counselor or principal—or a football coach. The lack of opportunity for advancement in teaching is in sharp contrast to other professions, where outstanding performance is rewarded. (p. 179)

## Inflation

The ethic of advancement is further frustrated when teachers realize how deeply inflation has cut into their paychecks. According to data from the National Center for Educational Statistics, the average annual salary for public school teachers increased nearly $10,000 dollars (from $9,269 to $19,157) between 1970–1971 and 1981–1982. After inflation, however, teachers suffered a 13% loss in purchasing power and a 14% loss from the salary peak in 1972–1973 (Plisko, 1984).

## Blue-Collar Advances

During the decade of real income decline for teachers, strongly unionized blue-collar workers fared much better. Between 1967 and 1978 the after-inflation income of coal miners advanced 31%, that of truck drivers 23%, and that of plumbers over 11%. Teachers who once prided themselves on their advancement into the middle class were alarmed to see that the incomes of many blue-collar workers equaled or greatly exceeded their

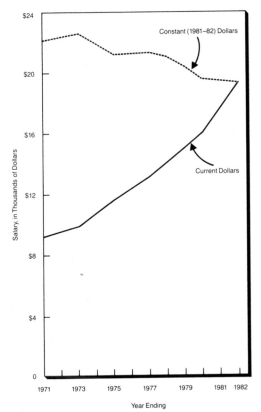

**Figure 2.2**   Average Annual Salary of Teachers in Public Elementary and Secondary Schools

own. Teachers' sense of self-worth and social location has been threatened by the real and comparative decline in their economic well-being. As Blumberg (1980) has shown, this problem is not unique to teachers; its effects are widespread within the middle class.

> Today, the middle-class struggle to maintain what have been for them appropriate income differentials is collapsing. Such salaried employees must inevitably develop the feeling that their income is no longer commensurate with their social worth. (p. 83)

Blumberg asks:

> In a society where money is the measure of social worth, what happens when clerical workers and retail sales people discover that factory workers are suddenly earning not merely slightly more, but 2–2.5 times more than they; when school teachers and librarians are being left behind in the factory dust; when unionized blue-collar workers are quickly closing in even on college professors who have invested up to ten years in graduate school . . . to prepare for a career. (p. 83)

He added ominously, "When rank—or imagined rank—no longer gets its due, social order is in danger" (p. 83).

There is, of course, no single answer to Blumberg's question regarding the long-term effects of status panic on the teaching profession. However, our interviews indicate that teachers are aware of and deeply concerned about their weakening financial situation and see a connection between income and social status in American society. For example, we asked one teacher if he would choose to become an educator if he had it to do over again. Although he acknowledged that teaching was important to him, he quickly added:

> But when I think about the way that society recognizes teachers, and the value of teaching, and the way they reward teachers ... [well] if I didn't have an outside income I would probably be very dissatisfied. Teaching is not recognized the way it should be. I feel that with my ability in mathematics I could just have easily become an engineer, any kind of scientist, a medical doctor, anything like that. I'm not sure I'd necessarily have been happier doing that ... but I would have more financial rewards.

It would be a mistake to suggest that money and status are primary and conscious motivators for all those who enter teaching. Studies indicate that people enter teaching and other helping professions for more altruistic reasons (NEA, 1982), but teachers did not expect teaching to be as financially precarious as it has turned out to be. Financial worries have discouraged many teachers and eroded their commitment to teaching:

> I do get discouraged on occasion. The pay is so low. So I ask myself, *Why am I doing this? Why did I ever go into teaching?* I feel embittered some of the time about the pay.

We asked the same teacher if she would encourage her daughter to go into teaching. She answered firmly that she would not because the pay was inadequate.

> It's too bad that we pay people who work with words so poorly. There's not much reward. My daughter has a high I.Q. and she is good in language and English. But I'm pushing her into math and science because there are more opportunities there.

Though altruistic motives bring many teachers to teaching, financial troubles encourage many to leave.

> I'm looking more and more to getting out of teaching. It's not so much that I don't like teaching. It's because I'm not making any money. I think I do too many things too well to sit around here [making $15,000] dollars a year when I can probably go and find some kind of business to get involved in and do much better than I'm doing. I think probably within the next three or four years I'll be out of teaching. It's the money. It's a real problem. I think we're just above the poverty line right now. We're just not doing well at all.

We asked a teacher what might be done to improve the prestige of his profession. Like many members of the middle class, the teacher saw a close connection between status and salary.

> I think the biggest thing they could do to increase teacher prestige would be to double the salaries. Double the salaries. People would place a higher value on what teachers do if they [teachers] had more money. If I had to pick one thing that would increase the prestige of teaching it would have to be an increase in the salaries.

## Declining Status

In addition to the problem of low pay, teachers are disturbed by the low status they are assigned nationally and in their home communities. Occupational status is one of the most widely studied components of the American social stratification system. Most studies derive from research conducted by the National Opinion Research Center in the 1950s. Since that time other studies have found a high degree of stability in the prestige the public assigns to most occupations. These studies show that teachers rank far below most other occupations (physicians, pharmacists, lawyers, and so on) and in the lower third of white-collar occupations. In a ranking system that gave status scores as high as 583 and as low as 30 to various occupations in America, Coleman and Rainwater (1978) found that high school teachers had a rating of 131, or just above the lowest level of managerial and kindred workers. Teachers are troubled by their low salaries and by the low status those salaries reflect.

Teaching has always been a marginal or semiprofession (Etzioni, 1969), but teachers worry that their status claims are being eroded by the public's declining faith in education in general and in the competence of teachers in particular. Between 1974 and 1981, for example, growing numbers of Americans expressed worry over the quality of public schooling. In a 1974 Gallup Poll, 32% of the American public assigned grades of C or below to indicate how they thought schools were doing. By 1984, as shown in Figure 2.3, 50% gave these low marks to the school, an improvement from 54% in 1981 (Gallup, 1984, p. 25). The reasons for the decline in public confidence have not been well studied, so its exact causes are not well known. However, national polls, scholars, critics, and the popular press frequently cite such factors as the prolonged decline in achievement test scores; the steady increase in educational expenditures (giving rise to the contention that the public is paying more for and getting less from its schools); increasing rates of school mischief, vandalism, and outright crime; the well-advertised though controversial claims that Great Society programs failed to improve the quality of education; increased union militancy; and the perhaps small, but seemingly growing, numbers of incompetent teachers. For the first time, the 1980 Gallup poll indicated that a majority of Americans (52%) would be displeased if a child of theirs became a teacher. This figure is up from 25% in 1969 (Gallup, 1980, p. 38).

The teachers we interviewed were aware of their flagging image in the

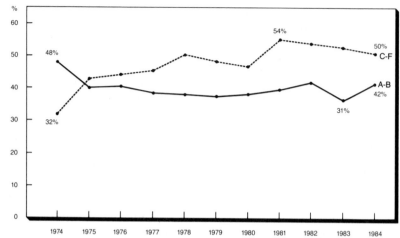

**Figure 2.3**   Distribution of Aggregate Good (A–B) and Bad (C–F) Grades for Public Schools

community and were disturbed that the public did not understand the problems facing educators or appreciate what they took to be the real accomplishments of public education. As one teacher told us:

> I don't think the average person knows what a teacher does. If I brought someone in [to the classroom and he] knew the content [of the course], he would still have a tough time physically and mentally doing the job.... Teaching is a physical and mental strain. It's exhausting.

Many teachers claimed that the public holds unrealistic expectations for education:

> Parents are demanding too much.... The whole society is demanding too much from the classroom teacher. We're not gods. We can't take a child that hasn't got it between the ears, a child that was born with poor genes, and make [him or her] pass a literacy test. We can't do that.

Teachers felt the growing pressure of accountability. Though their after-inflation income was declining, many teachers became convinced that the public and government officials were uninterested in the economic plight of teachers or in improving the quality of their work lives. "Let's face it," said one discouraged high school teacher.

> We're not paid what we deserve to be paid. We have a lot of responsibility and [the public is] demanding too much of us. When we ask for a raise they say, "Are you kidding?" Now if we grovel for a while, they may give us a raise [but it won't make up for what we lost through inflation].... Another problem is the teacher–student ratio. Teachers have talked about it. It's been in the papers.... Everyone knows ... if you want students to progress, you've got to lower that ratio. You can't have 38 kids in an English class and do a great job teaching writing. You just can't do it. That's one ... reason for teacher burnout; we have too many students [to do our jobs well].

Teachers felt squeezed between the high expectations the public holds for education and working conditions that made it difficult, if not impossible, for teachers to accomplish what the public demands. They worried about the media's willingness to highlight teacher inadequacies and the unwillingness to dwell on such teacher problems as low pay, poor working conditions, ineffective administrators, and the problematic home life of many students. One high school teacher said angrily during an interview:

> [The public is] demanding too much of teachers and not giving enough. . . . In the newspapers and all, we've lost a lot of respect. They blame the teachers because students don't do well on tests. We're getting the blame when a lot of the blame should be placed on the home. There needs to be a lot more demanded of the home and less demanded of teachers. Give us [fewer] students and then see what we can do. . . . Pay us as professionals and let administrators treat us as professionals and then see what we can do.

A National Education Association survey in 1981 asked teachers to indicate the factors and forces that have had a negative effect on their job satisfaction. Well over 50% of teachers surveyed indicated that the public's attitudes regarding schools, the treatment of education by the media, students' attitudes toward learning, low salaries, and the declining status of teachers have had a negative effect on teacher job satisfaction and professional morale (Dearman & Plisko, 1982).

## Lack of Recognition

Teachers complained that neither the public, the press nor their own school administrators adequately recognized their efforts and accomplishments. Direct or implied complaints were easy to come by, but compliments were not. When teachers taught a successful unit, took children camping for a week at a county park, took time to correct papers thoroughly or design imaginative lessons, or paid for supplies with their own money, the likelihood was great that these efforts would go unnoticed and unappreciated. The demand for service from teachers is infinitely elastic and will always stretch beyond whatever is supplied. In a sense then, no act a teacher may perform remains beyond the call of duty for very long. What is once offered is forever expected, and what is expected seldom merits the special attention of gratitude. Thus teachers who are already straining under the pressures of declining income and status are further burdened when their failures are advertised and their accomplishments go largely ignored. As one teacher confided:

> I think this year I suffered from what they call teacher burnout. There is very, very little recognition here. Even a dog needs to be patted on the head, but we don't get that here. It makes you question whether it's worth it.

Another teacher explained her frustration by saying that everybody needs to be "told that he or she does something well." She wished that administrators in her school would pay attention to her accomplishments and, on occasion, let her know that she was "doing a good job with these kids." She thought if she could just "hear that twice a year" it would sustain her and make her feel that her efforts were "worth it." She went on to say that no administrator had ever "been [in my class] to really see what I've done and that hurts. You try," she said, "you really try and you take your profession seriously; you don't just sit [down] on the job. But you never hear anything but complaints about your mistakes. You never hear anything that's worthwhile."

A remedial teacher reported that her husband was encouraging her to leave teaching because she was working so hard and getting so little in return.

> He sees how much teaching has devastated me over the years, and it has. A lot of these kids can break your heart. And he says I don't get much reward from teaching and I guess he's right; we certainly don't get much reward from the front office. We might get a pat on the back at a faculty meeting when the principal says, "You all have done a terrific job." But nobody comes in and says, "Thanks for stopping the riot at the basketball game"; that was something I did this year. And no one says, "Thanks for letting us know that such and such was going on." And no one says, "We think you're doing a terrific job." I don't know of anybody in this school who has ever gotten that kind of recognition.

If many teachers sensed that they lacked an appreciative public in the front office, they also felt that administrators did not fully appreciate the problems teachers faced and were unwilling to help or even listen to teachers who were having trouble. "My general complaint," said one teacher,

> is how quickly administrators forget what it's actually like to be working in a classroom. They forget some of the problems and frustrating times that you go through. They forget that you need some support and understanding and it's very seldom ... that you have someone [in the front office] who's genuinely interested and willing to to lend an ear and listen to your problems.

## White-Collar Blues

Teachers come to their work with aspirations for vertical mobility, but find little opportunity for advancement in their chosen profession. They come with the hope that they will earn an adequate income, but they find that their salaries are eroded by inflation and that the pay of many blue-collar workers equals or exceeds their own. They come with the expectation that white-collar work will afford them respectably high status in their community, but find that their prestige is damaged by the media reports of poor schools and unqualified teachers and by the declining public confidence in education. They come wanting to contribute to the learning and development of the young, but find that their efforts are unappreciated by administrators and largely ignored by the parents of the children they serve.

Not every one of the preceding perceptions was experienced by all teachers, nor were they perceived by all teachers with the same intensity. Teachers whose spouses earned a substantial salary were not as likely to be as distressed by low pay as, for example, teachers who, in 1981, were supporting a family on $16,500 a year. Females married to high-status professionals were less likely to feel the threat of status panic as deeply as teachers who were the sole support of their families. Teachers at some schools (the Middle School, in particular) found their administrators to be appreciative and helpful, whereas teachers at other schools felt ignored and at times harassed by the administration.

The point we are making in this chapter is *not* that all teachers are unhappy in their work. As we shall show in Chapter 4, many teachers find great satisfaction in what they do, feel that their work is vital and that they do it well, and would not consider leaving the classroom. We spell out the negative aspects of teaching because teachers mentioned them so often as ubiquitous and powerful impediments to job satisfaction. Some teachers, by dint of effort and/or accident of circumstance, are able to overcome these impediments and derive satisfaction from teaching. But for most teachers we observed and interviewed, the story of their careers was not one of simply overcoming or being defeated by the impediments just discussed. It was instead a tale of struggle—a battle to ignore problems they could not solve, to concentrate on attainable achievements, and to stave off disappointments and attendant sadness. It was a battle to convince and continually reconvince themselves that, in the final accounting, the good outweighed the bad and teaching was "worth it."

We want to emphasize that the problems discussed so far, and others to be discussed, confront all teachers. They are "social facts" that will not be wished away (Durkheim, 1966). Teachers do not simply choose to be satisfied on the job. They become satisfied only to the degree that they are able to deal with and successfully overcome the problems endemic to white-collar workers generally and to their own profession in particular. As our argument is developed in later chapters, we shall see that teachers can be assisted in overcoming the impediments to satisfaction—by attentive administrators, cooperative colleagues, effective teaching strategies, clear, schoolwide goals, schoolwide discipline policies, and an organizational structure that promotes professional interaction and shared decision making. But with or without such assistance, all teachers are faced with the problems endemic to their profession. Such problems make up the common cultural core of the teaching profession, and researchers or critics who ignore these problems ignore a significant portion of the teachers' real world. National Education Association data that show a steady rise in the number of teachers having second thoughts about their chosen profession (NEA, 1982) indicate the degree to which teacher dissatisfaction is no longer simply a personal trouble; it is a social issue that must be addressed if we hope to significantly improve American education. It is notable that roughly half of the teachers surveyed in a Gallup poll would prefer that their daughters not become teachers and only 31% would like to see their sons enter the profession (Gallup, 1985, p. 323).

The problems teachers face threaten their professional self-esteem and, for many, diminish their commitment to teaching. Increasingly, teachers appear to fit Vanfossen's (1979) melancholy description of low-level, white-collar employees. These workers, Vanfossen asserts,

> perform necessary work . . . and are essential to the running of bureaucracies. But they lack decision-making power and autonomy. Their jobs are relatively secure, but dead-end. Their incomes are sufficient, but minimal. They have to be gregarious and sociable to please both bosses and clients, yet they receive little recognition for their placating functions. They teach their children to get along with others and to get an education, for it is in these two ways that they themselves have moved away from their blue-collar origins. Their levels of self-esteem are higher than in the blue-collar stratum, yet they are prone to a chronic dissatisfaction with their jobs, their incomes, and life in general. They neither prosper nor perish. They truly are the epitome of the middle class. (p. 324)

## PROBLEMS ENDEMIC TO THE TEACHING PROFESSION

Up to this point we have been discussing problems that teachers share with many other white-collar workers. We now turn to a set of issues that are unique to teaching or, more accurately, to that broader strata of public service workers who, in the course of their jobs, interact directly with the public. Lipsky (1980), who studied this group in detail, gave them the unflattering and cumbersome title "street-level bureaucrats." Street-level bureaucrats work for the schools, the police, the welfare departments, the lower courts and the legal services offices, exercising, within narrow domains, a great deal of discretionary power "over the dispensation of benefits or the allocation of public sanctions" (p. xi).

### Uncertainty

"Street-level bureaucrats," wrote Lipsky (1980), "work with a relatively high degree of uncertainty because of the complexity of the subject matter (people) and the frequency or rapidity with which decisions have to be made" (p. 29). And so it is with teachers, who must make literally hundreds of decisions in the course of a day. These decisions often must be made without adequate knowledge or a shared technical culture (Dreeben, 1970; Lortie, 1975). The absence of professionally sanctioned goals and scientifically verified teaching techniques leaves every teacher free to make his or her own classroom decisions and ultimately to calculate his or her own professional competence. Although this allows educators some degree of autonomy within the classroom, it also leaves them vulnerable to self-doubt and arbitrary criticism from their many publics—students, parents, other teachers, administrators and, in extreme cases, the courts. Teaching provides few day-to-day (or year-to-year) assurances that a teacher's decisions have been wise and effective; that students are making progress academically, socially, or psychologically, or that the progress students are making is the result of the teacher's action and not the home environment, the work of other teachers, or the student's own maturation and native ability.

Lortie (1975) has written that "education is a tenuous, uncertain affair. It is necessary to keep such uncertainty in mind if we are to understand the psychic world of classroom teachers, for uncertainty is the lot of those who teach" (p. 133). To question teachers about their doubts unleashes "a torrent of feeling and frustration" (Lortie, p. 144). Some excerpts from our interviews confirm Lortie's point:

> It's not that [basic skills] students are bad. They are not discipline problems. But I feel ... they are not interested in coming to school, and I am not doing a good job of teaching them. I have not interested them to the point where they want to learn. I really feel like the class has been a waste.

> I gave a test at the end of the school year [that] reviewed material we had gone over since the fall. Most of my students didn't do very well. I felt as if [I were running] a diploma factory.

> For a while I thought I'd quit teaching. I just felt kind of useless because I was going through long periods of time thinking that I wasn't doing any good for anybody.

> With my brightest kids, the door is open and they can go to college. But with that middle group I have to ask, "What the hell am I teaching for?" They're not smart enough to go to college, and because of their color and their rural background, they're not going to get good jobs. So what the hell are they in school for?

> Sometimes I [worry] about whether I'm getting the point across. Maybe I should have presented [the material] another way. Are the kids listening? Do they care about this material as much as I do?

> I don't know that what I'm teaching will make any difference. It doesn't do my students a whole lot of good. It makes me sad to see some of my students leave, and I think: "Oh, boy, what's going to happen to you?" I ... feel they need some basics. But I wish I had something else to offer them.

> I don't think I've done a great deal of good. When they had to take a test [at the end of the year] they didn't do much better than they did at the beginning. That was when it really hit me. I tried to give a review assignment that would get them ready for the semester test. But they acted as if they had never seen the material before. And I just sat there and thought, "There has got to be a better way to teach."

Another teacher worried that she had lost the knack of teaching and that other teachers in her school were losing it as well.

I've been fairly successful up until the past two years. But these last few years have been frustrating. It bothers me that a lot of teachers come in to school and after a short while are just as jaded as the rest of us. You'd think that their enthusiasm would stick at least for two or three years. But it doesn't. That's not the way it was when I started teaching. I had six or seven years when I was involved in all kinds of activities. I had my greatest fun in working with kids after school. But now things are just the opposite. I get as far away from school as I can. It's totally different now. It's very sad to me.

Teachers come to their work with a commitment to public service (they want to help young people and serve society), and with high achievement aspirations (they hope to reach and teach all of their students) (NEA, 1982). Many teachers will fall short, often far short, of their own ideal conceptions of teaching, because the very nature of their work prevents them from achieving such lofty goals. As Lipsky (1980) explained, "Large classes or huge case loads and inadequate resources combined with uncertainties of method and the unpredictability of clients defeat [the] aspirations [of street-level bureaucrats]" (p. xii). Sooner or later, as Sizer (1984) has pointed out, all teachers must compromise. The compromise usually entails lowering one's sights and adjusting one's attitudes regarding student educability. In this way, teachers are able to maintain a sense of modest accomplishment in an environment where achievements are hard won and frustrations abound. A teacher's sense of personal teaching efficacy may decline with classroom experience, but it is likely to remain intact long after he or she has given up on the notion that all students are educable and deserve to be taught.

No teachers we talked with indicated that they had failed in their chosen profession. As we have seen, most admitted to teaching a lesson badly on occasion, planning a poor unit, and/or having difficulty with certain students. A few even said they had taught English or mathematics for a full year without noticeably lessening the ignorance of their pupils. But, even after such revelations, no respondent labeled himself or herself a "poor teacher." On the contrary, as the following excerpts from interviews indicate, teachers had a ready arsenal of assertions, anecdotes, and attributes they could draw on to affirm their professional competence:

I can relate to the kids, and most of the time I get across what I want to get across. [Of course] with my basic skills classes . . . even the smallest break-through is terrific.

I think I'm bright, and I think students pick up on that. I think I'm pretty good at . . . helping them get what I want them to get.

[It is rewarding] to see students graduate . . . get married, and get a job. The other day I was walking down the street and a girl came up to me and I didn't even recognize her. She had completed four years of [college] and was getting a job starting at $17,500. [That] makes me feel good.

I know one thing [that indicates I'm a good teacher]: I'm not scared. . . . I think I've accomplished a lot, and I think the students have learned a lot.

Maybe someone else could have succeeded [with my worst class this year], but I feel I haven't. [On the other hand] I think I did a better job than a lot of teachers would have done. I can name three teachers right here at this school who have gone home crying at the end of the day.

I care about my students. I don't feel that I'm going to work when I get up in the morning [and start off for school]. That's the truth. I swear to the Lord above. Now I get frustrated. I experience burnout from time to time, but I enjoy teaching. I was raised in a family of teachers. I guess I have teaching in my blood. And I have a lot of positive feedback.... People have told me that I'm a good teacher. I think I'm better than the average teacher. I really don't doubt my abilities very often. I do get discouraged on occasion.

The above comments of accomplishment and pride are similar to others teachers made during the course of our interviews. Although teachers in this study were bothered by such issues as poor pay and declining status, most reported that they found satisfaction in their work with students. However, such accomplishments often were hard to come by and difficult to document. Thus, even in these mildly self-congratulatory statements, one finds hints of uncertainty and evidence of the fragile nature of teacher satisfaction. In a compensatory education class, for example, the first teacher quoted above learned to be satisfied with even the most modest breakthrough.

We are not arguing against the claims of these teachers. Having observed in their classrooms, we are generally impressed by their diligence. Nevertheless, it is worth noting, as Jackson (1968) has done before us, that teachers do "not often turn to objective measures of school achievement for evidence of [their] effectiveness and as a source of professional satisfaction" (p. 126). The uncertain nature of their work encourages teachers to settle for softer, more subjective signs of success. Although mere assertions of competence are never strong enough to totally extinguish doubt, generally they are powerful enough to prevent teachers from directly confronting the realities of their own limitations or those of the teaching situation.

## Teacher Isolation

We might expect that the common problems teachers face would promote unity and cooperation in their ranks. We did not find that to be the case. In most of the schools we studied there was little evidence that teachers worked collectively to assuage one another's doubts or to bolster their flagging self-esteem. Instead, we found that teachers generally were isolated from those with whom they worked, and received little assistance or recognition from colleagues. One teacher explained that she and her fellow teachers were working "in their own little world[s]. Everybody is doing their own thing and nobody is helping anybody else." As a consequence, she contended, the school had become atomized and the educational enterprise hopelessly segmented. "Nobody is working [with other teachers] to make this a whole school. I don't think the school can be effective that way. We're all in the same boat together, and it's sinking."

Another teacher said he was troubled by his professional isolation and the insularity of his work. "I wish I had the opportunity to go around to other classes. I want to observe other teachers," he said, because he was sure he could learn from his peers. A high school English teacher lamented that teachers "don't help each other out." A colleague complained, more in resignation than in anger, that she had never

> gotten a lot of support from people [in her school]. You ask them to ... help you do something and they say, "I really don't have the time." They leave at 3:15 or 3:30 instead of a quarter to four. They go home and they don't take anything with them. They won't help anybody do anything.

Lipsky (1980) contended that street-level bureaucrats "work in isolation" and maintain norms of noninterference that "usually inhibit professionals from seeking guidance [from colleagues] in solving problems or providing services to clients, since to ask for help would be to admit to a degree of incapacity" (p. 203). How like Lipsky's insight is the following explanation for why teachers at one school do not cooperate:

> We have the chance but we don't do it. I don't know why that is. I ... think it would embarrass us if we hadn't thought of an idea ourselves and had to get it from another teacher.

Another teacher made the same point but added that she badly needed help:

> Anybody's input would [have been] a help. If they would just share some of the things they have tried. But you know teachers get hold of an idea and instead of sharing it, they hoard it. A lot of teachers are that way. They get some material and hoard it and won't let you see it. But I need some ideas and materials. I'm dying for information.

Teacher isolation and its attendant ideology of noninterference discourage teachers from offering help to colleagues even when they clearly need it (McPherson, 1972). A high school department chairman explained, "When teachers are having trouble, the rest of us generally ignore it. You can't come in ... and tell teachers what they should be doing. I mean you can't. You can't do it as a co-worker."

Not all teachers were bothered by their isolation from other teachers. One teacher said that her school offered no orientation sessions for new personnel. She had been teaching at the school for 5 months before she learned there was a modest instructional resource center in the school library. "After the new year, I learned that I could go down and get materials [from the library] instead of spending hours every night developing my own." We asked why her fellow teachers had not let her know about the materials and she shrugged and commented that at her school, "It's each man for himself."

The teacher quoted here was inconvenienced by isolation, but she was not opposed to it. "I'd rather stay on my own," she explained, "[because] I'm not the type of person who is cliquish." She assured the interviewer that she felt more comfortable being left to her own devices, even though it meant living with the fact that "nobody cared enough" to help her out. She felt there was greater safety behind her closed classroom door than there was likely to be in the more open, conflict-filled, and potentially judgmental world of cooperation. Another teacher said she was not bothered by "the loneliness of teaching" because, as she put it, "I'm basically a loner anyway. Maybe that helps."

A high school teacher was asked if he ever talked to his peers about common problems and concerns. "No," he answered, "because I never felt the need to do that. When I leave [the classroom], I leave my problems and try to settle them when I get back." Sharing problems, for him, was a sign of uncertainty, and he assured us that he was "not a wishy-washy person." He went on to say that he never saw his colleagues socially because "It's usually been my policy that my social life and my school life are two different things. [They are] geared differently."

Teacher insularity was so deeply taken for granted in one school that the administration neglected to introduce new faculty to other teachers. We asked a teacher who had been working at the school for over a year how her colleagues would describe her if they were being honest. She could not answer the question because, as she explained, "The majority of faculty don't know I'm here. The principal never introduced me. I don't even know the names of the teachers here." When we asked the same question of another teacher, she replied:

> I don't know. I don't know. [At my last school] I was very, very popular with the faculty and fairly popular with the students.... But here, I don't know.... I don't think they know whether I'm here or not.

If teacher isolation has its drawbacks, it also has its functions. On the psychological level, insularity functions to protect the professional image of individual teachers by placing a buffer between them and the criticisms they fear they might receive if others saw them at work. Isolation lessens the possibility that conflicts will develop among the faculty. For example, one teacher said that she was glad that she did not have to socialize with other teachers because isolation allowed her to avoid "the gossip and problems that teachers [who interact] probably ... have with each other. I'm sure there are personality conflicts, but I don't know about them because I'm not in on it."

The organizational function of insularity is to decrease institutional disruption when teachers are absent, resign, transfer to another school, or take a leave of absence. If teachers are self-sufficient and work independently, no teacher or group of teachers will ever become indispensable to the smooth operation of the school. Each teacher becomes a unit unto himself or herself and all units are functionally independent and, within specialties, interchangeable. The damage inflicted by all but the most grossly incompetent teachers is suffered by students but does not have an immediate or obvious impact on the day-to-day operation of the school. Thus a school can run smoothly even though it has a number of poor teachers on its staff.

## TEACHER ALIENATION

### Powerlessness

Sociologists have conceived *powerlessness* as a form of alienation caused by an individual's or group's perceived inability to affect the outcome of sociopolitical events (Levin, 1960). Within the sociology of work, however, powerlessness has a more restricted application. Shepard (1971) describes this form of alienation as "the perceived lack of freedom and control on the job" (pp. 13–14).

Teachers, like other street-level bureaucrats, enjoy a degree of autonomy in their work with clients. Though teacher autonomy is being restricted by the devices of accountability (competency testing, standardized behavioral objectives, legislated learning, and much more) (Wirth, 1983), many teachers believe they still have a good deal of freedom and control within their own classrooms. On matters outside the classrooms, however—issues of school policy, school board decisions, and state regulations—the teachers reported growing feelings of powerlessness. Not only were they unable to influence decisions in these areas, the decisions made by others were intruding on their small domain of freedom and control, the classroom. In the teachers' view, their work was being made unnecessarily difficult and their effectiveness was being severely undermined.

We found powerlessness to be a reoccurring theme in our talks with teachers. Most, even those who enjoyed good relationships with their school administrators, reported that they felt unable to influence decisions that would have an impact on the school and their classroom. As one experienced teacher said, "I haven't ever been involved in a school where I had much say-so." Another teacher suggested that administrators make poor decisions because

> there is too much of a separation between the administration and ... classroom teacher. [Administrators lack] actual feelings for [and an] understanding of what goes on in the classroom.

The interviewer probed for further information by rephrasing what the teacher had said: "So you have the impression that administrators at this school don't know what's going on in the classroom?" The teacher responded quickly, "Yes. Sometimes I have the feeling they don't care either."

Some teachers expressed frustration over their inability to influence the decision-making process. They complained that administrators didn't consult them or, worse, merely went through the motions of consultation. One teacher said, "We are sometimes consulted, but it never seems to matter." Another said:

> We talk [with administrators] to a certain extent, but I don't know that anybody listens. You tell your department head and he passes it on to the principal, but it doesn't help. The administration starts planning and they don't think about your problems. They have problems of their own.

Teachers in most schools reported that the administration treated them disrespectfully. They considered themselves to be professionals and were offended when they were treated like bureaucratic functionaries or naughty children. For example, on a teacher work day after students had been dismissed for summer vacation, the faculty at one school were grading exams, turning in grades, and straightening up their classrooms. Frequently during the day the principal used the public address system to remind his staff that "no one was to leave the school" until grades had been turned in and an administrator had checked the classrooms for cleanliness. Teachers were warned that a vice principal would come to each room and check everything, including the desk drawers and file cabinets, to make sure they were cleaned out. A teacher turned to a member of the research team and said in exasperation:

> I've taught at a lot of schools, and nobody has ever looked into my desk drawers, never! I feel it's rather an intrusion. They're saying I'm not professional. The biggest [problem at this school] is that we're being treated unprofessionally. We're talked down to. We're asked our opinion, but we know that it isn't going to make any difference. We all get talked down to at faculty meetings. If a teacher has done something wrong, then [the administration] should tell him. But the whole faculty shouldn't have to be lectured to.

Just as not all teachers were cognizant of or disturbed by their isolation from peers, not all teachers were conscious of, or apparently offended by, poor treatment from administrators. For example, a member of the research team was in the classroom of an English and art teacher (again at the end of the year, but at another school), when the principal entered and the following conversation ensued:

PRINCIPAL: You know I won't check you out until the art room is clean. (The principal turns to leave.)

TEACHER: But wait, wait, wait. I still have some art materials to store in there. I put some stuff in there yesterday. When I did, Horace said. . . .

PRINCIPAL: (Interrupts, speaking forcefully) Horace don't [sic] know how to to clean out stuff. He's not responsible—I am.

TEACHER: But he's my boss.... (Horace is the Department Chairman.)

PRINCIPAL: (Interrupting) No, I'm your boss, sweetie.

TEACHER: But I asked Horace, "Can I just leave this stuff [art materials] here [in the art room]?" He said, "Yes, you just leave it here."

PRINCIPAL: No. The answer to that question is no. Wait 'til I hit his office.

TEACHER: Well, he's not here [this afternoon].

PRINCIPAL: If he wants his paycheck, he'll have to get checked out. If I don't check him out, he doesn't get his paycheck. If he wants to wait until the end of the summer, that's fine. I'm just saying the room has to be cleaned out, and that is his responsibility.

TEACHER: But he's not here. If you can give me the key, I'll take some stuff up there after I've finished my grades. What should I do, put all that stuff in a box?

PRINCIPAL: (Angrily) I don't want you to leave that stuff in the front room.

TEACHER: Oh, I thought you were talking about the art room.

PRINCIPAL: No, that's fine as long as it's locked up. But the front room is your responsibility. You use it all the time, and it's filthy. Clean it up. You and Horace both.

TEACHER: (Relieved) Oh, you mean the room that has all those boxes?

PRINCIPAL: Boxes and art material and all that other stuff that needs to be put away in the back.

TEACHER: Well, if Horace isn't here [soon] I'm just going to throw it away.

PRINCIPAL: Don't throw it away. Give it to Reggie and let her lock it up for next year.

TEACHER: Okay, I can handle that. Where are you going to be?

PRINCIPAL: I'll be around.

TEACHER: But I have to get into the room to put away the art material.

PRINCIPAL: I'll be around. (The principal exits.)

Powerlessness is a *state of affairs*, a description of an existential reality. One has the power, or some power, to influence a class of events, or one does not. However, powerlessness is also a *status*. To say that someone is powerless is to suggest a lot about his or her position in a group and the value of the individual's task and talents to the institution. Within a hierarchically arranged organization, those who have power are treated differently from those who lack it. Power status, of course, ultimately affects how individuals define themselves, the organization, and their roles within it. Thus, powerlessness and powerfulness seep into one's consciousness and become *states of mind*, and eventually states of being.

When teachers described powerlessness in the school, they were describing multiple levels of an alienated reality. First, as we have seen, they described their inability to affect administrative decisions they said diminished the quality of their work and work lives. Second, they discussed how powerlessness was frustrating and occasionally humiliating. Their lack of power invited some administrators to "talk down to them" and to deny them the assumption of competence in the simplest of matters, such as turning in grades. Further, teachers were not only asked to do janitorial work, perhaps demeaning in itself, but their orders were delivered rudely, publicly (over the PA system and in front of school visitors), and with intimidating threats ("if you don't pass inspection, you don't get paid"). We turn now to the third level of alienation, powerlessness as a state of mind.

## Conformity and Self-Estrangement

Fromm (1963) suggested that when individuals doubt their professional competence, social status, and self-worth, an available haven from anxiety is found in what we are calling *the mentality of powerlessness*, and what he called *conformity to authority*. The art/English teacher quoted above was not affronted by the condescension of her principal; she merely wanted to understand the lines of authority and clarify what was expected of her. Insofar as isolation sets teachers adrift to deal with their own status insecurities and competence worries, it will (if Fromm is correct) promote an urge to conform to prevailing norms and to avoid questioning the assumptions on which those norms are based. Such teachers will seek security in an acceptance of the status quo. As one teacher said, describing himself as well as others, "I guess some feel that they should not rock the boat; they should just go along with things and forget about it."

As we have seen, many teachers were bothered by their inability to influence administrative decisions, but others accepted their powerlessness with adaptive resignation. For them, the acceptance of the status quo is so complete that they give little or no thought to the possibility of change. They have reified what they call "the system" and do not see it in their power (individually or collectively) to change it. Reified systems, by definition, as Gehlen (1980) has pointed out, "resist criticism and are immune to objections" (p. 145). Within reified systems all criticisms ultimately become self-criticisms or criticism of others, but seldom criticism of the system itself. Considerations of change are difficult to achieve. For example, a teacher who had spoken of low morale at his school was asked what might be done to improve the situation. He paused, shook his head, and answered, "I can't think of anything. These questions are hard to answer. They are things you don't think about very often."

When we asked the same question of another teacher, she replied, "I'd rather not get into that. I just won't get into that." Another teacher commented, "I don't feel like I'm part of a team. I feel decisions are being made someplace else." When we asked if this state of affairs was bothersome, the teacher replied:

> I guess I never thought about a question like that before. I'm sure that if there were a way I could better the program, I think I would be listened to. But as it stands now, I'm just kinda doing what I'm told to do.

When individuals accept (or are forced to accept) their own powerlessness, something vital is drained from the workers and the workplace. The institution has lost the creativity, vigor, and commitment of its members, and employees lose personal agency and become estranged from their work and themselves. Our discussions with teachers have convinced us that, for many, the conditions of their employment discourage professional involvement with their peers. Such conditions engender feelings of uncertainty, status panic, and self-protection through isolation, and create a mentality of powerlessness that sociologists refer to as *self-estrangement*. According to Blauner (1964), "When an individual lacks control over the work process and a sense of purposeful connection to the work enterprise, he may experience a kind of depersonalized detachment rather than an immediate involvement ... in the job tasks" (p. 26).

A sizable minority of the teachers we spoke with claimed that teaching was not fulfilling their needs nor tapping their potentials. One teacher said that she had been born too soon:

> If I were today's woman, I wouldn't be sitting here right now, and I'm not sure I'll be sitting here two or three years from now. I don't remember ever making a conscious decision to be a teacher. Never. I was a history major, and ... I was going to either go to law school or get a Ph.D. in history. I just picked up those education courses to have that teaching certificate. I never intended to end up here.

Another teacher said that if she had it to do over again she would not become a teacher because "I have capacities that I haven't tapped, that can't be tapped in teaching."

For these teachers and many more like them, teaching provides only a weak sense of accomplishment and satisfaction. Such teachers are estranged from their work. They feel they have given up an essential part of themselves to pursue a profession that provides scant recognition, social status, remuneration, or personal satisfaction. They do not realize themselves in their work and are haunted by the knowledge that they have not become all that they hoped to be. They reside in an occupational identity of powerlessness that further threatens their already beleaguered self-esteem. Blauner (1964) discussed the connection between lack of job satisfaction and self-identity:

> Self-estranging work compounds and intensifies [the] problem of a negative occupational identity. When work provides opportunities for control, creativity and challenge—when, in a word, it is self-expressive and enhances an individual's unique potentialities—then it contributes to the worker's sense of self-respect and dignity and at least partially overcomes the stigma of low status. Alienated work—without control, freedom, or responsibility—on the other hand simply confirms and deepens the feeling that societal estimates of low status and little worth are valid. (p. 31)

## CONCLUSION

Like most white-collar Americans, teachers desire success but have difficulty finding tangible signs of accomplishment. They work long hours, sometimes facing more than 150 students a day. The plan lessons, teach classes, counsel students, attend meetings, sponsor clubs, coach sports, correct papers, fill out forms, write report cards, meet with parents, decorate bulletin boards, clean their classrooms, and so much more. Yet, at the end of a day, week, or year, or at the close of a career, they have little way of gauging what they have accomplished. They are keepers of the American dream, strivers, carriers of middle-class values, but they have no tangible product to call their own. They are unsure of their accomplishments and generally are unsupported by colleagues, administrators, and members of the community. They have difficulty reconciling their aspirations with their accomplishments.

Lewis (1978) contended that most middle-class Americans are frustrated by the mismatch between actual achievements and personal expectations:

> If our quest for self-respect leads us to high aspirations, the chances are very great that in the overwhelming majority of cases there will be a considerable difference between what we think we are capable of and what it is we actually seem to be achieving. And if the maintenance of self-respect depends upon not only great expectations but great expectations realized, then such disparities are likely to pose a major threat to the self-esteem of many Americans. (p. 15)

Aspirations by themselves are relatively unproblematic. As Lewis pointed out, however, "convincing ourselves that we have indeed been successful—that our dreams have been realized and that consequently we may respect ourselves—is extremely problematic" (p. 15). The aspirations of teachers encourage them to lay claim to the "good life" and to personal achievement. But those same values make "any perceived failure ... a threat of significant psychological force to [their] self-esteem" (p. 14). Failure, or the hint of failure—in fact, anything but absolute assurance that our accomplishments have exceeded our aspirations—

threatens our self-esteem by causing us to doubt our character, our competence, or quite possibly both.... To the extent ... that our aspirations go
unrealized (whatever the reason), we are threatened and troubled by personal
guilt. Fearing that we have done less than we should, we are all too frequently
haunted by the sense that we have done ill. (p. 17)

Teachers are haunted in this way. They possess few personal or
institutional resources with which to exorcise the ubiquitous worry that
they have failed to fulfill their own middle-class success aspirations and
professional ideals. They are particularly vulnerable to the self-doubt and
the status panic that characterize so many white-collar workers.

Not all or even most teachers are estranged from their work. However,
the pressures of isolation, status panic, uncertainty, limited power, and
nonrecognition make it difficult for public school educators to avoid such
estrangement. The fact that, despite these conditions, so many teachers
find satisfactions that sustain them and remain dedicated to the students
they teach is powerful testimony to the commitment of successful teachers.
Critics who bemoan the quality of American schools too often forget the
enormity of the job we ask teachers to do and the difficult conditions under
which they are asked to work. Researchers who catalogue the behaviors of
effective teachers should consider the institutional and social conditions
that are most supportive of effective teaching techniques. The effective
school literature is a positive step in this direction.

The conditions of teaching discussed in this chapter are not merely
impediments to job satisfaction, they are also impediments to effective
instruction. Educators who suffer chronic status panic, uncertainty, and/or
estrangement are unlikely to muster the energy, innovation, and enthusiasm necessary to sustain a successful program of instruction for reluctant
learners. They are likely instead to "make do," that is, to select self-
protective practices that maximize the appearance of achievement and
minimize potential threats to their professional self-esteem. This goal shift,
from education to survival, is often accompanied by other attitudinal
transformations. Make-do teachers, who see that that their students are
not learning, are likely, as Lipsky (1980) has put it, "to seek and find the
explanation someplace other than in their own inadequacy" (p. 82). As we
have seen, the mentality of powerlessness will discourage teachers from
locating the problem within the school system. They are, therefore, likely
to blame poor student achievement solely on the students themselves or on
their home background. In the next chapter we'll discuss the efficacy belief
systems teachers hold and the classroom environments in which those
systems flourish.

# 3

## Teacher Efficacy Attitudes, Classroom Behavior, and Maintaining Professional Self-Esteem

### INTRODUCTION

Three days before Linda's graduation from the College of Education, she sat in her adviser's office. She was proud of her accomplishments and talked eagerly about the teaching career she would begin. Linda exuded the idealism typical of college students in the early 1970s but, through an appealing combination of naiveté and enthusiasm for life, she managed to avoid the self-absorbed dogmatism that afflicted many of her peers. She was already referring to herself as "a teacher" and spoke of the children she would meet in the fall as "my students." She had always wanted to be a teacher but only recently had become fully conscious of what had drawn her to a career in education. The classroom would provide a small arena in which she planned to work on what she called "the real problems": ignorance, prejudice, and poverty. Education, she claimed, could be an instrument of individual development and social reform. Yet, she was mature enough to recognize that her reasons for teaching were not wholly social and altruistic. She liked children and sensed that she would be happy only if she remained in close contact with the young. Few things brought her more joy, she said, than getting to know children well, helping them learn, and watching them tackle new challenges. Teaching offered her satisfaction and would allow her to continue her own development. An "ordinary, dull, routine job" would not help her to keep "learning and growing" and that was important to her because, she said, "I have not yet become all I plan to be."

Linda had done well in the college and had good reason to be proud of her accomplishments. Her grades were above average, recommendations strong, test scores more than presentable, and she had been offered the first two jobs for which she had interviewed. The professor who supervised her student teaching wrote in his final evaluation, "I believe, and the school teachers with whom she has worked all agree, that Linda is already a good teacher and, with experience, will become an outstanding educator."

Six years later, after observing in her class for three weeks, the Efficacy Project research team pondered the obvious discrepancy between the teacher we were seeing and the one Linda's professors, cooperating teachers, and indeed Linda herself had expected she would become. As a student, Linda was full of vitality and fueled by sense of purpose and personal efficacy. The teacher we observed had none of these characteristics. She went through her days mechanically and no longer spoke of social problems or individual development as motivating her work. Linda appeared unaware that her teaching had become just the kind of monotonous activity she had once been determined to avoid. Her classroom was drab, without decorations or examples of students' work. Visitors could not easily tell what subject was taught in her room and could see no physical evidence that those who worked within its walls shared a common commitment to their daily activities.

The relationship Linda had with students was subdued. Although she appeared to like the children in her classes and they, in turn, liked her, Linda had grown wary of those she taught and had learned to keep some emotional distance between herself and her pupils. Some, she explained, would take advantage of a friendship if they could, while others would "trash" a teacher emotionally if they were allowed to "unload their troubles." Linda had learned from 6 years of teaching how to stay close enough to her class to avoid conflicts and maintain order yet distant enough to remain emotionally safe.

Linda's teaching was unimaginative and field notes taken in her classroom would remind us later of Goodlad's (1984) description of classes where lessons were constrained, constraining, and monotonous (pp. 109 & 113). We were struck by the docility of her students and the routinized nature of their daily activities. Except for watching an occasional movie (often unrelated to the material under study), students did the same things every day; they plowed through a virtual avalanche of dittoed worksheets. "I have individualized instruction in here," said Linda the first day we visited her class. "You just have to with these students." Individualized instruction for Linda meant simply that her pupils did the same work, but completed it at their own pace. She monitored the class from her desk and was available to answer any questions students might bring to her. Seatwork was corrected, sometimes by Linda and often by the students themselves, but mistakes were never diagnosed and remediation seldom undertaken. No homework was assigned because, she explained, "these students just won't do it."

Linda's system of individualized instruction had its problems. The work students did each day was uninteresting, unrelenting, and unrewarding. To complete one's work was the occasion not for recognition, evaluation, praise, or even rest, but for the assignment of yet another thick packet of dittoed sheets. If there was an instructional sequence connecting one page of work to another, or one packet of worksheets to the next, Linda was unable to describe it convincingly and we could not discern it from studying the materials themselves. She liked her system, however, because it kept low-achieving students busy, minimized their frustrations, provided little opportunities for classroom conflict, and freed her from having to spend evenings and weekends planning lessons and correcting papers. After 6 years of teaching, Linda was just beginning to feel that she was in control of her class and of her own time.

The teacher we are calling Linda does not exist, at least not as a single person, and is the only fictitious individual we refer to in these pages. However, Linda has a powerful reality for us because she is a composite character who represents the activities, experiences, attitudes, and frustrations of many of the teachers with low sense of efficacy whom we observed working with low-achieving students. The events we describe all happened and the sentiments expressed are all real, but they are drawn from the activities and comments of a large group of teachers rather than from those of a single individual. Linda represents for us the discrepancy between the exciting potential so many basic skills teachers possessed and the less-exciting realities we observed in their classes.

What accounts for the fact that so many underachieving teachers work with low-level students? One reason is that principals in most of the schools we studied assigned first year teachers or veterans with the least academic and instructional skill to the lowest level classes in the school. Underachieving teachers were less visible in these classes and the parents of low-achieving children were unlikely to recognize, or effectively complain about, the poor teaching their children were receiving. Although the practice of assigning low-achieving classes to low-achieving teachers occurred at many schools, it did not involve more than one or two teachers at any particular school and, consequently, does not provide a full answer to the question just posed. A better answer is provided by Sizer (1984) in his book *Horace's Compromise*. Teaching low-achieving students is difficult and frustrating at best. It becomes nearly impossible when teachers continually are forced to compromise: to lower their goals, their expectations for students, their commitment to the educational system and the profession and, in the end, even their awareness that the system miseducates its least advantaged students.

Like Sizer's fictitious teacher Horace, Linda was forced to compromise. But to say that Linda, Horace, and all the teachers they represent, have made accommodations to the educational system is only to tell half the story, for compromises have consequences. The other half of the tale lies in the effects those compromises have on the attitudes, classroom behavior, and professional self-esteem of the teachers who make them and ultimately, of course, in their effect on students. These issues are the subject of this chapter.

In her first year of teaching Linda was assigned six classes of low-achieving students. She faced 134 students a day and, in the beginning, tackled her assignment eagerly. After her first month in the classroom, however, she began to appreciate the enormity of her mission and it slowly dawned on her that she was not going to accomplish all she had set out to do. Her students needed, indeed demanded, constant attention. They had learned well how to fail, but few had learned to succeed, and many lacked even rudimentary academic skills. Most suffered from a tangled combination of problems—undisciplined behavior, "bad attitudes," "lack of academic motivation," ill health, learning disorders, emotional troubles, the habit of school failure, low reading comprehension, single-parent homes, and poverty. Linda discovered that just keeping the lid on her classes required all of her attention and ingenuity. When she began teaching she had wanted to "get through" to even her most troubled students—to salve the wounded and heal the hurt, to help all her pupils work hard, trust their own abilities, and like themselves. In the end she settled for much less.

Horace and Linda both compromised with, and, to varying degrees, were compromised by the educational system. Sizer tells us that Horace understood the concessions he made, and, though distressed by the realities he confronted each day, he remained fundamentally unchanged by them. He recognized that the "gap between what would be nice and what is possible" was, in fact, a chasm that would not be vaulted (Sizer, 1984, p. 20). Nevertheless, he knew that the chasm should be vaulted and could be if only things were different.

Linda's compromises were more severe. She not only settled for less than Horace, she was less conscious of and less bothered by her concessions. No single compromise was large enough to stir her to anger or action, but when added together over time, her concessions were nearly total. Unless pressed by a researcher's impertinent questions, Linda would not talk of the past or future but focused instead on the present and what she took to be her most impressive accomplishments. She considered herself an excellent teacher, a "survivor." Unlike some who had quit teaching, Linda held on. Unlike colleagues who could not control their classes, Linda ran an orderly and quiet room. She seldom got angry at students and, though they occasionally tried her patience, they could no longer "trash me emotionally." Although some teachers in the school could not keep students in their seats, Linda managed to keep her pupils quiet and seemingly at work. True, she was not the teacher she set out to become, but she did not dwell on her past hopes because teaching had changed her and she had learned to lower her sights and to take pride in more modest accomplishments. Horace's tragedy lies in the objectives he held but could not achieve; Linda's is found in the goals she abandoned. Horace was angry, Linda merely resigned. Horace recognized sham and detested it, Linda contributed, albeit unconsciously, to the educational brummagem. Horace strove to achieve, Linda settled for the appearance of achievement. Horace was sure that his students could learn and become productive citizens, Linda was uncertain.

The tale of Horace and Linda, and the educators we are letting these fictitious characters represent, is not simply a story of good and bad, or successful and unsuccessful teachers. It is instead a tale of the quite different ways that two teachers adjusted to the realities of their profession. Horace and Linda do not represent all the options open to teachers, but our findings suggest that they do represent two of the most common kinds of compromises teachers make.

In this chapter we look not solely at the compromises made by individual teachers, but at the likely consequences of such accommodations on the motivation and behavior of teachers in general. Our aim is to look beneath institutional structures, administrative policies, questionnaire responses, and teachers' public presentations of self, and concentrate on what teachers actually do in the classroom, how they experience their work, and how they respond to those experiences. Though these issues are interrelated, we will discuss them separately and address their interconnectedness only at the end of the chapter. It should be kept in mind that we studied teachers who spent all or part of their day working with low-achieving students. Our findings are not generalizable to all teachers, or even to our own sample of teachers when they were working in different settings or in classes in which students enjoyed stronger academic credentials.

The findings reported in this chapter were drawn from 2 studies: (1) an observational ethnography conducted in 4 middle school and 4 junior high school classrooms, (2) an ethnographic interview study of 23 basic skills, high school teachers. (See Chapter 2 for a discussion of the methodology used in these studies.) The aim of both investigations was to discover the role definitions teachers held for themselves and their colleagues, the worries they expressed, the efficacy attitudes they developed, and, finally, how those worries and attitudes affected the quality of teachers' relationships with students, the discipline methods they employed, and the kind of instruction offered in their classrooms.

## THE ROLE EXPECTATIONS OF TEACHERS

We investigated the role expectations of teachers by asking, "Are there any poor teachers working in your school" and, if so, "How can you tell who they are?" Teachers' descriptions of poor teaching were vivid and detailed. We compared these descriptions with what teachers told us were the characteristics of successful teachers. What emerged from these two lines of inquiry was a remarkably consistent picture of the role expectations teachers held for themselves and one another. Though there were many components of teacher competence, most fell into one of three domains: relationships with students, classroom discipline, and instruction. In the schools we studied, teachers were considered "good teachers" by their colleagues when they accomplished the following:

1. Maintained pleasant relationships with students
   a. Cared about their students, enjoyed teaching them, and were genuinely concerned about their welfare
   b. Avoided incurring the long-term hostility or ill will of their pupils
   c. Maintained relationships with students that were neither aloof nor "unprofessionally" intimate
2. Maintained order in the classroom
   a. Had few confrontations with students
   b. Held students' attention
   c. Kept classroom noise within acceptable bounds
3. Instructed students effectively
   a. Knew the subject matter being taught
   b. Planned ahead, were well organized, and worked hard
   c. Presented lessons in a clear and interesting fashion
   d. Assigned tasks that students could and would do

It is reasonable to assume that such explicit criteria for good teaching would help educators assuage the competency uncertainties discussed in Chapter 2. If they could not always be sure that their pupils were advancing or that student advancements were the product of their own teaching skills, they could at least take solace in the fact that they were living up to the role expectations of their peers. However, we did not find that these explicit role expectations diminished teacher uncertainty. Instead we found teachers aware that their professional competence was under scrutiny and bothered by the fact that judgments were being made on the basis of fragmentary information and quick-glimpse observations. From an interview with John, a high school English teacher:

QUESTION: Do teachers make judgments about the competence of their fellow teachers?
ANSWER: Unfortunately, yes. They talk.
QUESTION: What kind of evidence do they use to make these judgments?
ANSWER: Generally what students say. Not just what one student but what a lot of students say. If something is said over and over again, we pay attention to it. We pay attention to the discipline methods used. If we walk by a class-

room and see students swinging from the ceiling, we know something is wrong. [We pay attention to] the materials ... teachers use [and] the tests and worksheets they hand out.

There are teachers I don't think are doing a very good job, and other teachers feel the same way. Now [we] haven't sat in their classrooms but we know what's going on. We know from what kids say how much time [the class spends] doing nothing.

From an interview with Janet, a high school mathematics teacher:

QUESTION: Do you know teachers who are not very good in the classroom?

ANSWER: (*The teacher lowers her voice.*) Yes.

QUESTION: How can you tell if they are not very good?

ANSWER: (*Again softly and after a long pause.*) Well, I guess from students, though they don't always know that they've got a bad teacher. But you hear students describing what they did in class and you hear other teachers and you can tell there are problems.... I guess I can tell when a teacher generates enthusiasm because you can see it in their students.

From an interview with Ted, another high school mathematics teacher:

QUESTION: Do teachers have opinions about the ability of their fellow teachers and, if so, how do they come to these conclusions?

ANSWER: I think we all have opinions based on informal observations. We pass by someone's room and observe what's going on. Sometimes they'll tell you about their evaluation of a student and you can compare that evaluation against your own.... And there's a lot of gossip, too. Kids will tell you about other teachers and they'll tell you about the attitude the teacher expresses. They may say that so and so makes them work hard but that they like her and her class is fun.

From an interview with Edward, a basic skills teacher who also teaches emotionally disturbed students:

QUESTION: You told me that teachers have opinions about one another's competence. Yet teachers here appear to have very little contact. Where do teachers get the information for their opinions?

ANSWER:    Well, I would say some of it is teachers' lounge gossip, but there is some truth in it. They know the teachers who order the stacks of three or four films at a time and they don't consider [showing films routinely] to be good teaching. And teachers judge the personal behavior quirks of other teachers. They'll make judgments if a teacher is always complaining or they'll evaluate the way a teacher is dressed.

The teachers we interviewed and observed were aware, sometimes keenly aware, that their colleagues were judging them. This awareness introduced a new level of uncertainty into their professional lives. A few teachers in every school we studied were judged to be incompetent by their peers. These judgments were public in the sense that they were discussed openly among members of the faculty. They were private, however, in the sense that negative judgments were never shared with the teacher being evaluated. Therefore, no teacher could be sure that colleagues respected his or her performance. We asked, "Do poor teachers know that they're doing a poor job?" In all but two cases, respondents said that poor teachers were unaware that they did not meet the role expectations of their peers. These answers are typical of what many teachers told us:

From an interview with Ann:

I'm glad you brought that up. I really don't think so. We've got one teacher in our department—no names, of course—who is not a good teacher by my standards, or by the standards of other department members, or by the administrators' standards. But she really doesn't know it. She sincerely does not know that she is [a poor] teacher.

From an interview with Jim:

I don't think that the bad ones know that they're being judged negatively. We don't make our criticisms public. We go out and tell other people what we think of them. Everybody else knows it, but the person doesn't know it. He'll go on doing what he's doing because he's so stupid.

The uncertainties of teaching are heightened still further when teachers realize that when they are having difficulty they probably will get no help from their fellow teachers or the administration.

From an interview with Edna:

QUESTION:    If a teacher is having trouble, how can he or she get help? Would anybody tell [such a teacher] what's wrong?
ANSWER:    I really believe someone should tell them. I believe that the principal, assistant principal, or department chairman should tell them.

QUESTION: What kind of help might the chairperson of this department be able to give a teacher who is having trouble?

ANSWER: I'm not sure. They might say, "Let me explain to you how I handle this problem." But that kind of help isn't [given] around here. When teachers are having trouble the rest of us generally ignore it.

QUESTION: Is there no ... way that a teacher can offer help to someone who is having trouble in the classroom?

ANSWER: It would be great if we could help. Really! If I were blowing it I would really want to know. I would want [to be told] in a nice way, and I'd want to get help. But it's almost impossible.

From an interview with Betty:

QUESTION: Do teachers try to help fellow teachers who are having trouble?

ANSWER: No. If they ask me, I will help them. But I don't want to say anything on my own. I wouldn't criticize or judge them either. It's not my place. All I know is that they are poor teachers.

*The fine art of impression management.* The teachers we interviewed knew that their competence was being judged by many publics, that these judgments were based on fragmentary information and would be kept from them, and that they probably would not get the help they needed to solve whatever problems they faced in the classroom. These realities heightened the uncertainty and sense of isolation that teachers already felt so acutely. Such conditions encouraged educators to camouflage rather than confront their shortcomings and to exaggerate, to themselves and others, what they took to be their accomplishments. Many fashioned an actor's sense of audience and continually monitored the impressions they made on students, parents, peers, and administrators. In a profession where anxiety runs high and it is difficult to find objective evidence of success, one may lessen uncertainty, and its attendant sense of vulnerability, by consciously working to create the impression of competence. Many teachers have perfected the fine art of impression management. Sometimes, as in the case of Linda, teachers settled for keeping their classes quiet and did not push their students because to do so was to risk student resistance and the appearance of trouble.

Teachers who employ impression management techniques understandably are reluctant to discuss the methods they use to tout their accomplishments. Admitting an interest in impression management undermines the very image of self-assured competence that a teacher is attempting to project. However, a few teachers were willing to discuss the pressure they felt and the techniques they employed to alleviate uncertainty. Others, though reluctant to discuss their own impression management efforts, were willing to talk about the practices of unnamed colleagues. One particularly open teacher explained that she had grown more "cautious" in her classes when she realized that other teachers "can tell an awful lot about what's going on" just by talking with students.

> I don't want anybody [saying] anything bad about what happen[s] in my class. I think that one thing keeps me on my toes more than anything else; more than the principal walking in . . . more than the assistant principal or anybody else coming in. I hear a lot of wild stories. You really hear some strange things [around here]. You hear an awful lot about what's happening in [other] classrooms. . . . You get an idea about how effective somebody is [by listening to their students].

Impression management techniques were employed outside the classroom as well. Teachers advertised their achievements, tempered their failures, and concealed their self-doubts. One teacher said that at her school it was well understood that you should "never let another teacher find a weakness or an area you need help in. Then you're vulnerable." Vulnerability increased uncertainty and further threatened the teacher's professional self-assurance. The teacher went on to explain:

> You can never go into a teachers' lounge and hear a teacher say, "Damn, I really failed . . . that kid today." You never hear that. You always hear how a teacher was on top of a situation. If there is any discussion of problems, teachers . . . make sure that their admissions are always equal. "Are you having trouble with Johnny? Well, I am too." Teachers are careful never to let another teacher get the upper hand.

Teachers attempt to lessen their vulnerability by asserting competence. As this teacher put it:

> Teachers aren't supposed to be vulnerable. In your classroom when you show vulnerability you lose control. You practice that attitude 8 hours a day. So how can you help having it affect your thinking outside the classroom.

The etiquette of the teachers' lounge limited the amount of overt boasting that teachers tactfully could employ. It was considered acceptable, a teacher in another school told us, "to let it be known that [you] require a certain amount of work from [your] students . . . and that [you] are a tough grader and all that." But such assertions should not suggest that you are more competent than your audience. A teacher at a third school elaborated on the etiquette of self-praise:

> Now we have some teachers who are boastful about their accomplishments and what they do. Other teachers don't like that. Don't brag, because we are all competitors and we all think we're very intelligent. (*The teacher laughs in mock sarcasm.*) We're the most intelligent people in the world, did you know that? We are, we know it all. (*The smile leaves her face.*) I don't, I really don't.

But every faculty I've been a part of, and this is my fourth, is made up of teachers who think they know it all.

These comments, and similar ones made by other teachers we interviewed, are consistent with McPherson's (1972) findings. At the school McPherson studied it was taboo "to complain too much or boast too much." By her account, the very uncertainty that encouraged artful boasting discouraged its overuse.

> Once somebody boasted too loudly or complained too bitterly, others began to look. To boast was to blow your own horn at the expense of other teachers. To complain was to expose vulnerabilities and insecurity. It encouraged competition and prestige jockeying, creating doubt in the minds of other teachers about their own standards and their ritual acceptance of the inevitability of what was. (pp. 201–202)

Nevertheless, in the absence of clear and public signs of competence, impression management was one of the few ways teachers could keep themselves motivated and maintain their sense of professional self-esteem.

*Maintaining professional self-esteem.* Teachers who employ impression management techniques are not engaged in acts of cynical showmanship. Instead, they are trying to convince others of what they themselves hope is true; that despite the doubts and uncertainties that plague them, they are good at what they do. Thus, in the give-and-take of impression management, teachers tend to be their own most attentive audience. Advertisements for the self may or may not convince a teacher's peers that all is well in the classroom, but they will have served an important function if they temporarily assuage the teacher's own uncertainties in that regard. An experienced high school teacher explained how impression management is connected to teachers' feelings of uncertainty and vulnerability and their desire for professional self-respect.

QUESTION: What about teachers who don't realize that they are poor teachers? Can you tell me about them?

ANSWER: Well, that's pretty sad. I don't know whether they *really* think they're good teachers or not. They talk a good game but that doesn't mean that they really are [unaware] of their limitations.

QUESTION: Do a lot of teachers "talk a good game?" That is, do teachers generally pretend to be more expert than they are?

ANSWER: Well, I guess it has to do with their self-esteem. You know, when other people think badly of you, it's hard to keep your self-image. [For that reason,] people are concerned about what other people think.

QUESTION: What are you saying, that teachers need to "talk a good

> game" so that other teachers will think well of them [and they can think well of themselves]?
>
> ANSWER: Yes, I think so. It's a matter of pride, I suppose.
> QUESTION: Do all teachers do that? Do they generally exaggerate their accomplishments?
> ANSWER: Pretty much so, I guess. [They do that] during informal discussions in the teachers' lounge.

What this teacher called "self-image" and "pride," we have called *professional self-respect, self-esteem,* or *sense of professional competence* (we use these terms interchangeably). The terms refer to the feelings teachers have about the quality of their work. A positive sense of professional self-esteem is achieved when teachers feel they are doing something worthwhile, that they are doing it competently, that it taxes their abilities (it is not something just anyone can do), and that their abilities are recognized and appreciated by others. If any one of these elements is missing, access to professional self-respect is jeopardized. As Rawls (1971) has written:

> When we feel that our [work is] of little value, we cannot pursue [it] with pleasure or take delight in [its] execution. Nor plagued by failure and self-doubt can we continue in our endeavors. It is clear then why self-respect is a primary good. Without it nothing may seem worth doing, or if some things have value for us, we lack the will to strive for them. All desire and activity becomes empty and vain, and we sink into apathy and cynicism. (p. 440)

Teachers' acts of impression management make little sense unless they are examined in the context of the teaching profession. Our study of teachers' sense of efficacy leads us to conclude that *the central social-psychological problem facing teachers today is how they can maintain a sense of satisfaction and accomplishment in a profession that offers so few supports for, and myriad threats to, their sense of professional self-respect.*

### TEACHING LOW-ACHIEVING STUDENTS

Maintaining a sense of professional accomplishment is difficult for teachers under the best of circumstances. Its complexities multiply geometrically when a teacher—even the most competent teacher—is assigned classes of low-achieving students. When we asked about the difficulties posed by such classes, teachers listed them effortlessly. Compared to average or above-average pupils, low-achieving students are more difficult to manage, more likely to show anger, and more likely to direct their anger at their classmates and the teacher. They are unlikely to work hard or show interest in class activities or assignments. Teachers must struggle to win their trust and friendship, and helping reluctant learners master academic material generally is an arduous affair.

When we consider the difficulties low-achieving students pose to their teachers and remember the competency criteria discussed earlier in this chapter, it becomes clearer why classes of reluctant learners are so threatening to the self-esteem of professional educators. Each of the competency criteria is more difficult to accomplish in classrooms dominated by low-achieving pupils. Thus teachers have much to lose and little to gain in classes of low-achieving youngsters. A teacher's reputation for competence and sense of professional self-esteem is threatened by students who are difficult to reach and teach. In such classes, teaching is more taxing, student progress is less dramatic, discipline problems are more frequent and more acute, and teacher–student relationships are more openly adversarial. Every teacher of low-achieving students must come to terms with the multiple threats such pupils pose to his or her sense of purpose and accomplishment and must find ways to minimize these threats. Not all teachers deal with competency threats in the same manner.

An efficacy questionnaire was administered to all teachers taking part in this study. The questionnaire administered to middle and junior high school teachers differed somewhat from the one administered to high school teachers (see Appendices A and C). However, both questionnaires contained the two Rand efficacy items discussed in Chapter 1 (see page 8). Responses to the efficacy items were tallied and an efficacy score was assigned to each teacher. A high efficacy score (8 or above) indicated a teacher's strong conviction that students from poor home environments can learn and that the teacher believes that he or she has the ability to get through to even the most difficult, unmotivated youngsters. Teachers receiving a high score on the two Rand items will be referred to as *high sense-of-efficacy teachers*. A low efficacy score (4 or below) indicated the teacher was not convinced that he or she had the skill to teach low-achieving students or that such pupils were capable of learning what schools had to teach. Those receiving a low score will be referred to as *low sense-of-efficacy teachers*. Eleven high school, basic skills teachers and three middle and junior high school teachers had high efficacy scores, whereas six high school, basic skills teachers and five middle and junior high school teachers had low efficacy scores.

In order to avoid observer bias, researchers observing in classrooms were not told the efficacy scores of the teachers they were studying. In fact, an ethnographic analysis of both interview and observational data was undertaken before results to the Rand efficacy items were revealed to the ethnographic research team. On the basis of that analysis the ethnographers accurately predicted which teachers had high efficacy scores on the Rand items and which had low scores.

***Competency threats and low sense-of-efficacy teachers.*** When many students in a class do not do their work well or at all, when they are difficult to manage and appear uncooperative, day-to-day classroom events threaten teachers' sense of professional competence. Low sense-of-efficacy teachers attributed classroom problems not to their own failings as teachers, but to the shortcomings of their students. They said that lack of achievement was best explained by the students' own (1) lack of ability, (2) insufficient motivation, (3) character deficiencies, or (4) poor home environments. We will deal with these four issues separately, though they are intertwined in the thinking of low sense-of-efficacy teachers.

Low sense-of-efficacy teachers were more likely than their high sense-of-efficacy counterparts to claim that low-achieving students did not learn in their classroom because they could not learn. These comments from interviews are typical of the views expressed by all low sense-of-efficacy teachers in our study:

> I don't know if they [low-achieving students] will ever get it [basic skills] no matter how hard you work them. Partially [that's due to] immaturity and lack of motivation. I'm sure some of it has to do with their mental ability and capacity. I'm sure of that.

> There is only so much we teachers can do with students when they come to us in the ninth grade working at the third stanine. I guess we really don't believe we can bring them up to the eighth stanine. That's a big problem. You've got to consider what's coming in [to this school].

> You can't do much with [basic skills students]. I don't know why that is, but there are things they just can't do. So you don't see much progress and you don't feel much is going on.

Ability, of course, is a factor in student achievement, so we should not be surprised that teachers mention low ability as a deterrent to student learning. However, low sense-of-efficacy teachers use mental ability to explain why some students *cannot be taught* rather than why these students have difficulty learning. The two perspectives are quite different. If teachers believe that some students are incapable of learning, they are not likely to waste energy working to help such pupils along. On the other hand, if teachers believe that low-achieving students can learn but have difficulty learning, they are likely to expend extra effort to assure that their students have mastered the material being taught.

Motivation is another factor associated with student achievement, and low sense-of-efficacy teachers had much to say on the topic. Some examples:

> I can tell them every day that they have to do well in English, but they don't seem to care. And I don't think it's me.... You can't stand there with a cattle prod to keep them awake.

> I have some [students] in there who just don't care about school at all. [They are] totally turned off. They don't care. I don't think they belong in school.

> They're not interested in coming to school.

> A lot of these kids don't have the internal, academic motivation they need to ... pursue an education for education's sake. That's not in their values.

Here again, low sense-of-efficacy teachers saw lack of motivation as an explanation for why some students could not learn in school. Such explanations freed teachers from responsibility for student learning because they thought ability and motivation were beyond their control.

Furthermore, teachers with a low sense of efficacy were likely to be offended by the behavior of low-achieving students. Poor behavior was offered as the cause of low achievement and as a reason why teachers should not be held responsible for the student failure. One teacher said:

> Regular students are just more vivacious and want to excel. They want to do well. But compensatory education classes will bring you down because of discipline problems.... If one student looks at another ... the wrong way, they'll start arguing. They try to make the teacher look bad if they can.... I don't know why, but they will. I'll admit I look forward to Wednesdays when I don't have to teach my fifth period comp ed [compensatory education] class.

Teachers with a low sense of efficacy often attributed low achievement to the poor home environments of their students:

> It doesn't do any good to call parents of comp ed students. I've never gotten a response.... I don't think the parents care. They don't think education is important.... They think school is just a place for kids to go ... and to socialize.

> You know [compensatory education students] don't have dinner table conversations. They don't [talk] in the evenings with their families. They don't converse on an intellectual level.... It's just chatter, and that's all it is. That's all they know is chatter.

> I wish somebody cared at home. I'm not saying they're not loved or cared for, but I wish somebody cared [about the kids'] education.

> You can tell whether these students come from a decent home with both parents ... and someone in an authority position. With the decline of ... family life you're going to run into more and more learning [disability] problems. [There is not much a teacher can do.] I mean you can work with them for a time, but whether they learn is dependent on the parents' authority.... I've seen the homes half of these kids live in and [it's] no wonder they can't [learn.]

Low sense-of-efficacy teachers were frustrated and sometimes angered by the attitudes and behaviors of their low-achieving students. Such youngsters offended the moral sensibilities of teachers and violated their image of what students should think, be, and do. One high school math teacher told us she was shocked by the students in the first basic skills class she taught:

> I thought compensatory education students would be willing to work because they needed help. But I had a number of very, very extreme behavior problems in the class. I had some students ... who really plugged at it, but [I had] some do-nothings and forget-abouts who would only talk about food, or

boys, or what to wear. Some kids were . . . out of it. What could I do? They were constantly being suspended, or if they weren't suspended, they were truant, or in fights, or in the courts. I don't think teachers are prepared to deal with students like this. That's what made teaching these classes unpleasant for me. I was robbed by some students in the class.

I don't think a lot of the basic skills students are motivated. So I think it's too much to ask of a teacher that students pass [the state assessment] test. I think a teacher could nearly kill herself trying to motivate some students. [We should] motivate but we shouldn't have to push and push and push. Outside factors are telling kids, "Why bother?" [They know that] so-and-so can get a job without a high school education, so-and-so can rip people off. [A student] can burglarize people . . . and make a fortune. Teachers are dealing with so many externals that make teaching too hard.

I cannot get kids to come in and make up skills they've missed. They have no excuse but I can't force them. People need to look at the kind of students who are actually going into basic skills classes. They are putting kids with low scores on the Metropolitan Achievement test in these classes. Kids have gotten zero on [the state assessment test] and no one is asking why their test scores were low. I think the test scores were low because kids were away from school a great deal, . . . were in trouble constantly, or were creating problems in class.

The teacher was convinced that many of the students in her basic skills classes were too psychologically troubled to be helped at school:

I think that kids surely need help. They deserve some type of help. But I think the kind of help they need is far more than what a regular teacher can give in a classroom. They need psychological help and they need disciplinary action. I really don't feel comfortable teaching them.

To a great degree, this teacher's discomfort arose from the fact that she found her basic skills students morally unacceptable:

I have a value conflict with the students. I don't believe there are degrees of cheating. I don't believe that it's right to take something, just because somebody else has it and you don't. I'm constantly faced with that [attitude] in my basic skills classes. "I haven't got it and I want it . . . so I'm going to take it." They think that's all right. It's an issue of the haves and the have nots.

I don't like them to say hurtful things to students or to say hurtful things about someone's mother. I abstain from that kind of thing in my classroom. But many times I get to a point where I think of [hurtful] things to say to students, and at times I have [said them]. But I do that in order to protect another student. I have had to put down students because they were giving that kind of treatment to someone else. I find that sometimes that's the only way you can handle it.

This teacher did not want to teach angry, low-ability children who came from the wrong side of the tracks. She wanted to teach "motivated . . . better-than-average students." She found the latter to be "self-confident and kind. They don't need to lash out at me. A lot of them feel better about school and have school spirit. And they pull together on some things." She thought that below-average students were so difficult to work with, were so unmotivated, so hurtful, and so uneducable that they did not deserve her time:

> In some instances I'm not sure I care. Sometimes I feel, "What's the use?" Teaching can be very frustrating. I'm not going to mince words about it. That's the way I feel. I feel threatened, too. I can see where a lot of these classes could be very threatening.

This teacher describes herself as "burned out" and said she was considering a career move to administration. "I'm tired of walking into the same classroom, facing the same kinds of students, and getting the same kind of results."

To sum up, teachers with a low sense of efficacy did not share responsibility for the academic failures of their low-achieving students. They expected these students to fail and were not surprised when that expectation came true. Such students, the teachers insisted, were not bright enough, not well enough behaved, or well enough brought up to succeed in school. This "silk purse–sow's ear" argument absolved teachers of responsibility for student learning and student behavior. In effect, it circumvented the role expectations for good teaching. Low-efficacy teachers were untroubled by the failure of low-achieving students because they were sure there was nothing they, or any other teacher, could do to help such students succeed. The responsibility for student failure lay with genetics, the home, and/or with the students themselves and thus did not overly threaten the teacher's sense of professional competence. Note the fatalism expressed by low sense-of-efficacy teachers:

> I don't think any of us ever blame ourselves [for student failure). I mean all of us have our doubts, we have our bad days. We all feel we could put more into it, or [we feel] if we cared more we could get students motivated. But we don't blame ourselves for the problems here.

> I tell the students, "You have the right to fail and I will do nothing to disturb that right."

> You don't want to sit down and continue to work ... with [compensatory education students] when you know they're not going to remember it. I feel you can sit down with some of these students and go over [the material] and they'll know it right then and there. And you get up and leave and come back 5 minutes later, and they've forgotten how to do it completely.

> I don't reach Edward ... and I accept the fact that I'm not going to move Jim along. It took me a couple of years to say that about [students]. But I'm not going to move them all. I think an awful lot of teacher energy is wasted with those [students] who do not do anything.... There's the question, Is it worth it, spending hours and hours for just 12 compensatory education students? It takes a lot of time, a lot of time for very few kids.

> I learned that most students did not enjoy reading at all. They liked to sit in a

classroom situation and read a play with each student taking a part. But that takes a long time. And they would get frustrated and . . . lose interest or miss the whole point. We finally read a novel . . . that my intern found. It took [the class] 8 weeks to get through it. They hated it. As a matter of fact, I guess only about four [students] finished it.

*Competency threats and high sense-of-efficacy teachers.* Teachers with a high sense of efficacy were more likely than their low-efficacy counterparts to define low-achieving students as reachable, teachable, and worthy of teacher attention and effort. Although low sense-of-efficacy teachers were threatened by the lack of discipline, motivation, and achievement they saw in their classes, teachers with a high sense of efficacy were more able to rise above these threats. In fact, many high sense-of-efficacy teachers took pride in their ability to teach the very students their colleagues defined as unteachable. They were not oblivious to the problems low-achieving students brought into the classroom. They accepted those problems as real and thought them tragic. Yet, they also thought these students' problems were at least partially surmountable and felt it was their responsibility to help students over the hurdles that life had placed before them and that students sometimes placed before themselves. The following quotes are typical of the hopeful determination that high sense-of-efficacy teachers expressed to us during interviews.

> You see, [low-achieving] kids need teachers. They probably need them more than any other students. They need a teacher who will work with them and who will care. I don't mean to be derogatory, but they don't need a first-year teacher who doesn't know what she's doing. They need someone who knows what's going on. The kids with the most problems need the best teachers. We have to be tough on kids all the way around. I have grandiose plans. Half the time they don't work out. We start a new unit and I think it's going to be terrific and then it falls on its face. But I say, "Well . . . that's tough. I'll try again."

> I don't believe it's right to give up on anybody. I guess that's why I keep trying. A student can fail every day in the week [but] I'm not going to accept it. . . . Most students start doing some [work] and they . . . see results. They're not going to be math wizards, but they're going to be able to do something [before they leave this class].

> I think I'm lacking a bit in my basic skills classes because this is my first year of teaching. After a while I think I can start getting those [test] scores up. I think the longer [basic skills] classes are around, the more successful we'll become. Eventually the [test scores] will get better. With a bit more work, we can have better results.

> I enjoy basic skills [classes]. The students definitely need the assistance. They need my help. Most really want to master these skills. I think most of them work fairly well. I think I can tell fairly well whether a student is putting sufficient effort [into his or her work]. I may give students an F [when I think]

their progress is too slow. Last [marking period] I gave several students Fs and I saw a very great increase in their progress during the last 9 weeks.

The efficacy issue provides insight into the differences between Horace and Linda, the two teachers described at the start of the chapter. Something in Linda's experience caused her to lose faith in the efficacy of schooling for low-achieving students. Confronted with difficult classes, she began to question whether she was made of the "right stuff" for teaching and whether the students she faced were capable of learning. Slowly, and probably unconsciously, she came to the conclusion that the problem resided not with her, but with her students. She no longer aimed at improving the academic achievement of her pupils but prided herself instead on smaller accomplishments, such as keeping her pupils quiet, under control, and marginally engaged in low-level, academic work.

Horace saw the school in a different light. Like Linda, he was frustrated by his students and by the conditions under which he taught. However, he traced the root of his frustrations not to the limitations of his students or even to his own shortcomings, but to a schooling system that made teaching and learning almost impossible. The conditions of teaching angered him and he worked hard to fight the cynicism and despair he felt growing inside him.

Of course, the teacher that Sizer described in *Horace's Compromise* did not face the same problems Linda confronted each day. He did not spend 6 years working with low-achieving students from poverty families. Horace taught average-ability students from average homes and his dissatisfaction came from the fact that he had to settle for average results. He wanted more from his students, from himself, from his school, and from his profession. Although Sizer placed Horace in a typical school and a typical classroom, we found teachers just like Horace working under much tougher conditions in the schools we studied. They too were determined to make an academic difference in the lives of their students. They knew that what they offered in the classrooms would not, by itself, break the cycle of failure and poverty that characterized the lives of their students. However, the fact that they could not do enough did not become an excuse for doing nothing.

In the next sections we will continue to spell out the attitudinal differences that separate teachers with a high sense of efficacy from those whose sense of efficacy is low. We will also draw on classroom observation data to show that efficacy attitudes appear to affect the relationships teachers have with students, the classroom management practices they use, and the instructional strategies they employ.

## THE STUDENT–TEACHER RELATIONSHIP

The teachers we observed and subsequently interviewed said they derived their greatest satisfactions directly from the pupils they taught. We asked teachers to describe their most rewarding teaching experiences. Though the teaching situations they related were superficially quite different, all shared four important characteristics. In every rewarding teaching situation described by these teachers (1) students shared the teacher's goals for the class, (2) students shared the teacher's definitions of what it means to be a teacher and to be a student, (3) the students and the teacher were willing to help one another achieve the class objectives and to fulfill the responsibilities of their respective roles, and (4) both students and the teacher shared a sense of pride in what they had accomplished together. These exemplary experiences were remembered fondly by teachers. They described the situations enthusiastically, as if the memory of past success temporarily refueled their enthusiasm and reminded them of what teaching could be. Although teachers said that successful teaching came easily when the situation was right, they also said that such situations did not come often. Everyday classroom life usually is made of duller stuff and teachers typically had to settle for realities that fell far short of the ideal. The kind of realities for which teachers settle was mediated by several factors, an important one being the efficacy attitudes that teachers adopted as they struggled to maintain a sense of competence in a difficult and uncertain profession. Nowhere is the power of the efficacy factor more apparent than in the teaching domain we have labeled the student–teacher relationship.

***Low sense-of-efficacy teachers' relationships with students.***    As we saw in the previous discussion, teachers with a low sense of efficacy tended to be distrustful of their pupils, or at least of the lowest achieving, most misbehaving students in their classes. Such students threatened their sense of professional competence. Low sense-of-efficacy teachers dealt with this threat by putting classroom discipline at the center of their thinking and teaching practices. Some were ineffectual classroom managers, others were quite effective. No matter how effective they were or were not, *all low sense-of-efficacy teachers defined the classroom situation in terms of conflict.* Those who controlled their classes effectively took pride in that accomplishment. Linda was such a teacher. Those who could not control their classes blamed their failure on the incorrigibility of their students.

Weber (1958) made a useful and now classic distinction between positional and personal authority in modern society. According to Weber, these two modes of authority grow from different sources and are maintained by different methods. *Positional authority* resides in the status an individual holds in a given organization. It is bestowed by the organization and, in effect, is on loan to a status holder. Positional authority comes with the job and disappears when an individual leaves his or her post. *Personal authority* is of a different order. It grows from the personality and demonstrated competence of the individual and is bestowed voluntarily by others. Personal power must be earned and cannot be bestowed by an organization.

Educators with a low sense of efficacy found security in the positional authority they inherited from the teaching role. They jealously guarded their authority and were reluctant to establish relationships with students that might jeopardize their positional power. A researcher made the following notes during a conversation with a low sense-of-efficacy teacher.

> Laurie commented that building rapport with students was essential. However, she said that sometimes she had to get herself out of conversations [with students when she thought] she might "incriminate" herself. She said that personal relationships sometimes interfered with [a teacher's authority] because students try to get away with things. She said that close relationships with students sometimes made it difficult for her to know what she was [supposed] to do.

Another low sense-of-efficacy teacher explained that it was important to "act like a teacher" with students and to avoid becoming too familiar:

> I started off like a sweet angel and had all these wonderful ideas, but they laughed me out of the room. So I cried a lot my first year because I was so upset. I finally realized that the fewer times I would smile the better off I would be. To them, smiling was a sign of weakness.

*High sense-of-efficacy teachers' relationships with students.* Teachers with a high sense of efficacy had a more benign view of students. Though they too believed that youngsters can and will disrupt a class if given free rein, they thought that disruptive behavior could be avoided if teachers made clear and fair classroom rules; enforced those rules consistently and without anger; and if they tempered enforcement by establishing friendly relationships with students, expecting them to behave well, and treating students in accordance with that expectation. Teachers with a low sense of efficacy relied heavily on positional authority, but those with a high sense of efficacy were more likely to establish and utilize personal authority. Teachers in the latter group were more willing to demonstrate to students that they cared about them and were concerned about their progress and their problems. For example, one high sense-of-efficacy teacher said she wanted to help students develop knowledge and skill, "but along with that I try to be a friend to them. I try to be someone who understands." Another teacher said:

> Students come and talk to me and I listen. I don't put myself in the role of counselor but sometimes I'm there and I have to do that job. So if a girl comes in on drugs or is having family problems, I'll try and do something about it. I think my students would describe me as somebody they enjoyed. They like being in my class.

A third teacher explained that what she liked most about teaching was forming informal relationships with students, having friendly conversations, and getting to know what her pupils were doing and thinking.

> I appreciate students who initiate conversations with me and who I really get to know. They know me as a person and talk about things you don't have to talk about with your teacher. They don't talk about their homework or their assignments; they talk about what happened to them at home or [about] a movie they saw, or they ask me if I had a nice weekend.

High sense-of-efficacy teachers built warm relationships with their students. They did not think that such relationships challenged their authority or threatened their professional self-esteem. Indeed, they contended that friendly relationships in and out of class strengthened their authority and made teaching more enjoyable and classroom management easier.

### CLASSROOM MANAGEMENT STRATEGIES

No single variable distinguishes the classroom management techniques of low sense-of-efficacy teachers from those with a high sense of efficacy. Teachers within a particular category do not employ exactly the same discipline methods, so it would be a mistake to assume that efficacy attitudes carry with them specific recipes for classroom management. Nevertheless, some useful generalizations can be made when we look across the different methods employed by teachers within a particular efficacy group.

*Classroom management strategies of low sense-of-efficacy teachers.* Although teachers with a low sense of efficacy often ran orderly classes, from the teachers' point of view, disorder was an ever-present and thoroughly disagreeable possibility. As indicated earlier, low sense-of-efficacy teachers defined the classroom situation in terms of conflict. One discouraged teacher explained that she had to be vigilant in her class:

> You have to be constantly on your guard because you never know if someone is going to say something that's going to get somebody else mad. If someone laughs at a student, you've lost him for the period.... Doggone it, there are always four or five people that will throw things off. Maybe you couldn't go over what you've done the day before because they didn't bring [their work] to class, or they left their books at home, or something [happened] to them. [Some students] don't seem to care.

Another teacher made a similar point:

> God, the abuse you have to put up with. Well, it's not that you have to put up with it, but it still comes back every day. Discipline problems burn you out and make you feel useless. You've already reached the kids you're going to reach ... during the first 5 minutes of the class. You spend the next 20 minutes worrying about discipline.

It was commonly contended that a single student could disrupt an entire class and badly damage the teacher's authority. One teacher took an observer aside before the start of class to explain "there's a student in this class who ruins [everything]." Later the teacher said that her job was made unbearable by students

> who cannot or will not concentrate [or are] concerned with socializing or being flirtatious.... Their attention span is very, very short.... They do not contribute to motivating themselves. They are easily diverted. They are easily upset sometimes by conditions they have caused themselves. Unless they will help themselves, how can [teachers] go the extra mile?

The teacher went on to say that students sometimes united against her and refused to tell her when their classmates were secretly misbehaving. She complained that too many students have "the attitude that they shouldn't rat on each other." Such an attitude not only made life difficult for the teacher, it was, as she put it, "bad for society."

The perception that low-achieving students will try to disrupt the class led low sense-of-efficacy teachers to work diligently to "keep things under control." Controlling the class was a primary aim and they employed a variety of techniques to accomplish it. One technique frequently used by low sense-of-efficacy teachers was to publicly embarrass students who misbehaved. This tactic served both to punish the transgressing student and to discourage other pupils from similar misbehavior. A few examples drawn from field notes and from interviews of the embarrassment tactic:

> A student says to the teacher, "Why don't you put the answers up on the board as we go along?" The teacher responds, "If you want to run the class, you can. Otherwise, shut up."

> The class is being noisy. A visitor comes into the room to remind students that they will need permission slips if they are going on the swimming field trip. The teacher tells the visitor [while the class listens], "It's all right with me if you take them and drown them."

> When students misbehaved, I'd get a message to the dean. I think it has a better effect if I go with them ... and witness what the dean says to them. When somebody ... fusses at you and a third person is watching, it's a humiliating experience. I think it has a better effect.

> Most of the time I had to be real, real, real mean. Real rough. I would single out [a student] and that would make him mad. I'd say, "Allen, I've given up on you...." That would make him mad, but it wouldn't change his ways.

> There is noise in the room. The teacher says, "You'll have to use self-discipline. I'm not allowed to use strait-jackets."

> The teacher says angrily, "Turn around and be still or I'll tape your mouths shut."

A few low sense-of-efficacy teachers were adept at turning class opinion against students the teacher thought were getting out of line. A particularly severe example of this technique occurred when a teacher handed back a test and was reviewing the answers with the class. A student we'll call Jenny had lost points for a question she believed she had answered correctly. She asked the teacher to explain, but the teacher merely restated the answer and moved on. Jenny objected and asserted that her answer was preferable to the one the teacher proposed. The teacher ignored the comment until Jenny complained, "But Mrs. Smith, I was right." The teacher did not answer Jenny but said to the class, "We aren't going to lunch until we finish [going over the test.]" The class was eager to get to lunch and immediately put pressure on Jenny to abandon her question. The researcher's field notes describe what happened next.

> Some students commented, "Yes, let's get on with it." Jenny appears upset and looks down at her paper. The teacher asks, "What's the problem?" Jenny replies softly, "I don't get it." Other students comment angrily, "She gets an A and she's complaining about her grade. She should see what I got." Jenny says sadly, "It's not the grade, Mrs. Smith; I just want to understand. I don't understand why this is wrong."
>
> [Some other questions come from the class and the teacher answers them. She then turns to Jenny and says that there is a difference of opinion on what the right answer should be on this particular kind of question.] However she indicates that her [the teacher's] answer is correct. [Mrs. Smith reads the question and then the answer she contends is correct.] She asks, "Jenny, do you understand now?" The teacher has not explained the answer. She has merely asserted it. Jenny answers, "I just don't think that this [word] is an adjective and that my answer is correct."

Jenny was upset and and looked down at the desk to hide her face from the teacher and the class. Her classmates were impatient and did not want their departure for lunch delayed any longer. Jenny dropped the issue and the class continued to review the test. A few minutes later, the teacher noticed that Jenny was still looking down at her desk. She stopped the review and brought the class's attention back to Jenny. Her comments are recorded in the researcher's field notes:

> "If you're going to cry and be upset about it, Jenny, I'm sorry." The teacher's comments gave no hint of empathy. She has pointed out to the class that Jenny was crying, a fact that Jenny was trying to hide by keeping her head down.

Another classroom management device used by low sense-of-efficacy teachers was to separate "difficult students" from their classmates. We call this process *excommunication*. In its simplest form, excommunication entails sending potential troublemakers out of the room. An example from field notes:

> Students on the right side of the room are participating in the lesson. Students on the left are supposed to be participating but instead are engaged in their own activities. The teacher ignores them. [When the noise from the left side of

the room gets quite loud] the teacher tells three students, "Go!" One asks, "Where?" The teacher answers, "I don't care where, just go."

The excommunication device was frequently used during periods of instruction and will be discussed again in a later section of the chapter that deals with teaching techniques.

*The classroom management strategies of high sense-of-efficacy teachers.* If the classrooms of low sense-of-efficacy teachers were characterized by an undercurrent of conflict, the classrooms of high sense-of-efficacy teachers were characterized by relative harmony. High sense-of-efficacy teachers made fewer and less negative comments about the students in their classes. We observed no cases where they used embarrassment as a punishment and seldom saw excommunication employed as a classroom management technique. The atmosphere in most classes was relaxed and friendly. As one high sense-of-efficacy teacher told us:

> It has to be a relaxed situation. I don't like . . . a strict, regimented type of teaching. If students are relaxed and the teacher is relaxed . . . there is more learning occurring. I read somewhere recently . . . that if students laugh . . . they learn.

Of course students misbehaved in classes taught by high sense-of-efficacy teachers. These teachers, like their low sense-of-efficacy counterparts, found it necessary to correct misbehavior and to make sure tomfoolery did not get out of hand. However, high sense-of-efficacy teachers appeared to have fewer instances of misbehavior, and when problems occurred they were able to handle them quietly and directly, without negative affect, sarcasm, or embarrassment. They were not likely to perceive students as desiring to misbehave and less likely to think that rule infractions challenged their authority. Their corrective remarks to students tended to be firm, to the point, and without emotional embellishments. They were not accompanied by references to the student's character or to past transgressions. Some examples from field notes illustrate the kind of corrective and directive comments made by high-sense-of-efficacy teachers:

> Move up a seat and stay there.
>
> I want to see you after class.
>
> Those of you at the door, please come back and sit down.
>
> If you don't listen you're going to miss this.
>
> Now who's whistling? Cut it out, you'll have all weekend to whistle.

If teachers are to maintain their professional self-esteem, it is essential that they remain in control of classroom situations. A large percentage of both high and low sense-of-efficacy teachers appeared able to accomplish this goal. However, these two groups were likely to define classroom events in differing ways and to handle them in differing manners. Low sense-of-efficacy teachers defined their classes in terms of conflict and potential disruption. Misbehavior threatened their professional self-confidence and they worked hard to keep potential troublemakers in line. They reacted to problematic events more harshly and were willing to "put students in their place" by embarrassing them in front of their classmates.

High sense-of-efficacy teachers defined student misbehavior in less threatening terms and thus reacted to it less harshly and with less emotion. Their corrections and directions were short and to the point and, perhaps as a consequence, invited quicker compliance and less "back talk" from their students. Their manner was more relaxed and their classrooms efficient and friendly. Slightly problematic situations seldom escalated into major confrontations.

The differences we are describing here are differences in degree rather than kind. High sense-of-efficacy teachers sometimes lost their tempers and defined students in negative terms. They sometimes spoke harshly to their classes. However, our analysis of qualitative data suggests that high sense-of-efficacy teachers engage in these behaviors less frequently than do those with a low sense of efficacy. In a later portion of the study we used systematic observation instruments to measure teacher and student behavior in high school basic skills classes. The hypotheses generated in the qualitative portion of our research were confirmed by our quantitative findings. High school teachers with a high sense of efficacy were more likely than low sense-of-efficacy teachers to run warm and friendly classrooms and to avoid the use of negative affect. See Chapter 5 for a discussion of findings from the quantitative portion of our research.

INSTRUCTIONAL STRATEGIES

Although teachers are free to choose their own teaching methods, there are certain instructional imperatives that are built into the organizational arrangements of most junior high schools and high schools. For example, the day is segmented into periods and the curriculum organized around specified subject areas. Students are assigned to specific teachers and are expected to study specific subjects in specified time slots. These taken-for-granted facts of school life build rhythms of order and disorder into the day. At the ringing of a bell all students in the school gather their belongings, enter the corridors that connect classrooms, and make their way to their next class. Between classes they socialize, visit the lavatory, or dash to their lockers to retrieve books needed for the next class.

It falls to teachers to restore order at the start of the next period. Before the class ends 55 minutes later, the teacher is expected to have taken attendance, made necessary announcements, gained students' attentions, sparked their interest, oriented them to the topic of the day, maintained order, instructed the class, checked to see that all students understood what has been taught, reinstructed when necessary, made assignments, kept students on task, and ended the class on schedule and in an orderly fashion. On a loftier level, we like to assume that the teacher knows the subject matter well, that what was taught was worth learning, that it was taught accurately and efficiently, and that it interested and challenged students, advanced their knowledge, and contributed to their ability to think.

How successfully teachers deal with the instructional imperatives and the loftier goals just listed depends on many factors. Successful teachers are efficient classroom managers and are able to maintain pleasant relationships with their students. Although these skills are necessary for classroom success, they are not sufficient. Successful teachers must also be knowledgeable and successful instructors. They must have information, know how to impart it clearly, have a flair for making learning interesting, and must tenaciously insist that students master what is being taught.

As we shall see in the next two sections of this chapter, low sense-of-efficacy teachers find it difficult to be effective teachers in classes with low-achieving students. The teachers' belief that some students cannot or will not learn undermines whatever possibility for learning might have existed in their classes. High efficacy attitudes made teaching and learning more likely, but did not guarantee that learning would take place.

*Instructional strategies of low sense-of-efficacy teachers.* No single strategy is employed exclusively by low sense-of-efficacy teachers; however, certain patterns are discernible when data are analyzed across the low-efficacy group. The distrust low sense-of-efficacy teachers have for their students colors the instructional techniques they employ. They are likely to view their work in terms of containment and control rather than teaching and learning. They tend to believe that low achievers do not learn, either because they won't ("thinking is just something they are too lazy to do"), or because they can't ("it has to do with a lack of mental ability"). Thus low sense-of-efficacy teachers do not spend much time trying to teach low achievers because, in their view, such an effort would produce many frustrations and few results. A classroom observer made these comments in his field notes:

> The teacher told me how difficult it is to teach [students who are on] different levels. She feels she has to ignore those who won't learn and try to teach those who will. This, she said, was the advice of her principal. At first it was shocking but now she realizes [that it contains] a great deal of truth.

Other teachers made similar comments during interviews:

> I guess it is a first-year mistake [to think] you have to reach everybody. But there's no way you can and you've got to realize that.

> It didn't take me long after I came to this school to see that students were

slower [than average]. So I didn't try to accomplish a great deal. I don't feel the students listen or care.

The teacher said her main concern was just controlling disruptive students. At this point she's not real concerned about their getting work done as long as they don't disrupt the rest of the class.

Low sense-of-efficacy teachers categorized students by ability and dished out instruction in portions proportionate to each pupil's perceived mental capacity. They were frustrated, however, when they faced classes with students of differing abilities.

The way we have classes set up makes it really hard. We've got total illiterates sitting next to people who are gifted and we're supposed to teach them all.

I have everything from the very bright to the very dull here. That white boy in the brown shirt over there is almost LD [learning disabled].

Many low sense-of-efficacy teachers suggested that low-achieving students should not be in school:

"I don't think they belong in school. I think they need an alternative, or that they should be reassigned to another teacher's class." The teacher said that next year she would not teach a class like this [with many low-achieving students]. She said she told the principal that she would work at the school again only if she could teach French . . . for several periods during the day. She explained that she did not want to work with the same kind of students she is teaching now.

Though classroom observers did not objectively measure student–teacher interaction during the ethnographic phase of this study, a review of field notes indicated that low sense-of-efficacy teachers called on low-achieving students less often, and seldom pushed or encouraged such students to do their work, do it well, or hand it in on time. Frequently the work assigned to such students appeared trivial and designed to keep them busy so the teacher could teach "the brighter ones." For example:

The teacher divided the class into two groups. One group is . . . diagramming sentences while the others are working on [an exercise that deals with] irregular verbs. She describes the [irregular verb] assignment and tells the students that they can go to the library to do their work. . . . The nine students leave the class. All six black students in the class are in this group.

At the end of the class the observer talked to the teacher and recorded the following in his field notes:

I asked what assignment she gave to the library group. She responded, "I gave them an assignment on irregular verbs. It's hard and they won't get it. Most won't even do it. And that's OK with me. I just had to give them something to do so I could work with the rest of the class on diagramming sentences." I asked, "Will you teach diagramming sentences to those students during another class?" She responded, "Are you kidding? They can't learn that. They can't learn verbs either for that matter."

The following day the teacher again taught a lesson on diagramming sentences. The group that had been sent to the library sat quietly in the back two rows of the classroom. They did not take part in the lesson. The observer's field notes describe the day's events:

All the interaction between the students and the teacher comes from students in the first three rows. Students in the back two rows hardly participate at all. They are not disruptive, but they are not a part of what is going on. The teacher sets the first three rows to work on a grammar exercise. . . . She turns to Ester, a black female, and says, "You be the teacher today for your group." She gives the Warriner Manual to Ester and sends the group to the back table. These are the same students who left the class for the library yesterday; the group the teacher said would not be able to do the work she had assigned. They received no instruction on irregular verbs and are now grading their own papers. I can't tell from where I'm sitting if they are correcting work, doing it for the first time, or changing the answers.

Sending low-achieving students from the room or ignoring their presence in the room while the teacher works with higher achievers is another form of the *excommunication* tactic discussed earlier. In fact many low sense-of-efficacy teachers paid little or no attention to their lowest achieving students as long as the students were well behaved. Not all low sense-of-efficacy teachers excommunicated students as blatantly as the teacher just described. Some simply stopped trying to teach such students because they had not responded to the teacher's earlier efforts at instruction. Some examples from field notes:

A white male at the head table talks to the white male next to him. The teacher asks if the white male has done his assignment. He gives her a blank look. The teacher asks, "Don't you know if you've done your work in the past week . . . ? Don't you care?" The student answers, "No." The teacher responds, "Then sit quietly and don't disturb anyone else because they do care. . . ." The student takes out a paperback book and flips through its pages, closes it, and starts tapping quietly on the table with the head of his pencil.

The teacher is leading the lesson. The boy the teacher identified as "illiterate" during lunch sits silently in the back of the room. He takes no part in the class discussion, speaks to no one, and is not called on by the teacher. He merely looks into space. Finally he puts his head down and goes to sleep. [The teacher had said], "I can't get through to some students. He can't read at all; well, maybe at the third-grade level. I tried to help and when my intern was here she tried, too. I'm going to try and get him switched to another class."

When teachers sort and stratify their classes according to ability and give preferential treatment (more instruction, more interaction, more appropriate praise and feedback, more assignments, and so on) to some while neglecting others, all pupils are likely to learn where they stand in the teacher's pecking order. In an advanced class, students made mosaics to illustrate the Greek myths they had been studying. The teacher asked if the students would take their products around to other classes but the students were reluctant to do so. The teacher encouraged them saying, "But they're your peers." A student reinforced the teacher's request by saying to the class, "Yeah, you've got to prove you're above them." The teacher nodded in agreement.

A week later the same teacher was working with a heterogeneously grouped social studies class. The teacher asked a question of the entire class and a student from the lowest group volunteered an answer. The teacher said the answer was correct, to which the student replied, "See, we're not so dumb."

A guidance counselor interrupted another class and asked a student to come to her office. The teacher said to the student and to the class:

> "You might as well go, Jim, you're not learning anything anyway." The student leaves and another student asks, "Are you calling us dumb?" The teacher replies sarcastically, "No, you're wonderful."

The attitudes, statements, and classroom practices of low sense-of-efficacy teachers stigmatize some students and run the risk of convincing these pupils that the teacher is right—they are not bright enough to learn what is being taught in school.

Up to this point we have been discussing the teaching practices of low sense-of-efficacy teachers who ran generally orderly classes and, at least with their better students, were generally competent teachers. Some other low sense-of-efficacy teachers had difficulty controlling their classes and were not successful at teaching even high-achieving students. This group was small, and though they shared the characteristics of other low sense-of-efficacy teachers, their problems were more extreme. These teachers had not mastered any of the imperatives of instruction. They did not get classes started smoothly or on time and could not get and keep students' attention. Their classes constantly misbehaved. We seldom found them greeting students at the start of the period or engaging them in informal conversation during the day. Class periods were so chaotic that serious instruction often was impossible. These teachers sometimes showed movies, not for their educational content but because they kept students quiet. These teachers devalued students' work by allowing some students to do no assignments at all, by failing to keep adequate records of student progress, and by not controlling their classes. In one teacher's room, for example, a student was giving a report and the teacher allowed so much noise that the student gave up in disgust saying, "Oh, the heck with it." The teacher, seeing it as futile to try to control the class, gave students free rein for the rest of the period.

***Instructional strategies of high sense-of-efficacy teachers.*** High sense-of-efficacy teachers had less trouble managing their classes than did teachers with low efficacy attitudes and appeared to have fewer and less severe altercations with their pupils. They expected students to be seated at the start of class, to have their materials ready, to take the class and their work seriously, and to treat the teacher and one another with respect. They communicated that class time was valuable and should be well spent, and that school work was important and should be done carefully. Almost everything these teachers did and said during class communicated and enforced these expectations. For example, high sense-of-efficacy teachers usually greeted their students at the door and talked with them informally before class. When the bell rang, however, they got their students' attention and went directly to work. Some examples from field notes:

> Let's have your attention please, this is going to be a great day. We're going to get a lot done. I don't want anyone to miss a thing.
>
> The bell has rung. Everybody should be in their seats.
>
> The first thing we're going to do is to work on the final draft of your papers. I know these papers are going to be wonderful. Today we're going to practice the skill of writing a good paragraph.

The remarks high sense-of-efficacy teachers made to their students at the end of classes reinforced the teachers' belief that school work was important and their expectation that students should take their work seriously and master what was being taught:

> Your deadline is approaching. When is your paper due? I'm not going to give you additional time on Friday. It's due at the beginning of the period.
>
> Do you have any questions you want to ask before you go home today?
>
> Remember, there is a test coming up. Study hard and show me what you can do.

High sense-of-efficacy teachers tended to exhibit what educational researchers have come to call "with-it-ness"; that is, they stayed aware of what was going on in their classrooms. They seldom overlooked infractions and, when they occurred, they took immediate action to curb the inappropriate behavior. Further, they stayed on the scene long enough to make sure the reprimanded student stopped misbehaving and went back to work.

Teachers with a high sense of efficacy kept their students on task and stayed on task themselves. They did not use class time to grade papers, did not leave the classroom often, did not socialize with students or other adults during class time, and seldom engaged in behaviors or activities that were unrelated to instruction or learning. They gave students assignments to do in class and frequently walked around the room answering students' questions, checking student progress, and offering encouragement. Assignments were checked and teachers kept a record of how students were doing. The following excerpt from field notes nicely illustrates the classroom behavior of a typical high sense-of-efficacy teacher:

The teacher went to the board and began to illustrate a point she was making about a particular aspect [of the assignment. The students begin their work.] She moves from the the board to two students and talks briefly with them. She moves over to Tom ... observing and checking students' work as she moves around the room. She went from Harry to Betty to Paul to John. She said to Emmit, "How are you doing?" She looked at his paper and moves on.... She stops at Sally's desk and answers a question. She moves to her own desk and looks through a folder and answers another student's question as she does so. She is looking for a paper that is related to the report Harry is writing. She seems unable to find the paper and asks Harry to look in his locker. The teacher moves to Harriet. Another student asks a question and the teacher moves on to Barry. Ellen goes to Barry's desk and leans across it to say something to Betty. The teacher looks up, looks around the room and says, "I like the way John, Beverly, and Ron are working." Ellen goes back to her seat. The teacher continues to work with two other students.

High sense-of-efficacy teachers spent more time on whole-group and individual instruction. They encouraged their students more frequently, monitored student behavior and work more attentively, coached them more carefully, praised them more often and more appropriately, and generally ran happier and more efficient classes. They demonstrated their concern for student learning. Effective monitoring did not take the form of harping or reprimanding. Statements such as, "I like the way Sally, Bev, and Ron are working," enabled teachers to reward appropriate behavior and to extinguish negative behavior without embarrassment or anger.

## CONCLUSION

In this chapter we have discussed the attitudes of teachers with high and low sense of efficacy. We have concentrated on the relations between those attitudes and teachers' behaviors and beliefs in each of three areas: (1) relationships with students, (2) classroom management strategies, and (3) instructional methods. We focused on teachers with the highest and lowest efficacy scores and found that efficacy attitudes were related to a host of teacher behaviors and beliefs. Low efficacy attitudes were related to a distrust of low-achieving students; discomfort in low-achieving classrooms; a control orientation in discipline matters; a reliance on positional authority; the use of embarrassment and excommunication as behavior management devices; the sorting and classifying of students by ability; a willingness to ignore the lowest achievers in the room and to send them from the class; a deemphasis on instruction and the importance of learning; an inability to ignite student interest in academic work; and an unwillingness to push students and to closely monitor their academic progress.

High efficacy attitudes were related to a belief that all students can learn and want to do so; efforts to establish warm and encouraging relationships with students; the conviction that students will behave well if

treated fairly, firmly, and with consistency; a reliance on personal authority; the use of direct, nonemotional management techniques; a reluctance
to embarrass students; an effort to treat all students as capable and
trustworthy; an emphasis on instruction and the importance of learning; an
effort to keep students on task, interested, and aware of their individual
accomplishments; a willingness to teach all students in the class, to push
them, and to monitor their work; and the determination not to accept
student failure.

For purposes of analysis and presentation of results, it was useful to
separate high sense-of-efficacy teachers from low sense-of-efficacy teachers
and to compare activities and attitudes within various categories such as
how they teach, relate to students, and discipline their classes. However,
this device oversimplifies matters that are exceedingly complex. The
categories of teaching are not separate in teachers' thinking or in the experience of students; they are of a piece. How teachers relate to students
influences their methods of discipline and instruction and these methods
in turn influence the behavior and attitudes of students. What students
do in the classroom influences the behaviors and attitudes of teachers. All
these variables are reciprocally related. Therefore, it is misleading to see
a teacher's efficacy attitudes as the first and causal link in a linear chain of
events. Efficacy expectations are powerful and deserve the attention of
anyone interested in the improvement of education. However, it makes
little sense to look at the consequences of efficacy attitudes without also
looking at the causes of those attitudes and the contexts in which they
emerge.

There are other complications as well. We have compared teachers
with extreme efficacy scores so that differences in their behavior and
attitudes would be easier to see and describe. The differences that emerged
were severe and should interest researchers, teachers, and policy makers
alike, but it must be kept in mind that most teachers do not fall into these
extreme categories. We can take some comfort in the fact that the average
teacher scores moderately high on the Rand efficacy items and displays
more of the behaviors associated with high efficacy attitudes than behaviors associated with low efficacy attitudes. On the other hand, it is
discomforting to note that although the efforts of teachers with high
efficacy attitudes were admirable, few high sense-of-efficacy teachers ran
classes that we would term innovative or went much beyond the direct
instruction, teach-and-drill methods suggested in the process–product
literature. Although these methods are worthwhile and certainly preferable to the methods employed by low sense-of-efficacy teachers, they
probably are not sufficient to advance the critical thinking skills of
low-achieving students.

Still another difficulty that comes from comparing high sense-of-
efficacy teachers with low sense-of-efficacy teachers is that the research
findings invite us to simply associate positive efficacy attitudes with good

teaching and negative attitudes with poor teaching. The policy implication of such an association might be that we only should train and hire teachers with high efficacy expectations. In fact, however, we already are doing just that. Most teachers leave college with a high sense of efficacy, Linda being an excellent case in point. But as neophyte teachers adjust to the complexity of classroom reality, many lose the positive expectations they held for themselves and their students. Before rushing to policy judgments on the basis of teacher efficacy research, it would be wise to inquire into why so many teachers are unable to maintain high efficacy attitudes today. The fact that so many teachers are unable to maintain positive expectations and suffer from a diminished sense of professional self-esteem is a major impediment to the improvement of education in the United States.

There is also danger in associating in too absolute a way low efficacy attitudes with poor teaching. It must be remembered that our research focused on how teachers dealt with low-achieving students. Some teachers did a dismally poor job teaching low-achievers, but were efficient, and occasionally outstanding, when teaching average or advanced students. The transformation in the behavior and demeanor of low sense-of-efficacy teachers as they moved from one class to the next, or from one student to another, sometimes was startling. Although this was not the case for all low sense-of-efficacy teachers, such changes appeared often enough to remind us of the contextual nature of efficacy attitudes and the error of considering them to be fixed traits.

We are confident that efficacy attitudes result from teachers' experiences on many levels of the social system. At the macrosystem level, efficacy attitudes are influenced by the culture's dissatisfaction with the quality of education in the United States, by the popular assumption that human intelligence is a fixed trait, and by the widely held view that schools are arenas of competition where talented youngsters who learn academic material easily are separated from untalented youngsters who do not. At the level of the exosystem, efficacy attitudes are affected by the declining buying power of teachers' pay checks and by the declining status of their profession. At the level of the mesosystem, efficacy attitudes are related to the organizaton of the school and to the degree of teachers' isolation from or cooperation with colleagues. These variables were discussed in Chapter 2 and will be examined more completely in Chapter 4.

A number of microsystem variables affect teachers' experience of teaching and, ultimately, their efficacy attitudes. For example, the sense of personal efficacy teachers bring with them into the profession may affect the sense of teaching efficacy they develop over time. How teachers experience the uncertainties of their work, their initial experiences in low-achieving classrooms, their perceptions of how students and other teachers judge their competence, and the perceived effectiveness of their impression management efforts, all have an effect on the compromises they make with their profession, their students, and themselves.

Certainly some teachers are more able than others to maintain high efficacy expectations even under severely difficult teaching conditions. We do not know what enables them to hang onto their high hopes when other teachers, working under the same conditions, gradually lose their determination, optimism, and teaching skills. There is reason to question whether the teaching profession can retain its most determined, high sense-of-efficacy teachers. It is worth remembering that Horace is an unhappy teacher, dissatisfied with his performance and with the conditions under which he works. He is angry at a system that does not allow him to do his job well and he is impatient with administrators he thinks are not doing enough to improve the quality of education. Horace often is tempted to get out of teaching.

Linda, on the other hand, has adjusted to the realities of school life. She thinks her pay is too low and would like a smaller class load, but views such changes as luxuries, not necessities. She is satisfied with the job she is doing, thinks she is teaching her students as much as they are likely to learn from anyone, and gets along well with her principal. She is happy and has no plans to leave the classroom.

Although we do not know precisely what keeps Horace's efficacy attitudes intact or what caused Linda to lose faith in the efficacy of teaching, we do have some leads that we will follow in the next chapter. It is a shame when dedicated teachers leave their profession in disgust. It is no less a shame that teachers like Linda gradually lose their talents, dedication, and efficacy expectations. A profession is in grave trouble when it does not protect the professional self-esteem of its membership, cannot retain the most talented people in its ranks, and does not develop the potential and increase the talent of those who work within it. We think the teaching profession is in trouble.

# 4

# School Organization and Teachers' Sense of Efficacy

## Written with Nancy Doda

## INTRODUCTION

A number of previous studies (Fuller, Wood, Rapoport, & Dornbusch, 1982) indicate that school organization can significantly influence teachers' feelings of effectiveness. For example, Bidwell's (1973) work shows that the school organization can limit the opportunities that teachers have to establish spheres of personal influence that might help them effect changes in their schools. Meyer and Cohen (1971) found that teachers in open-spaced schools had greater autonomy and felt more able to influence peers and administrators than did teachers in more conventionally organized schools. The researchers attributed these feelings of autonomy and influence to the collegial interaction fostered by the team teaching in open-spaced schools. Little's (1982) focused ethnography of four relatively successful and two relatively unsuccessful schools showed that norms of collegiality and experimentation prevailed in the successful schools. Unsuccessful schools were more often characterized by teacher isolation. Thus, organizational differences can influence student achievement and teachers' beliefs about their own effectiveness.

Teachers' sense of efficacy may contribute to the relationship between school organization and school achievement. Teachers whose work environment fosters, rather than destroys, belief in their own effectiveness maintain an academic focus and work to establish friendly and productive relationships with students. As a result, students will experience school more positively, maintain faith in their own ability to improve academically, work harder, and ultimately improve their achievement test performance. The purpose of the Middle School Efficacy Study was to refine the conceptual framework of teachers' sense of efficacy by examining the relationship between school organizational structure and teachers' efficacy attitudes.

Three objectives guided the design of the Middle School Study: (1) identification of school organization factors that are related to teachers' efficacy attitudes, (2) clarification of the processes by which school organization influences the efficacy attitudes of teachers, and (3) further delineation of the teacher efficacy construct.

Because the objective of the study was to understand how patterns of teacher thought and behavior are influenced by school organization, two middle schools with major organizational differences were selected for this phase of research. The first school was organized like a traditional junior high, whereas the second adhered closely to modern middle-school concepts (Alexander & George, 1981). The two schools differed in the following ways:

1. *Interdisciplinary teams versus departmental organization:* Subject specialization was the primary organizing feature of the junior high school. Teachers were assigned to departments and classrooms according to the subjects they taught. Thus, grade-level social studies teachers worked in one wing of the school, grade-level English teachers in another, and grade-level math teachers in still another. On a typical day, a teacher in the English department might not see or interact with any of the other people in the school who teach the children in her English classes.

   In the middle school, teachers were organized according to the students they taught in common rather than the teachers' subject specialization. Teams of four or five teachers from various subject matter fields were assigned to work with groups of between 120 and 170 students. Teaching teams were assigned neighboring classrooms and a common planning room, and followed similar daily schedules. They coordinated their curriculum planning, designed lessons around common themes, diagnosed the learning problems of specific students, and made team decisions on how best to solve those problems.

2. *Multi-age versus single-age grouping:* Junior high school students were grouped by grade level. As they progressed through the sixth, seventh, and eighth grades, the chances were good that they would face a whole new group of teachers each year.

   Middle school students were assigned to multi-aged student groups when they entered the school and remained in their group for 3 years. A team of teachers from various disciplines was assigned to work with each group of students. Teachers remained with their student groups throughout their students' middle school careers. Thus, in a typical middle school math class there were approximately 24 students—8 in their first year of middle school, 8 in their second year, and 8 in their third year. The purpose of the middle school arrangement was to provide consistency and continuity in both personnel and instruction. Teachers got to know students well and, over time, devised instructional and counseling strategies that teachers thought were best suited to individual students. An effort was made to establish an esprit de corps among teachers, among students, and between both groups.

3. *Homeroom versus adviser–advisee programs:* In the junior high school the first period of the day was called *homeroom*. In fact, the homeroom period was simply the first academic period of the day. Attendance was taken and school announcements were made during the first 5 minutes of this class. There was no expectation that homeroom teachers would form special relationships with their students or serve in an advisory capacity.

In the middle school, multi-aged groups of students were assigned a teacher–adviser with whom they met for 25 minutes each day. Advisers acted as liaisons between the parents and the school and served as counselors and omsbudsmen for their advisees. In most instances students retained the same advisers for 3 years.

The Middle School Efficacy Study was conducted in two phases: (1) a questionnaire study designed to compare the efficacy attitudes of teachers in the two school settings and (2) a microethnography that investigated the classrooms of two teachers in each of the two schools. The second phase was designed to explore the relationship between school organization and such variables as teachers' efficacy attitudes, collegial relationships, experiences of stress, and teaching styles. In order to highlight the significance of the school organization variable, care was taken to select schools that were organized differently but otherwise were quite similar. The schools were about the same size and served students from similar racial and socioeconomic backgrounds. The racial composition and percentage of poverty students in the two schools are presented in Table 4.1.

TABLE 4.1.  Racial Composition and Percentage of Poverty Students in Participating Schools

| | Students | | | | | | Free or reduced lunch | |
| | Total | | Black | | White | | | |
| *School* | *N* | *%* | *N* | *%* | *N* | *%* | *N* | *%* |
|---|---|---|---|---|---|---|---|---|
| Middle school | 971 | 100 | 327 | 33.7 | 644 | 66.3 | 455 | 46.9 |
| Junior high | 945 | 100 | 342 | 36.2 | 603 | 63.8 | 418 | 44.2 |

## THE QUESTIONNAIRE STUDY

The questionnaire investigated the relationships among teachers' sense of efficacy, school organization, and several variables that previously had been shown to be related to effective teaching. These variables included school climate, teachers' feelings of job satisfaction, their experience of stress, commitment to teaching, and perceptions of the teacher role. Each of these variables and research pertaining to them are discussed below.

### School Climate and Teachers' Sense of Efficacy

A number of important studies challenge the Coleman et al. (1966) and Jencks et al. (1972) conclusion that one school is about as effective (or as ineffective) as another in educating the children of the poor. Though the studies that challenge this conclusion vary in their perspectives and methodologies, they have produced surprisingly consistent results. One of the most interesting of these findings is the relationship between school climate and student learning. When the climate of a school supports student achievement and is intolerant of misbehavior, students are likely to learn more in their classes, perform better on achievement tests, engage in less disruptive behavior, and be more satisfied with their schooling.

The work of Brookover and his colleagues (Brookover, Gigliotti, Henderson, & Schneider, 1973; Brookover & Lezotte, 1977; Brookover et al., 1978, 1979) suggests that the negative effects of low socioeconomic status on academic performance can be reduced if the school climate fosters high academic expectations and rewards achievement. Ellett and Masters (1978) studied the relationship between teachers' and students' perceptions of school climate and concluded that an educationally effective climate can be constructed out of different combinations of organizational, interpersonal, and sociopsychological factors. Thus, a variety of different school climate configurations could be associated with high student achievement.

A major study in Great Britain has substantiated the findings of school climate research in the United States. Rutter and his colleagues (Rutter et al., 1979) reported that student achievement was related to the overall ethos of the school. According to Rutter, a positive school ethos is achieved by the accumulative effect of such factors as a strong academic emphasis, high expectations for student achievement, clear incentive and reward systems, continual monitoring of student work, and providing students with corrective feedback. Like Ellett and Masters, Rutter concluded that an effective school climate is not achieved by any specific teaching strategies or particular mix of school factors. A number of different configurations of the variables mentioned can produce a positive school climate and improvement of academic achievement.

A number of teacher-related factors have been shown to be related to school effectiveness and student achievement. Strong collegial relations among faculty members (Ellett & Masters, 1977), teachers' perceptions that students' academic performance can be improved, and teachers' ability to communicate high performance expectations to their students (Brookover et al., 1979) all appear to contribute to the improvement of school ethos and to student achievement. In addition, Cohen (1979) reported that school organization can affect the degree of intergroup conflict among students, creating another variable that may influence teachers' efficacy attitudes and student achievement.

The mounting evidence showing that school climate variables relate to student achievement suggests that research is needed to identify the processes by which school-level influences are translated into student performance. Teachers' sense of efficacy may be an important mediator of school climate influences. If aspects of the organization (for example, team teaching or multi-age grouping) sustain teachers' sense of efficacy, then teachers may be more motivated to teach and their students more motivated to learn.

## Job Satisfaction and Teachers' Sense of Efficacy

Teachers' general satisfaction with teaching was expected to have a reciprocal relationship with their sense of efficacy. If teachers doubt their competence as teachers, it is unlikely that they will be satisfied with their chosen profession. Similarly, if teachers are dissatisfied with teaching, they may come to question their professional competence. Unfortunately, there seems to be rather general dissatisfaction among teachers at present (Dearman & Plisko, 1982; Lortie, 1975).

Research on job satisfaction offers some clues as to why teaching is not perceived as a highly satisfying occupation. From an extensive review of the research on the determinants of job satisfaction, Vroom (1964) concluded that the most significant factors contributing to job satisfaction include "high pay, substantial promotional opportunities, considerate and participative supervision, an opportunity to interact with one's peers, varied duties, and a high degree of control over work methods and work pace" (p. 173). As we indicated in Chapter 2, teaching offers little in these areas that would make it a personally rewarding profession.

The uncertainty that Jackson (1968) and Lortie (1975) have shown as endemic to teaching also must be considered in the study of job satisfaction and teachers' sense of efficacy. Lortie reported that teachers were generally uncertain about their effectiveness, and discussions on this topic evoked more emotion from respondents than any other issue in his study. In fact, direct questions about their feelings of effectiveness led to such emotional "flooding" that Lortie had to phrase his questions in gentler terms. He wrote:

Thus a seemingly simple question on problems of evaluating progress unleashed a torrent of feeling and frustration; one finds self-blame, a sense of inadequacy, the bitter taste of failure, anger at the students, despair, and other dark emotions. The freedom to assess one's own work is no occasion for joy; the conscience remains unsatisfied as ambiguity, uncertainty, and little apparent change impede the flow of reassurance. Teaching demands, it seems, the capacity to work for protracted periods without sure knowledge that one is having any positive effect on students. Some find it difficult to maintain their self-esteem. (p. 144)

This tormented sense of uncertainty must be a significant concern in identifying factors related to sense of efficacy. For example, how do teachers cope with the uncertainty in a way that enables them to maintain their sense of efficacy? Although teachers traditionally have not used collegial support groups to help them improve their teaching or elevate their educational aims, group support may function to help teachers live with professional uncertainty and the realization that they are not going to accomplish all they set out to achieve when they began teaching (Lortie, 1975).

School organization may influence job satisfaction by providing opportunities that foster teachers' sense of efficacy. For example, a school organization that encourages collegial interaction among teachers may create an atmosphere of support that increases teachers' collective sense of efficacy. Our comparison of two schools differing in organizational structure was designed to investigate this question.

## Teacher Stress

Teacher stress and burnout have been prominent topics in the discussion of teaching in recent years. Kyriacou (Kyriacou & Sutcliffe, 1977) defined *teacher stress* as

a response by a teacher of negative affect (such as anger, anxiety, or depression) accompanied by potentially pathogenic physiological changes (such as increased heart rate, or release of adrenocorticotrophic hormone into the bloodstream) as a result of the demands made upon the teacher. (p. 299)

A number of factors contribute to teacher stress:

(1) the degree of role conflict or role ambiguity involved,
(2) the degree to which the teacher[s] perceive that [they are] unable to meet the demands made upon [them],
(3) the degree to which the teacher's ability to meet the demands is impaired by poor working conditions,
(4) the degree to which the demands are new or unfamiliar, and
(5) the degree to which the teacher[s are] already experiencing stress resulting from sources outside [the teaching] role. (Kyriacou & Sutcliffe, 1977, p. 299)

The second factor, "the degree to which teachers perceive that they are unable to meet the demands made upon them," is conceptually similar to teachers' sense of inefficacy. Thus, it is reasonable to propose that teachers' sense of efficacy is related to teacher stress. To the extent that teachers are confident that they are having a positive impact on student learning, teacher stress should be reduced. However, there is ample evidence indicating that teachers' sense of efficacy is not the sole factor contributing to teacher stress. Inadequate pay, excessive clerical work, and discipline problems all contribute to making teaching a stressful profession (Raschke, Dedrick, Strathe, & Hawkes, 1985).

The relationship among stress, efficacy attitudes, and environmental factors probably is reciprocal. Bandura's (1982) analysis of self-efficacy suggests that negative emotional states that are brought on by environmental factors can wear down a person's sense of personal competence. Thus teachers who experience stress caused by low pay, overwork, and/or student misbehavior are likely to question their own abilities: "How effective can I be when I'm paid so poorly, when I get so far behind in my work, or when students behave so inappropriately in my classes?"

Many teachers have become disillusioned with teaching. For example, Sparks (1979) reported that 46% of the teachers he questioned were dissatisfied with their careers and would not choose to teach if they had it to do over again. Inability to deal with the stresses of teaching is likely to be a major contributor to teacher dissatisfaction and ultimately to the lowering of teachers' sense of efficacy.

## Teachers' Commitment to Teaching

Teachers' motivation to perform well in the classroom is a function of their commitment to their profession and of their sense of efficacy (Fuller et al., 1982; Vroom, 1964). A variety of factors have been found to influence teachers' commitment. These include sex, age, and marital status (Lortie, 1975). Aspects of school structure also may influence teacher commitment. Because commitment to teaching is likely to interact with efficacy attitudes and the effort teachers spend in helping students learn, the relationship of school structure to teacher commitment was investigated.

## Teacher Role Perceptions

Teachers vary in their perceptions of their professional role responsibilities (Metz, 1978; Mitchell, 1983; Rohrkemper & Brophy, 1979). For example, some teachers assume it is their job to impart information, whereas others concentrate on developing the self-esteem and citizenship of their students. Such differences of opinion have classroom consequences, and psychological results as well. Teachers with different aims are likely to employ quite different criteria in judging their own competence and assessing the educability and progress of their students.

Differences in teachers' role perceptions have been attributed to a variety of factors, including teacher personality, the absence of a technical culture of teaching (Lortie, 1975), and the characteristics of students being taught (Cohen, 1972). The organizational structure of the school also may influence teachers' role perceptions (Fuller et al., 1982). To examine the relationship of school structure and teachers' role perceptions, we compared the perceptions of teachers at the middle school with those at the junior high school.

## Research Participants

Teachers at the two schools were asked to spend 2 hours completing a questionnaire designed to investigate their perceptions of teaching. Each teacher was paid $10 for taking part in the study. Approximately half the teachers at each school completed the lengthy questionnaire: 29 teachers from the middle school and 20 teachers from the junior high. The final sample of teachers consisted of 35 white females, 5 white males, 7 black females, and 2 black males. The teachers ranged in age from their early twenties to their late fifties, though the majority of the teachers were between 25 and 35 years old. Because the questionnaire return rate was roughly equivalent, it was assumed that the samples were similar; however, generalizations drawn from the data must be viewed cautiously because teacher participation was voluntary and the questionnaire return rate was low.

## Questionnaire Measures

*Teachers' Sense of Efficacy.* The two Rand items, utilizing five choice Likert scales, were used to measure the efficacy attitudes of teachers at the two schools. (All questionnaire items can be found in Appendix A.)

*Teacher Expectations.* Teachers completed two teacher-climate measures—Present Evaluations and Expectations for High School Completion and the Teacher–Student Commitment to Improve—both developed by Brookover and his colleagues at Michigan State University (Brookover et al., 1973). The two measures, each consisting of five items, had been found by Brookover to be significantly related to student achievement.

*Collegial Relations.* A six-item subscale of the School Survey (Ellett & Masters, 1977) was used to measure colleague relationships. Teachers were asked to indicate the extent of cooperation and positive work relationships within their schools.

*Student Conflict.* Eleven items from Deslonde's Multicultural Social Climate Scale (Cohen, 1979) were used to assess the level of intergroup conflict among students at each of the two schools. These items asked teachers to indicate the frequency of aggressive behavior, ranging from pushing and name calling to stealing and extortion.

*Job Satisfaction.* Teachers were asked to indicate their satisfaction with their job on a 7-point Likert scale, with responses ranging from (1) *I am extremely satisfied with teaching as my occupation* to (7) *I am extremely dissatisfied with teaching as my occupation.*

*Stress.* Teachers were asked to respond to the question, "In general, how stressful do you find being a middle school teacher?" The response choice ranged from (1) *not at all stressful* to (5) *extremely stressful.*

*Commitment to Teaching.* Three items were selected to investigate teachers' commitment to their profession. First, teachers were told to imagine that a circle divided into eight sections represented their life interests. They were then asked, "How many of the eight sections would you say "belong" to your work as a teacher?" Second, teachers were asked, "How important is teaching to you?" Responses on a 4-point scale ranged from (1) *extremely important* to (4) *not important at all.* Third, teachers were asked, "If you had it to do over again, would you choose to become a teacher?" Teachers circled *yes* or *no.*

*Teacher Attributions.* To explore the relationship of school organization and teachers' attributions of responsibility for students' failure, teachers were asked to complete the statement, "When my students fail to learn a lesson that I have taught, their failure is probably due to _____." Responses were categorized as being either an attribution to self (e.g., students didn't learn because the teacher failed to prepare the lesson or explain it clearly) or an attribution to the student (e.g., students didn't learn because they lacked ability or didn't try).

*Teacher Role Perceptions.* To examine the range of responsibilities that teachers accept as part of the teaching role, the following question was adapted from Fox, Jung, Schmuck, Van Egmond, and Ritus (1970):

> All of us have certain things about our role performance which we think are important. There are 10 numbered blanks on the page below. In the blanks, please write 10 verbs or short descriptive phrases, each referring to the statement, "As a middle school teacher, I do the following things."

## Results

The mean responses for teachers in each school to each questionnaire item are presented in Table 4.2. A one-way analysis of variance revealed a trend

TABLE 4.2.  School Means and Standard Deviations for Questionnaire Data

| Item[a] | School | N | Mean | SD | Minimum score | Maximum score |
|---|---|---|---|---|---|---|
| Efficacy 1 | Middle | 28 | 3.43 | .96 | 2 | 5 |
| | Junior | 20 | 2.95 | 1.15 | 1 | 5 |
| Efficacy 2 | Middle | 29 | 3.76 | .79 | 2 | 5 |
| | Junior | 20 | 3.50 | .79 | 2 | 5 |
| Teacher expectations[b] | Middle | 29 | 23.86 | 4.10 | 15 | 35 |
| | Junior | 20 | 26.65 | 3.47 | 20 | 33 |
| Colleague relations | Middle | 29 | 14.79 | 2.51 | 10 | 18 |
| | Junior | 20 | 16.75 | 2.07 | 11 | 18 |
| Student conflict | Middle | 29 | 41.52 | 7.08 | 17 | 51 |
| | Junior | 20 | 43.65 | 8.04 | 26 | 56 |
| Job satisfaction[c] | Middle | 29 | 2.21 | .82 | 1 | 4 |
| | Junior | 20 | 2.95 | 1.19 | 1 | 5 |
| Stress | Middle | 29 | 3.34 | 1.01 | 1 | 5 |
| | Junior | 20 | 3.10 | 1.12 | 0 | 5 |
| Teaching/interest | Middle | 29 | 3.97 | 1.30 | 1 | 7 |
| | Junior | 20 | 3.55 | 1.64 | 2 | 7 |
| Teaching/importance[d] | Middle | 29 | 1.52 | .51 | 1 | 2 |
| | Junior | 20 | 1.90 | .55 | 1 | 3 |

[a] Unless otherwise indicated, the higher the score, the stronger the attitude.
[b] Lower score indicates higher expectation.
[c] Lower score indicates greater satisfaction.
[d] The lower the score, the more important teaching is to the teacher.

approaching significance, indicating that middle school teachers had a higher sense of efficacy than did junior high teachers, as measured by the total score on the two Rand Efficacy items, $F(1, 46) = 2.28$, $p < .10$. Although the school effect on teachers' sense of efficacy scores failed to attain statistical significance, the fact that middle school teachers did have higher mean scores on both items suggests the need for further study of the relationship between efficacy attitudes and school organization. The skew and limited variability ($M = 8.66$, $SD = 1.51$) of the Rand Efficacy measure restricted the possibility of discovering real differences in teachers' sense of efficacy due to school differences. Examination of the response distribution of answers to the Rand items revealed that 50% of the middle school teachers scored 8 or above compared to 30% of the junior high teachers; in contrast, 32% of middle school teachers scored 6 or less on the Rand items compared to 55% of the junior high teachers. These data suggest that real school differences in teachers' sense of efficacy may exist that could be detected with a larger sample and a more reliable (longer) instrument.

Coefficient alphas calculated for items measuring teachers' expectations (Brookover et al., 1973), colleague relations (Ellett & Masters, 1977), student conflict (Cohen, 1979) and school climate were .61, .84, and .59, respectively. These coefficients were considered sufficiently high to warrant use of a total score for each. One-way analysis of variance indicated that middle school teachers had higher expectations of academic success for their students than did junior high teachers ($F = 6.18, p < .05$). Middle school teachers reported more difficulties with collegial relations than did junior high teachers ($F = 8.24, p < .01$). No significant differences in student intergroup conflict were reported.

A Wilcoxin test of school differences in job satisfaction revealed that the middle school teachers reported being more satisfied with teaching than junior high teachers ($x^2 = 3.85, p < .05$). The middle school teachers considered teaching to be more important to them than did the junior high teachers ($x^2 = 7.69, p < .01$). The school differences in measures of teacher stress and teaching as a life interest were not statistically significant.

Teachers' responses to the item asking for attribution of responsibility for student failure also suggested a potentially important difference between the teachers in the two schools, though statistically significant differences were not detectable. It can be seen in Table 4.3 that middle school teachers were much less less likely than junior high teachers to blame students for poor academic achievement. Thirty-five percent of junior high teachers but only 14% of middle school teachers attributed academic failure to their students. Forty-one percent of middle school teachers and 30% of junior high teachers attributed student failure to the teachers' poor performance.

The teachers' responses to the role perception question were sorted and categorized. The frequencies with which the responses occurred are reported for middle school and junior high school teachers in Table 4.4.

The results were surprising in that there was so much variety in the teachers' responses. Traditionally accepted role responsibilities, such as evaluation and curriculum design, were not mentioned frequently by either group of teachers. The most frequently mentioned responsibility, occurring on 51% of the questionnaires, was classroom management. The second most frequent response was instruction. The third referred to teachers' emotions (experiencing positive and negative affect). Other role responsibilities mentioned by a third or more of the teachers were to motivate students, plan lessons, help students emotionally, and listen to students.

TABLE 4.3. Teachers' Attribution of Responsibility for Failure

| | Middle school | | Junior high | | Total | |
|---|---|---|---|---|---|---|
| | # | % | # | % | # | % |
| Self | 12 | 41 | 6 | 30 | 19 | 38 |
| Student | 4 | 14 | 7 | 35 | 11 | 22 |
| Self and student | 9 | 31 | 7 | 35 | 16 | 32 |
| Other | 4 | 14 | 0 | 0 | 4 | 8 |

TABLE 4.4.    Teacher Role Perception Categories

| Categories | Middle school % | Junior high % | Total % |
|---|---|---|---|
| Manage classroom | 48 | 55 | 51 |
| Instruct/help students learn subject | 38 | 65 | 49 |
| Experience positive affect | 48 | 40 | 45 |
| Experience negative affect | 41 | 45 | 43 |
| Motivate | 34 | 45 | 39 |
| Plan | 38 | 35 | 38 |
| Help students emotionally | 41 | 30 | 36 |
| Listen | 41 | 25 | 35 |
| Adapt teaching to student's ability | 17 | 50 | 31 |
| Grade (evaluate) | 31 | 20 | 27 |
| Work with colleagues | 28 | 20 | 24 |
| Understand | 28 | 20 | 24 |
| Develop personal relation with students | 41 | 0 | 24 |
| Care | 28 | 15 | 22 |
| Work with parents | 17 | 30 | 22 |
| Work hard | 31 | 5 | 20 |
| Talk | 14 | 15 | 14 |
| Teach responsibility | 14 | 14 | 14 |
| Keep records | 10 | 20 | 14 |
| Act as a role model | 24 | 0 | 14 |
| Help students learn social skills | 6 | 20 | 12 |

Managing the classroom and experiencing emotion were a part of what teachers did at both schools. However, teachers at the middle school and the junior high did not always agree on what teaching entailed. For example, 41% of middle school teachers said that "establishing personal relationships" was part of their work, but no junior high teachers made such a claim. Twenty-four percent of the middle school teachers said they acted as role models to students, but no junior high teachers mentioned role modeling. Less dramatic, but nevertheless consistent, differences were found in such affective areas as "helping students emotionally," "listening to students," "understanding," and "caring." Middle school teachers put much greater emphasis on the affective domain than did their counterparts in the junior high school. In contrast, junior high teachers emphasized instructional concerns. Sixty-five percent of junior high teachers mentioned that it was their job to teach students subject matter, whereas only 38% of middle school teachers mentioned instruction.

Fifty percent of junior high teachers and only 17% of middle school teachers mentioned adapting their teaching to fit the ability level of different students. The latter finding is interesting because the organizational differences between the two schools, specifically the multi-age grouping at the middle school, suggest that middle school teachers would be confronted with greater ability differences in their classes than would the junior high teachers. Yet, middle school teachers were less concerned with ability issues than were junior high teachers. The explanation for this finding is probably related to a theme that will be developed in the next section of the chapter—namely, that the junior high school had an individualistic orientation that encouraged teachers to look for differences among students and to sort students according to achievement and ability. The middle school orientation, on the other hand, was communal rather than individualistic. Teachers were more impressed by what students held in common than by what separated or appeared to separate them. Thus it is not surprising that middle school teachers had significantly higher expectations of academic success for their students than did junior high teachers and tended to have higher efficacy scores as well.

Also of interest is that 31% of middle school teachers but only 5% of junior high teachers mentioned "working hard" on their list of what they do as teachers. This too is probably related to the organizational differences between the two schools. Middle school teachers worked in teams and shared in decision making and the governance of the school to a much greater extent than did their counterparts in the junior high. Not only did this mean that middle school teachers had extra layers of responsibility and had to put in many hours of committee work, but the team orientation increased the points of contact and possible points of conflict among teachers. Thus it is not surprising that middle school teachers reported more difficulties with colleagues than did junior high teachers.

# A MICROETHNOGRAPHY OF MIDDLE SCHOOL AND JUNIOR HIGH SCHOOL TEACHERS' PERSPECTIVES AND PRACTICES

## Introduction

The questionnaire study indicated that teacher attitudes at the two schools differed markedly in some areas. In order to better understand the structural features of the two schools and how they might be related to teacher attitudes, an exploratory microethnography study was designed.

## Methodology

The nature of the research task required a methodology capable of examining teaching and its contextual determinants and of generating hypotheses for further research and theory. An understanding of the processes through which school organization influences teacher thought and action required a methodology that goes beyond a mere description of what teachers do in the classroom and what they profess to believe. What was needed was a methodology that would allow researchers to describe the complex meaning systems that people use to understand their roles, their work, and the organizations in which they work (Spradley, 1980).

Because of its usefulness for these purposes, the ethnographic method of participant observation was chosen as the appropriate methodology for the second stage of the middle school/junior high study.

Participant observation entails sharing the cultural environments of the group being studied. As Becker, Geer, and Hughes (1968) explain,

> The participant observer follows those he studies through their daily round of life, seeing what they do, when, with whom, and under what circumstances, and querying them about the meaning of their actions. In this way [the researcher] builds up a body of field notes and interviews that come nearer than any other social science method to capturing the patterns of collective action as they occur in real life. (p. 13)

Limitations of time and resources made it impossible to undertake a full-fledged organizational ethnography of both schools. It was decided, therefore, that a microethnographic study of two middle school and two junior high teachers' school lives would be conducted. The goal of the analysis was to produce an ethnographic account of the four teachers' perspectives and practices in the two schools. More importantly, however, the goal was to discover cultural themes that connected attitudes to actions and had explanatory power. Attention was paid to teachers' behaviors, their beliefs regarding the teaching role, the organization of the two schools, how teachers perceived the organization, and how school organization was related to the beliefs and behaviors of teachers.

Two teachers from the middle school and two from the junior high were observed over the course of an academic year. A researcher visited their classrooms and observed their interactions with colleagues, administrators, and students. Each teacher was observed a minimum of 12 times. Care was taken to insure that the number and timing of visits were roughly equivalent for all four teachers and that all periods of the day were represented. The teachers were interviewed at various times throughout the year and were questioned about classroom events, student behavior, curriculum decisions, teaching methods, and their educational aims. The following criteria were used to select the four teachers in this part of the study:

- Two or more years of teaching in their present positions
- Previous teaching experience at another school
- Willingness to participate in the study
- Identified as "good classroom managers" by the school principal
- In the case of middle school teachers, membership on the same team
- In the case of the junior high school teachers, membership in the same department, but teaching different grade levels.

These criteria were established to reduce those teacher differences that were least likely to be related to school organization and to highlight those differences that were most likely to be related to the organization of the school.

All data collected in the field were recorded in fieldnotes. Following each day in the field, the researcher transcribed and expanded her fieldnotes on audio tape. Within a few days, the content of the tapes was typed onto 5" × 8" cards. The primary analysis of data was the responsibility of one member of the research team, but findings were discussed with and verified by other team members who were working in the two schools and, at times, with the same four teachers.

The primary methodological strategy employed for data analysis was *cultural theme analysis*—a process for identifying domains that can serve as categories and provide a system of meaning for the individuals within the cultural setting. Spradley (1980) defined a *cultural theme* as "any principle recurrent in a number of domains, tacit or implicit, and serving as a relationship among domains; any system of cultural meaning" (p. 141).

## Results

The major cultural themes that distinguish the teachers at one school from those at the other are described in the next section. Theme descriptions are followed by a discussion of school organizational factors and their apparent relationship to teachers' beliefs and behaviors.

*Conceptions of teaching: An exalted or burdened profession?* Teachers' attitudes about teaching were sharply different at the two schools. At the middle school, teachers perceived the work of teaching as a demanding but important job. Though frustrated because there never seemed to be enough time to do all that needed to be done, they said teaching was personally challenging and socially significant. Despite daily hardships, they found deep satisfaction in what one teacher called the "exalted" profession. A measure of these feelings is captured in this middle school teacher's comments:

> I think that teaching is an inspired profession, I really do. For philosophical and religious reasons, I feel teaching ... teaching is a gift and a unique opportunity to help other individuals.... It's a great contribution that we can make to our fellow human beings and our society.... [We're working not only with students'] intellect, but [with] their total being over a period of years. We're spending ... as [much time with students] as their parents do.... We're entrusted with their development and that's a great responsibility and yet, a great opportunity. I see it as both. I consider my position an exalted one ... and I think that's one of the reasons I have stayed with [teaching. I] realize my rewards are ... not ... financial [but] I feel good about what I'm doing. I feel I'm really contributing to society and my fellow man. Maybe that's much more worthwhile than the dollar. So I guess that is a basic assumption; ... that I feel [teaching] is a calling....
>
> One of the things that helped develop the idea [that teaching is a] calling

or the exalted position is the Middle School concept. I think if you taught at a high school or let's say in a junior high school situation, the stress is [not] on the total development of the child. . . . You see yourself as instilling a certain amount of intellectual knowledge. Now if you only perceived your role that way, it doesn't give you this full feeling [of accomplishment]. Still it is a tremendous responsibility. But when you think about the total development of the child, [as we do in the Middle School, you're] talking about his moral development, values, how he relates to other people, and [whether or not] he is going to be a contributing member of society. We're talking about a lot more things than just the mind. That makes [teaching] much more fulfilling.

The belief of middle school teachers that teaching is a noble profession was supported by an equally strong belief in the efficacy of their own teaching and of the teaching enterprise in general. They were convinced that they could make a significant contribution to the lives of children and were publicly and personally committed to doing so. They thought it necessary and possible to teach students to assume responsibility for their own behavior. The strength of this conviction was expressed by one middle school teacher when she answered a question about her teaching goals.

First, before you can teach [students] anything, you have to teach them how to live, if they don't know how yet. Unfortunately, a lot of them don't. And you have to teach them to take responsibility for their own actions. You can't ever let them . . . blame anybody else for their performance in school. [That's] something that *they* have to take responsibility for. I really feel . . . that's true. The thing I want to teach them is how to continue learning after they leave me or . . . leave school. I don't want them to just do things because they get a grade for it. . . . That's why I really stress . . . recreational reading. And I think it's very important to teach them how to get along with each other—not just in the school setting but in other . . . settings too. It's unfortunate that we have all the responsibilities that we do. Because you can't teach kids how to read or do math or anything else if they don't know how to live. And though some of them do, many of them don't.

I didn't have this orientation in the beginning. At the beginning I thought I was supposed to go in and teach language arts. And that was all I was going to do. . . . This was when I taught at another middle school [that] wasn't very organized. I had just eighth graders then. I soon began to realize that [kids had] lots of behaviors that they learned other places, [behaviors] that really interfered with their learning [in school]. There were lots of things they were bringing from home—lots of problems and things that interfered with their learning. [At first] I thought that what I needed to do was ignore those other things. I really thought that was my job—to ignore problems and to go ahead and teach. . . . But I found out that you couldn't. You can't let the problems be an excuse for why kids don't learn. But you . . . have to take the other problems and extraneous things into account or you can't teach. [You can't use] those things as an excuse and say. . . . "This kid can never learn, . . . look at his home life." I totally disagree with [that]. But I still think you need to look at those [problems] and work with those things before you teach the kids.

This teacher's commitment to reach all her students is also reflected in her description of the kinds of students in her classes.

> I have some kids who don't come from a supportive environment. So when ... they get to school, before they can learn anything, they've got to have a supportive environment established at school. Nobody at home is telling them that it's important for them to learn.... So I have to first ... convince them that [learning] is important and they must trust me enough [to] want to learn whatever it is that I have to teach them. So, besides ... the kind of stuff I'm teaching other kids, I also have to teach them [to value] learning.
>
> And then there are kids who you not only have to teach values about learning, but also ... about life values. They don't know that there is a way to live without fighting or [how to] take responsibility for [their own lives]. You really can do things about your life. They have to be shown that the things they do have consequences and that they can control their own lives. So ... you have to teach them that learning is important. You have to teach them that they can control their own lives and you also have to teach them [subject matter]. Yes, I would say that's really been the major way that I differentiate [my students]. I have found that it really doesn't have that much to do with economics at all.

At the junior high, the teachers did not describe teaching in lofty terms or express ambitious goals. Although they said they "liked" their work, they described teaching as a "burdened," "trying" profession. Questions about teaching were answered briefly and without excitement or inspiration. Their answers contrasted sharply with the lengthy, philosophical responses of middle school teachers. When asked to define teaching, one junior high teacher said simply, "Teaching is teaching a child how to use all his skills." The second junior high teacher answered the question in much the same way. "Teaching," she said, was "helping children learn to become, to grow as individuals, to become all they can be."

For middle school teachers, work with students offered an unambiguous opportunity to change the course of their pupils' lives. Junior high teachers thought the most they could do was develop capacities and skills that were already present as clear potential in their pupils. The futures they envisioned for their students were constrained by their pupils' present abilities and circumstances. They were uncertain that schools could set students off in new, more promising directions. At best, teachers could accelerate a student's course along an already established path.

The junior high teachers could recall a time when they viewed teaching as an opportunity to change students' lives. The glow of that ideal, however, had faded, and teachers acknowledged their past perspective as naive. They now set simpler short-term goals for their classes and themselves, and they defined themselves as agents of the curriculum and not as agents of student development. They viewed this shift as practical and realistic, and though they did not express displeasure, they did not describe their activities with enthusiasm or vision. When asked if there were things they looked forward to each day, one teacher responded:

> No. I think I kinda do look forward to each class as it comes in. I don't think I look forward to any one thing in particular, because I usually try to change the pace during class so I won't get bored. I try not to bore myself. Sometimes I do ... after six classes.

To the same question, the second junior high teacher replied:

> Oh, well, I don't know. Most of the days I don't. I mean, I don't ever ... well, maybe Monday mornings, maybe if I'm really tired or something like that, or just don't feel good [I might not look forward to work], but most of the time I don't [dread work]. I hardly ever dread [coming in] unless there's some other kind of pressure.... And if there is, oh, I don't know....

The junior high teachers were somewhat fatalistic about their students' potential academic performance. They felt they had limited power to improve the academic performance of their students and even less power to influence the course of their pupils' lives. Some, they thought, would improve over the course of the year, others would not. They believed that there was little a teacher could do to alter this natural course of events. The response of one junior high teacher to the question, "Have you ever had a child who was not interested in school activities?" was as follows:

> TEACHER: Well, there's quite a number of those, and some of them are, you know, lacking. I can deal with some, and some of them leave exactly as they came in.
>
> INTERVIEWER: What works with kids like that?
>
> TEACHER: Just explaining ... "I know social studies may not be one of the things that you really like, but ... I think you can try. I think you can do something." Sometimes it helps. Sometimes it doesn't.

With this focus on curriculum matters in their teaching, the junior high teachers viewed students' potential in terms of their pupils' academic performance (i.e., good grades and subject matter mastery) rather than their social and emotional development (getting along with others, learning to value learning, and taking responsibility for their own actions). Moreover, they worked to fit their students to the demands of the curriculum, rather than working to tailor the curriculum to the different needs of their students. Thus teachers were frustrated by county regulations that disallowed streaming, that is, assigning all students to classes by the pupils' academic ability.

> INTERVIEWER: How does your teaching situation affect your capacity to achieve your teaching goals?
>
> TEACHER: First of all, ... [the] kids aren't grouped; ... [that] makes it difficult for teaching. Some [students] are

INTERVIEWER:

TEACHER:

capable, and some of them [aren't]. You know, you've got everything from an ESE kid (just one slot out of EMR) to a gifted [kid] in the same room. It's very difficult to handle the needs of those kids when the range is so huge. Meeting the needs of this great disparity . . . that is totally beyond me.

Can you give me an example of how you might change some part of your teaching or grading or expectations [to meet the individual needs of students?]

Well, . . . if I assign a written report . . . I don't expect as thorough [a job from some students]. In many instances, I don't expect what you would really call a report from certain students. I mean if they copy something straight out of an encyclopedia I feel lucky.

Junior high teachers defined their role in terms of the academic goals of the school but did not believe that all children supported the teachers' academic aims. In particular, the teachers considered student motivation a problem. As one teacher explained:

They are more supportive of their own little social thing. . . . My thing is not that important. It's important to me; it's just not important to them. They're not trying to keep from doing it, but it's just not that important to them. It's a minor thing in their lives.

To sum up, middle school teachers gave effusive descriptions of their profession and the opportunities it provided for contributing to the lives of students and the future of society. In contrast, junior high teachers were less optimistic about their ability to influence the academic performance of some students or the future lives of most.

*Teacher role perceptions: Student development versus academic instruction.* Job attitudes were closely linked to teachers' role perceptions at the two schools. At the middle school, teachers saw themselves as responsible for providing instruction but viewed that role as secondary to their most important obligation: "helping students." They saw themselves as agents of social development, responsible for advising, guiding, encouraging, and caring for their pupils. One related goal was to teach students how to "get along in the world." To achieve this goal, they worked to form strong personal relationships with all students and especially with their advisees. Moreover, they worked collaboratively with members of their teaching teams to broaden their knowledge of students. Teachers claimed that the three elements of the teaching role (helping students, enhancing teacher–student relationships, and team membership) are complementary, and all are part of a conception of teaching and learning that is socially rather than individually based. The intellectual and social development of children is important, but it is to be achieved through a team effort, in an environment of trust, caring, and hard work. The comments of the two middle school teachers reflect the social orientation of their school:

> This school is set up . . . around teams and AAs [adviser-advisee relationships] and . . . it means that one of the most important things at this school is making sure . . . that kids are happy and comfortable here and [that] they feel safe. When [students] feel that, that's a really important thing. You feel better about spending time trying to make it happen. You don't feel like you're shortchanging the kids. I think there are probably a lot of schools where the subject matter . . . overrides any other concern. I would say that at least on this team, and probably across the school, that we . . . make sure that the kids are happy first. Otherwise they aren't going to learn anything, anyway. . . . We have to recognize that [and] do something about it.

The second teacher explained:

> I . . . feel that if you're going to have any really effective development [at] the emotional level, you have to have a program that is laid out very clearly and then is encouraged. That's basically what the adviser–advisee program is all about. It's a format where certain types of activities are set up so that you can work with students' values and help them clarify what they think is important in their lives, and it also works with their self-concept, which is extremely important to an adolescent because they go through a lot . . . at this age. A lot of times it is easy to picture oneself as "the ugly duckling," unacceptable, a social outcast, or whatever. . . . We help a student realize that there are good things about him, and having a positive self-concept and a positive self-image is extremely important. It is hard even to work at an academic level if you are frustrated with yourself and what's happening in your life. [The adviser–advisee program gives us] a means of dealing with . . . these types of problems.

In contrast, teachers from the junior high school defined their work in terms of instruction, grading, and discipline or classroom management. The importance of these three aspects of teaching is evident in the response a junior high teacher gave to the following question:

> INTERVIEWER: How do you evaluate students?
> TEACHER: Test scores, teacher tests (not Metropolitans), and sometimes self-evaluation kinds of things, I've used those too. But . . . the academic mark . . . is mainly based on tests and classroom work. Now with the behavior part of it, that's based on, well, observations, marks for one particular thing or another; like [if they were caught] with gum, or if they were sent to the office, or [if I told them to do something] more than once, or if I had to write their names on the board [because they weren't] where they were supposed to be.

A second teacher gave a shorter answer to the same question. "Easy," she said, "three ways: tests, homework, and classwork." The junior high teachers viewed themselves primarily as agents of the curriculum, responsible for the effective dissemination of knowledge. Athough they hoped to influence students' social and emotional development, this was not viewed as a legitimate goal to be pursued actively with all students.

Classroom observations revealed that teachers from the two schools employed teaching methods that were compatible with their perceptions of the teaching role and their goals for education. Middle school teachers employed a variety of instructional strategies, focused on "understanding over completion," and frequently grouped students in an effort to meet individual needs. Teachers at the junior high relied on variants of a single teaching method; teachers lectured, students listened and supplemented their understanding by reading the text. Tests were given to determine how much information the students had retained. Exams and quizzes were not diagnostic, and a poor performance by individuals or the class was seldom followed by reinstruction. Despite the teachers' dislike of heterogeneous grouping, the class was taught as a whole. Teachers emphasized the need to get through the text and to get students to complete their work so that it could be graded.

*Organizational features of the schools and teachers' sense of efficacy.* Middle school teachers' interactions with students demonstrated their belief that students could learn and that teachers could positively affect the lives of their pupils. The behavior of the junior high teachers, on the other hand, indicated that they were less confident that all students could be taught or that teachers could have a lasting impact on their students. Three organizational features of the middle school appeared to support teachers' efficacy attitudes: (1) team teaching, (2) the sharing of decision-making power by the principal with the staff, and (3) multi-aged grouping that allowed teachers to work with students from the time they entered school to the time they graduated. The nature and apparent influence of these three features are discussed in the following sections.

*Teaming, departmentalization, and collegial relations.* At the middle school, teachers were organized into interdisciplinary teams. Four or more teachers shared responsibility for a multi-age group of students from the 6th, 7th, and 8th grades. The teaching team worked together in the same part of the building, shared the same planning room, worked within the same daily schedule, and shared resources and supplies. Teachers at the junior high had autonomous responsibility for their classes. Formal membership in a subject-area department was the primary unit of collegial association. However, the departmental structure at the junior high school was not designed to promote daily, task-related interactions or shared decision making.

The roles teachers played in decision making at the two schools varied considerably. At the middle school, problems were discussed in team meetings, consensus was hammered out, plans were made, and decisions were referred to the principal usually for final approval but sometimes for further discussion. The process, one of shared responsibility and group participation, was in keeping with the predominantly social orientation of the middle school.

Decision making at the junior high occurred at the administrative level of the school and was in harmony with the school's predominantly individualistic orientation. Departmental chairpersons sometimes were consulted by the principal and suggestions from individual teachers were considered when offered. Occasionally, the opinions of individual teachers were solicited. Decisions were made, however, in the principal's office, not by teachers in group meetings. Faculty suggestions came from individuals as expressions of personal opinion and preference, seldom from departments or groups of teachers. Little effort was made to arrive at a group consensus through open discussion at department or faculty meetings.

The organizational differences at the two schools promoted quite different relationships among teachers at each of the schools. What follows is an account of how the organization of the school produces an atmosphere of individualism and isolation at the junior high and one of community and shared commitment at the middle school.

Evidence of teamwork and community showed itself at the start of each day at the middle school. Before the first bell, faculty gathered in the teachers' lounge to sign in and check the mail for announcements. This gathering was an occasion for sharing news, anecdotes, and companionship, and for starting the day on a note of communal enthusiasm. During the day, teachers spent most of their time in their classrooms but, when the schedule allowed, they used the team planning room for parent conferences, meetings with students, coffee breaks, or formal and informal meetings with members of their team.

Planning rooms were the hub of collegial activity at the school. Teams arranged their rooms to facilitate interaction and decorated them to express group cohesion and to advertise their collective identity. The following excerpt from fieldnotes describes a typical planning room at the middle school.

> Just outside the planning room there is a display on the wall. A large sign reads "Courtesy of the Dynamos." *Dynamo*, it turns out, is the team logo. Below the sign are seven posters, each with a picture and short autobiography of a teacher. Inside the small room, rectangular tables have been fitted together to form a single, large table, surrounded by chairs. On the wall hangs a bulletin board on which is posted a sign that reads "D Team Planning Room." On the other side of the room there is a wall of cabinets containing, as a sign announces, "Team Supplies." Taped on the cabinets are seven large message-envelopes, each with a teacher's name written in magic marker. On a second

bulletin board, near the door, are displayed birthday cards, cartoons, and various notices. Above the board hangs a poster for the film *Stir Crazy*. A picture of two men in bird costumes is captioned, "Two Birds of a Feather." The *Two* has been crossed out and replaced by a "Seven." Along a third wall is a small table. On it is a coffee pot, cups, and the ingredients for instant coffee, tea, and cocoa.

The classrooms of most teachers on the team were in close proximity to one another and to the team planning room. Time for team planning was built into the school schedule at the beginning and end of the work day. In addition, teachers had a common lunch period and each teacher had an individual planning period every other day. Room assignments and the schedule at the middle school were designed to assure that teachers would share both time and space with their fellow team members. Teachers valued their time together, as one teacher explained:

> Lunch time is our big social time. As a matter of fact we even have special lunches. About once a month, we all bring in some things and eat together. We get a lot accomplished at lunch time talking about the kids. We don't necessarily sit there with the intention of talking about the kids but when you have just spent 4 hours with them, that's what you're thinking about. So that's what we talk about.

Sharing reponsibility for a group of students contributed to the unity of the teacher teams. Even in the more private world of the classroom, teachers were never fully separated from their colleagues. Teachers moved freely in and out of one another's rooms and, even when teaching alone, felt connected to others by a shared curriculum and a common concern for students. In one teacher's words:

> I just feel ... there is no time here at school when we're not talking about something that'll benefit the kids in some way. It's not that we plan it that way; it just happens that way. That's where our concern is.

Teachers shared their problems and frustrations with one another, and as one teacher explained, this commonality of experience provided a powerful sense of team unity:

> After the students leave [at the end of the day], I usually sit [in the classroom] for 2 minutes and collect myself. Then [the teachers] usually get together as a team. There is a lot of communication about [our] frustrations and what's succeeding and what's not.... We talk about [everything]: "This is driving me crazy," or "I'm about to lose my mind." That's when the team becomes very important. When a particular teacher is having a bad day, we really pull around and lift her spirits. There is always a lot of that going on. There is [also] a lot of pat[ting] on the back [when a teacher] has a particularly good day, and if something is really successful.

Common responsibilities gave teachers a common focus and a common sense of accomplishment. Formal and informal, planned and unplanned team experiences became interwoven and shaped the behavior of teachers—who, in turn, shaped the character and direction of the team. In the end, teams were held together as much by friendship as they were by the formal organization of the school. As one teacher put it:

> Everybody in the school is aware of the fact that a team, in order to do its job, has to work smoothly and cooperate and learn to get along. As a result, some things just happen spontaneously, and other things we sort of plan. At Christmas and other times we have special get togethers; after school we get together socially, and the team builds that kind of relationship. We're very close. I care a lot about my team.

Teams also were a source of support and a resource for solving problems. When a student was having a problem, teachers brought the situation to the attention of the team:

> If I become aware of a problem, it is very important for me to communicate with ... my team about the student and the problem. On our team, we're constantly involved in the process of trying to help students. [Because we all teach] the same students [we can provide and get] lots of help.

Teams were the main resource that teachers had for providing help to students and getting help for themselves. Teachers reported that teams made their jobs easier because they provided consistency, not only in curricular matters but in the area of discipline as well. One teacher explained that all the students on her team knew that their teachers "are very strict; we're very firm with the kids on certain things—mainly behavior. We just don't allow them to behave like animals, and they know that. It makes my teaching a lot easier."

The same teacher went on to say that teams made her counseling more effective:

> A lot of counseling goes on in this team. Kids find somebody on the team to whom they can talk, and ... different kids [choose] different teachers. Whenever they need to talk to a teacher about something, the others will always try to cover [so] that teacher will have some time to spend with this one student.

Working in teams was highly valued by middle school teachers. As we have seen, teams provided direction, fellowship, help, advice, support, group identity, continuity, and a sense of pride and shared accomplishment. Teams diminished isolation and uncertainty—two problems endemic to the teaching profession. Shared decision making took time, however. Differences of opinion inevitably surfaced and had to be rectified. Though teams were sources of energy and inspiration, they were also taxing. Some teachers, who did not take part in the microethnographic portion of the study indicated that though they loved teaching at the middle school, they realized that someday they would run out of energy and would have to transfer to another, less-demanding school.

Teacher relationships at the junior high school were of a strikingly different nature than at the middle school across town. Once again faculty roles and relationships were connected to the organization of the school. From the start of the day at 8:15 until the end of the workday at 3:30 teachers saw themselves as individual members of the staff doing separate jobs with relative independence. They decided on their own how they would teach and, within the confines of the school and county curricula, what would be taught. They shared few responsibilities with other teachers, nor did they want to, for they valued their relative autonomy. Their successes were their own and others learned of their problems only to the degree that teachers themselves wished to reveal them.

The individual orientation of teachers and the junior high organization that supported it were evident in many aspects of school life. A teacher's schedule was viewed as a personal assignment and was not designed to put that teacher in daily contact with colleagues. During free periods teachers were usually found working alone in their classrooms rather than with other adults.

Faculty, departmental, and grade-level meetings were infrequent and were formally organized around set agendas. Normally such meetings took place after school and were conducted with an air of hurried efficiency. A "good meeting" was one in which individual tasks were defined and assigned quickly and where discussions were brief and well focused. Typically, faculty and department meetings occurred two or three times a month. There was no need for more because teachers were not actively involved in decision making at the school.

When junior high teachers were asked if they took part in school decisions, they invariably said that they did. For example, one teacher said that "at department meetings you definitely can participate in decision making." The example she gave was indicative of the limited decision-making role teachers tended to play in the junior high school. She said a teacher who had decided to show a film might ask colleagues if they would like to show the film to their classes on the same day. Decisions would be made concerning "who's going to do what" and individual teachers "would have input."

Not all incidents of teacher decision making were as trivial as the above example might indicate, but most showed the same individualistic orientation. For example, a committee of three teachers was formed to decide how much material from a new textbook would be covered over the course of a year and at what rate the material would be presented to students. The committee met, assigned the task to the most experienced teacher, and agreed to meet again when the work was completed. As a teacher on the committee explained:

> Sally had been teaching world history for a long time and so she said, "If you want me to, I'll set a schedule up for us," and we all said all right.... We hadn't been [teaching history that long] and definitely not with this book, this

new textbook. So she set up the schedule, and we had input in that we could say that this is not good.

The teacher just quoted was willing to assign the task to someone she assumed knew more than she did, but her real preference was that the committee not be formed in the first place and that the questions of content and scheduling be left to individual teachers:

> We had input . . . but until you go through [the teaching of the text] you don't know what's good and what's bad. So I really think that a teacher is better off if she sets up her own time schedule.

That same committee worked to prepare for an upcoming evaluation visit. A time was set for daily meetings and for a while teachers worked together on their assigned task. Before long, however, the group decided that specific tasks should be assigned to individuals to complete on their own. As a committee member explained:

> We started off meeting . . . together each day, each third period. And then things broke down so that. . . . Sally was doing some things with language arts and reading [with which] Francis and I weren't familiar [and] couldn't do. Francis was worrying with the Science Fair and the science curriculum. And then I started doing social studies. We sort of all branched off. It was just easier to go our separate ways.

Individuals going their separate ways was the common pattern at the junior high school even when teachers served on committees together. Committee work did not provide a sense of common purpose or collective achievement and did not provide the occasion for exploring one another's educational beliefs. When asked if teachers at her school shared a philosophy of education one teacher replied, "I don't know. I really don't know about that; I can't tell." There was nothing in the organization of the school or the tasks of teaching at the junior high that necessitated a sharing of educational philosophies. Thus it did not trouble the principal to say that there were "40 teachers in the school and about as many different philosophies." When he was asked what qualities he looked for in hiring new teachers the principal answered, "knowledge of subject matter." He did not mention the ability to cooperate or collaborate.

There were few opportunities to share ideas at the junior high. Outside of brief lunchtime encounters and infrequent faculty meetings, teachers rarely saw one another. When they did have occasion to talk, conversations were seldom related to the tasks of teaching. Decision making did not necessitate faculty discussions because school decisions were made by administrators, and classroom decisions by individual teachers. Even committee work, as we have seen, tended to be divided into separate tasks that were performed by individuals working independently.

Teachers were not brought together by common responsibilities, shared time, or communal space. Formal meetings were viewed as time consuming, not always necessary, and never a prerequisite for successful teaching. Neither the work teachers did nor the manner in which it was organized promoted the development of personal or professional relationships among the staff. Though friendships existed, they were usually initiated and/or maintained outside the school.

> I have a particular group of friends . . . that usually go out, just the girls, once a month right after payday. These relationships have built up over the years partly from outside of school. One [friend] is my neighbor and one's ex-husband works with my husband, and [I] go to the same church with some others.

Teachers took pride in their ability to manage orderly classrooms, keep students on task, and be liked by their former and current pupils. These goals of junior high teachers were similar to those of middle school teachers, though these goals were achieved individually rather than collectively. Teaching was defined as an individual skill, and a good school as a well-organized collection (rather than collectivity) of talented teachers doing their work independently and well.

*The principal.* The different orientations of the two schools were reflected in the attitudes and behaviors of their principals, the decision-making procedures the principals established, and their perception of the teacher role. The middle school principal described a good teacher as one who "cares about kids, can communicate effectively, and is a good role model for students." He expected teachers to share in school decision making and delegated a good deal of decision-making power to teacher teams. He was convinced that he needed the ideas of teachers to improve his school and to keep it running smoothly. The staff enjoyed a semi-collaborative relationship with the principal whom they viewed as a co-worker.

The middle school was governed by a steering committee comprised of administrators, team leaders, and teacher representatives from special areas such as physical education. School policy decisions were made by this committee during biweekly meetings. Often, however, the principal would defer a decision with the suggestion that committee members "take this back and discuss it with your teams." The committee considered advice from teams before coming to a final decision. At other times the committee only raised issues and then asked teams to make their own decisions.

The middle school principal expected teachers to take part in school governance, and the relationships he built with the staff reflected that expectation. He spent a good deal of time talking with teachers, soliciting ideas, and asking about their concerns. When the principal was asked what skills a teacher needed to work in his school he answered:

> Well, the major thing is communication skills because I don't think . . . a lot of other things are possible without good communication skills. Teachers are all

encouraged to do well on their own, but most important, they must cooperate and get along well with other staff.

Teachers echoed this priority. For example, a team leader described her relationship with the principal as being

> about the same kind I have with teachers. You know, we talk sometimes about kids. We talk about the organization of the school, a lot of maintenance type things, about what I am allowed to do and not to do. And we also talk about ourselves, too, you know, I meet him as a person as well as a principal.

Because the participation in group decision making was deemed important in the school, the principal established a number of channels through which teachers could contribute their ideas and concerns. He described the communication set-up this way:

> On the individual level, anybody can come and speak to me or a team leader by themselves. But their next step is on the team basis [where] seven or eight teachers get together and talk about things. Often decisions are made on the team level. Then another step up is the Program Improvement Council, where team leaders or any individual can come with concerns. [Ideas] can be expressed there which have an umbrella effect [of spreading information] over the entire school. Administrators are a part of [the Council] too. So everyone hears [the idea] directly or indirectly.

The administration worked to promote both formal and informal teacher interaction. Before each school year started, and again during the Christmas season, the principal held a party for the staff. During the year he occasionally initiated "T.G.I.F." gatherings where teachers got together at a local bar for a few hours on Friday afternoons. Teams often traveled to the bar together. The principal thought such occasions important because, he said, "People who play well together will work well together." The principal's concern to build bonds of community and friendship within the school typified his essentially fraternal relationships with his faculty and staff.

The junior high principal described a good teacher as "one who is really knowledgeable about the subject matter to be taught and really excited about teaching it, a good classroom manager, and someone who understands [early teenage] students." He expected teachers to be prepared for their work in the classroom and able to make decisions in that domain. Teacher opinions and ideas were sometimes solicited on school-wide matters, but the decision-making responsibility rested unambiguously with the principal and his administrative staff. The principal's relationship with the teachers was one of friendly paternalism. He worked to protect his staff against classroom intrusions, to make teaching as easy and pleasant as possible, and to generally reduce faculty friction and stress. He visited teachers' classrooms regularly and often complimented teachers on what he saw going on there. He demanded little of his teachers outside of the classroom. He seldom called on teachers to help him make decisions, in part to spare them extra work and in part because he saw decision making as his responsibility. In the principal's view there was a clear division between the work of administrators and teachers.

The junior high principal was aided in his work by two assistant principals. When an assistant was asked how decisions were made at the school he answered, "Ted [the principal] says you're going to do that, and it gets done." He went on to say that the principal did discuss decisions with his assistants:

> We're kind of like the team management concept. Although Ted is in charge, he will never—at least I don't think he will—make decisions without consulting us. We sit down and hash [decisions] out and talk ... and give our views. I look at things a certain way and [the second assistant principal] looks at things in a certain way. We sit down and [offer] our input. He [the principal] will even go out and solicit input from teachers.

*Multi-Age Grouping.* The middle school teachers viewed the multi-aged grouping as the most positive and satisfying part of their work because it allowed them to get to know their students well and to trace their development over time. Teachers witnessed dramatic developmental changes over the 3 years they worked with students and were able to feel that they contributed to their students' emotional and mental growth. Strategies could be worked out to solve problems students were having, and knowing students well increased the likelihood that such strategies would prove successful. Teachers thought they were less likely than teachers working at other schools to write off students who were difficult to reach. A teacher explained:

> The big advantages [of multi-age grouping] are, first, it takes a long time to find out what really makes some students click and [to devise] successful techniques [for] working with them. A lot of times it takes a half a year or longer. You're going to have half a year working with them and then the next teacher has to go through the same thing [again. In a typical junior high school] there really is no communication between the sixth- and seventh-grade teachers. [One teacher might say to another,] "Oh boy, there are real problems now" or [some other] negative things. Or a teacher might say off-handedly, "I successfully did this" or whatever. But there is no established [system] of communication between the grade levels. So by having [students] for 3 years, I may be able to find out what will be successful and then institute it for [perhaps] 2½ years.
>
> The second advantage ... is when you run into a problem in most schools with a student that just seems to frustrate you at every hand, you [are tempted to] write him off. If you get through 6 months ... and you haven't succeeded you say, "Well, all I have is [3 months] to go," and you slide through the rest of the year. You can't do that here because you know you've got [another] 2½ years to face [with that student]. I don't think we've got the same inclination [to give up on a student here], however. I think you have much more

encouragement [when you have 3 years to work with a student]. Maybe [if] after 2½ years ... you haven't succeeded, you aren't going to succeed. But sometimes 6 months is all you really need to find out what [will be] successful. Therefore, [we're] encouraged to institute [our own programs for students] rather than write [students] off.

Middle school teachers focused on long-term goals and made a concerted and cooperative effort to make the school an environment that encouraged development and happiness among students. The chance to get to know students well and the school ethos of pervasive caring encouraged middle school teachers to share responsibility for students' school experiences. Time was spent decorating hallways and classrooms and working with students in nonacademic settings. Teachers felt they knew their students well, took pride in their pupils' achievements, relished the friendships they formed with students, and gained support from team members with whom they shared friendships, responsibilities, accomplishments, and common educational aims.

Unlike the middle school teachers, junior high teachers who only taught students for 1 academic year found it difficult to observe developmental changes in their students over the course of 9 months. Teachers focused instead on short-term improvements in test scores and mastery of subject matter and took pride in student achievements in these areas. Teachers did not often work with students in nonacademic settings nor take upon themselves much of the responsibility for students' learning.

## CONCLUSION

One function of qualitative research is to provide promising hypotheses for future quantitative study. Another function is to investigate the human dynamics that underlie quantitative findings of statistical significance. The microethnography reported in this chapter serves both these functions. The findings lead to the hypothesis that school organization, leadership, and ethos contribute to the establishment and maintenance of teachers' sense of efficacy. Teaching teams, adviser–advisee programs, multi-aged grouping, and clear and shared educational aims appeared to lessen teachers' self-doubts and to diminish the self-protective, low-efficacy ideologies that accompany such doubts.

This hypothesis is bolstered by the comments of a middle school teacher responding to the question, "How does your teaching situation, that is, [school] organization, affect your ability to achieve your teaching goals?"

There is no way it hinders it. It only furthers it. The AA [adviser–advisee] program helps tremendously in getting close [to students] and being able to teach some lessons I want to teach about being a total person. The interdisciplinary cooperation between team members helps us do things we would otherwise be unable to do. The multi-age grouping gives me a student for 3 years. I really get to know him, can really help him, can really influence his life. So, I can't think of any way that [the school organization] has hindered; it has only furthered my teaching goals.

The microethnography has furthered our understanding of the questionnaire data drawn from teachers at the middle school and junior high school. An analysis of those data showed that the middle school teachers tended to have higher sense-of-efficacy scores than did the junior high teachers. The middle school teachers also had higher expectations for student progress, were more satisfied with teaching as a career, and valued teaching more than did junior high teachers. In addition, middle school teachers were less likely to blame students for their failures and were more likely than the junior high teachers to accept personal responsibility for their students' academic troubles. Finally, we observed that the middle school teachers felt responsible for students' personal development, and junior high teachers emphasized teachers' instructional responsibilities. The microethnography offers suggestions for why these differences were found. At the middle school, the team teaching organization, the multi-age grouping, and the adviser–advisee relationship between teachers and students fostered a sense of community. Teachers shared a commitment to the school's "modern middle school" philosophy and were encouraged to share their concerns about students with team members. The participation in school decision making helped the middle school teachers perceive themselves as part of a communal effort. This sense of community helped sustain teachers' enthusiasm for their profession and their beliefs that students, even students from difficult home backgrounds, can succeed in their academic work. In contrast, the junior high teachers taught in a more traditional, individualistic school environment. Their school lives were characterized by the sense of isolation that Lortie (1975) described so effectively. Having only their short-term, individual achievements with students to bolster their commitment to the profession, the junior high teachers were less able to maintain their enthusiasm and their expectations for student achievement.

## Cautionary Afterword

The study of two organizationally different schools tempts researchers and readers to select one school as inherently "better" than the other. The comparative nature of the microethnography invites this kind of either-or choice. Yet such comparisons are misleading and in some ways unfair. To use the word *best* makes little sense without reference to specific educational aims. A school that is "better" at achieving one aim is not necessarily "better" at achieving another. At present, there is no generic category of "better" or "best" in education.

In the case of this study, certain values were suggested in the very framing of the research question. When we asked, "Does school organization have an influence on the maintenance of teachers' efficacy attitudes?" we built into the research the assumption that efficacy attitudes are important and worth supporting. Therefore, each findings statement reported in this chapter carries with it the not-so-subtle suggestion that one school provided a better environment for maintenance of teachers' sense of efficacy than did the other. Although it appears that the middle school did a better job of supporting the efficacy attitudes of teachers, it is going too far to say that the middle school is, therefore, a better school. Rather than clutter the ethnography with caveats and qualifiers that were not directly relevant to the study of efficacy, we chose to end the chapter with a few cautionary comments that may be helpful when considering the findings we have reported in this study.

First, microethnographic studies have the modest aim of developing hypotheses for further research. The conclusion (that the middle school was more conducive to the maintenance of teachers' efficacy attitudes than was the junior high) is put forth tentatively, not conclusively. After all, only two schools were studied and, in this portion of the research, only two teachers in each school were observed and interviewed over the course of a school year. We conclude that the efficacy–organization connection is important and warrants further investigation.

Second, there is nothing in the findings of this study that should lead us to conclude that the junior high school was inferior to the middle school or that teachers at one school were less talented or dedicated than teachers at the other. Teachers at the two schools had different aims but both faculties reported finding satisfaction in their work, liking their principals, and approving of the organization of their schools.

Third, both schools possessed strengths that, if combined, might produce an exceptionally effective educational program. The middle school's teams, multi-aged grouping, adviser–advisee programs, and shared decision-making power engendered in teachers a high degree of energy, dedication, and mutual support. Close relationships with students were formed and an emphasis on student development was maintained. The junior high school's concentration on discipline and academics encouraged some teachers to adopt direct-instruction teaching techniques that research has shown correlate with achievement gains among low-achieving students. It appeared that the middle school could benefit from developing a greater academic emphasis and, perhaps, from modifying the teachers' assumption that an academic emphasis was incompatible with its focus on student development.

Fourth, there were some problems at both schools that are worth noting here. The middle school teachers reported that their work was satisfying but draining, and they worried that they would not be able to keep working at this pace for long. Shared decision making brought conflicts to the surface that had to be discussed and worked out. Such conflicts seldom surfaced at the junior high and, as a result, teachers there reported less friction among faculty. Researchers gathered the impression that the middle school organization was effective but precarious. Because it so taxed the energies of teachers, it demanded close bonds of friendship and careful leadership to keep it running effectively. If, however, the school lost a critical mass of teachers through normal turnover or lost its autonomy through mandates from the school district's central office, only the shell of the former organization might remain. Teachers would still be working hard, but the esprit de corps that made such work rewarding might disappear.

# 5

# Teachers' Sense of Efficacy, Classroom Behavior, and Student Achievement

## INTRODUCTION

Our ethnographic observations in classrooms in the Middle School Study (Ashton, Webb, & Doda, 1983) suggested that high- and low-efficacy teachers differed in their interactions with students, especially in their contacts with low-achieving students. Teachers with a high sense of efficacy seemed to employ a pattern of strategies that minimized negative affect, promoted an expectation of achievement, and provided a definition of the classroom situation characterized by warm interpersonal relationships and academic work. Teachers with a low sense of efficacy appeared to establish a pattern of strategies that heightened negative affect and promoted an expectation of failure for low-achieving students. Low-efficacy teachers stratified students into competent and incompetent groups and defined classroom situations in terms of conflict rather than warm interpersonal relationships. Academic achievement often was emphasized but only for those students whom the teacher defined as able and worthy of the teacher's attention. To substantiate our ethnographic observations, we conducted a classroom observation study, using systematic observation techniques developed in previous process–product studies of classroom interactions.

## METHODOLOGY

Basic skills mathematics and communications classrooms were selected for this study, because we expected that of all teaching situations we could choose to study, teachers' sense of efficacy would be most likely to have an impact on teacher behavior in these classrooms. Because teachers with a low sense of efficacy doubt their ability to teach, they would be most likely to demonstrate their sense of inadequacy when teaching a class of low-achieving students who had a long history of school failure. Students were placed in basic skills classes because of low scores (below the 30th percentile) on the annual Metropolitan Achievement Test. These students were selected for special remediation because they had failed or were expected to fail the state competency test administered to all 11th graders in the state. Thus, to maximize the likelihood of observing behavioral correlates of teachers' sense of efficacy, we conducted our observational study in high school basic skills classes.

## Participants

Forty-eight basic skills teachers (mathematics and communications teachers in four high schools in a southeastern university community) participated in the study. One basic skills class of each teacher was observed at least twice, and most were observed three times during a 2-month period in the winter of 1980–1981. Because the curriculum of the classes was similar across grades, to the extent that students of different grade levels were combined in several classes, observations were conducted in 9th, 10th, and 11th grade classes. Major portions of the data were available for 45 teachers, although that number varied somewhat from analysis to analysis, due to missing data.

## Process–Product Measures

*Student achievement.*   The mathematics, language, and reading subtests of the Metropolitan Achievement Test (MAT) were administered to the basic skills students in the spring of 1980 and 1981.

*Teacher attitudes.*   Teachers completed a questionnaire (see Appendix C) that included the two Rand efficacy questions, an eight-item forced-choice measure of teaching efficacy (developed for this study and hereafter referred to as the Webb efficacy measure), a measure of personal teaching efficacy comprised of 15 vignettes (hereafter referred to as the Efficacy Vignettes), two items regarding stress experienced by teachers in teaching basic skills classes and the level of stress they experienced in teaching in general, and a question regarding the degree of responsibility they felt for their students' learning.

*Classroom observation measures.*   Three instruments were used to collect classroom process data. The Climate and Control System (Soar & Soar, 1980) was used to measure the classroom climate; the Teacher Practices

Observation Record (Brown, 1968) was used to gather information about the teachers' instructional styles, and the Engagement Rate Form (Squires et al., 1983) was used to measure students' attentiveness.

*The Climate and Control System (CCS).* The CCS (see Appendix E) is a 1980 revision (Soar & Soar, 1980) of the Florida Climate and Control System (Soar, Soar & Ragosta, 1971). The instrument provides a record of the climate and control aspects of the classroom, by noting the classroom organization, the teacher's control strategies, the pupil's response to the teacher's control, and, in turn, the teacher's response to pupils' reactions to their control strategies. In addition, climate is measured in terms of the expression of both positive and negative affect of teachers and pupils.

The CCS instrument consists of two coding sheets. The matrix on the top half of the first page is used to record interactive sequences between pupils and teachers in terms of the three contexts: teacher initiation and pupil response, and two types of follow-up, either by teacher or pupil initiation. The bottom half of the first page is used to record information about the teachers' organization of the classroom, for example, the type of groupings and the degree to which students are engaged in the classroom tasks. The second page of the CCS instrument is designed to measure the expression of affect on the part of both the teacher and the pupils. In addition, the instrument distinguishes between negative and positive and verbal and nonverbal affect.

*The Teacher Practices Observation Record (TPOR).* The TPOR was designed by Brown (1968) to analyze the instructional methods utilized by the teacher in the classroom. It consists of 62 items describing teacher behavior; half of the items reflect a progressive or experimental approach to instruction, as represented by the philosophy of John Dewey, and half reflect a traditional or "direct instruction" approach to the classroom. The types of observations included in the TPOR focus on the nature of the classroom situation, the nature of the problems the teacher presents to students, the processes the teacher uses in developing students' ideas, the teacher's use of subject matter, the teacher's evaluation and motivation strategies, and the extent to which the teacher differentiates instruction and evaluation to meet individual student needs.

*Research for Better Schools Engagement Rate Form.* A practical and simple procedure for determining student engagement rate developed by Research for Better Schools (RBS) (Huitt & Rim, 1980; Squires et al., 1983) was adapted to estimate student time-on-task in basic skills classrooms. On the engagement rate form, the observer noted the number of students engaged and unengaged. According to RBS directions, approximately 15 observations should be recorded during a class period at time intervals ranging from 1 to 3 minutes. Because our previous observations in middle school classrooms led us to the hypothesis that teachers' sense of efficacy is related to teachers' use of the entire class period for instruction, we were most interested in the engagement rate at the beginning and end of class periods. Consequently, observers were instructed to complete the engagement rate form at the end of the first 5 minutes of the class period, 5 minutes before the end of the period, and then at intervals occurring after coding of a set of TPOR and CCS observations. Generally, this procedure resulted in five engagement rate observations per class period.

## Observational Data Collection Procedures

Observations were carried out by five observers who were each trained in the use of the instruments during an intensive 2-month training period by Robert and Ruth Soar. Each observer began each classroom visit by completing a data sheet indicating the number of students present in the class and other classroom identifying information. After observing for 5 minutes, the observer noted the engagement behavior of the class on the RBS instrument, then spent 3 minutes coding the teacher's verbal behavior on the CCS form, and 2 minutes observing the teacher's nonverbal behavior; this was followed by recording of the affective climate of the classroom on the CCS instrument. Subsequently, the observer noted the teacher and student behavior for a 5-minute period and then completed the TPOR observation form. Then the observer noted the engagement rate again, completing the same sequence of observations until 5 minutes prior to the end of the period, when the student engagement rate was noted for the last time and the observation period ended. The observers obtained at least three sets of observations for almost all classroom visits. Three classroom visits were sought for each teacher, though this goal was not met for all teachers due to scheduling difficulties.

## RESULTS

### Classroom Environment Factors

In an earlier study, Soar and Soar (1978) reduced the observation data obtained from the CCS and the TPOR by factor analysis to a set of factors representing a paradigm of the classroom environment for learning. The paradigm delineates four independent dimensions of classroom behavior: (1) emotional climate, (2) teacher management of pupil behavior, (3) teacher management of learning tasks, and (4) teacher management of thinking processes. In addition to the compelling rational argument that teacher behaviors do not occur in isolation but rather in clusters that support or moderate each other, the use of factor scores is preferable to individual items because of the low reliability of individual observation items and the reduction in the large number of relationships that must be tested (Soar & Soar, 1978).

Although the internal consistency of the measures was lower than in Soar and Soar's earlier study, the results were considered generally supportive. The correlations of items with the measures of which they were a part were .50 or greater for 59% of the items and .39 or greater for 75% of the items. Correlations were strongest for measures of affect expression (84% were .50 or greater), weaker for the remaining measures. The original measures were developed on self-contained elementary school classrooms; therefore, the low correlations for some of the items were not surprising, because the behaviors (e.g., "Teacher touches, pats") were not likely to occur at the secondary level. Other low correlations seemed reasonable because the classes were remedial, reducing the likelihood that higher level thinking activities would be encouraged.

## Reliability of Process Measures

Reliability of the process measures was estimated using intraclass correlation that treated as error both teacher variability from occasion to occasion and differences between observers—the most stringent estimate of reliability. The intraclass correlation coefficient was used as the computing procedure because it is sensitive to differences in average amounts of a

TABLE 5.1. Intraclass Correlation Estimates of Reliability of Classroom Process-Factor Measures

| Classroom process factors | Mean square between (MSB) | Mean square within (MSW) | MSB–MSW | (MSB–MSW)/MSB |
|---|---|---|---|---|
| Teacher negative affect | .017 | .010 | .007 | .41** |
| Teacher positive affect | .019 | .014 | .005 | .26 |
| Pupil negative affect | .011 | .010 | .001 | .09 |
| Pupil positive affect | .010 | .008 | .008 | .50*** |
| Teacher strong control | .005 | .003 | .002 | .40** |
| Teacher moderate control | .0044 | .0048 | | .00 |
| Pupil disorder versus control | .04 | .02 | .02 | .50*** |
| Pupil follows routine | .043 | .038 | .005 | .12 |
| Teacher central and directs activity | .023 | .010 | .013 | .57*** |
| Differentiated activities | .010 | .007 | .003 | .30* |
| Guided discovery | .0065 | .0066 | | .00 |
| Narrow, one-answer interaction | .032 | .022 | .010 | .31* |
| Guess or hypothesize | .0094 | .0057 | .0037 | .39** |
| Interest–attention rating | 1.23 | .65 | .58 | .47*** |

\* $p < .05$.
\*\* $p < .01$.
\*\*\* $p < .001$.

given behavior recorded by different observers, in contrast to product-moment correlation which is not (Soar & Soar, 1982). The intraclass correlation coefficient is estimated from the sums of squares from standard analysis of variance computing procedures (Algina, 1978; Bartko, 1967; Rowley, 1976; Soar & Soar, 1982). Because the intraclass correlation reflects differences due to occasions as well as differences due to observers, it is expected to be much lower than the traditional observer agreement statistic, which represents only observer differences. In fact, Soar and Soar (1982) reported:

> It is not unusual to find reliabilities on the order of .5 to .6; indeed, in a study of ours a measure with a reliability of .38 was one of the most powerful in terms of accounting for pupil gain. (p. 31)

The intraclass correlation coefficients for the process-product paradigm of learning factor scores are presented in Table 5.1. The low correlations are probably attributable in large measure to the great similarity across teachers in teaching strategies in the basic skills classes and to the infrequency of occurrence of some behaviors, such as pupil negative affect and guided discovery.

## Process–Product Analysis

Analyses of the process–product relationships were calculated with the class as the unit of analysis. Partial correlations between teacher attitude and classroom process variables and students' 1981 Metropolitan mathematics test scores were computed, holding spring 1980 scores constant. The results of this analysis are presented in Table 5.2. Significant relationships with students' mathematics achievement were obtained for Rand Efficacy 1 ($r = .78$, $p = .003$), teacher negative affect ($r = -.60$, $p = .01$), pupil negative affect ($r = -.52$, $p = .03$), and teachers' use of strong control ($r = -.66$, $p = .004$). Interesting trends emerged for the Webb Efficacy measure ($r = .50$, $p = .10$), the engagement rate measure ($r = .45$, $p = .07$), and guided discovery ($r = .44$, $p = .08$).

To examine the unique contributions to students' Metropolitan mathematics achievement, of the Rand and the Webb Efficacy measures, teacher strong control and pupil negative affect, a stepwise multiple regression analysis was computed. To control for entering ability, the students' Metropolitan mathematics achievement scores were first regressed on their previous year's test scores; the remaining variables then were entered in single steps determined by the respective contribution of each variable to reducing unexplained variance. Two steps in the multiple regression were completed before the additional predictor variables were deemed insignificant ($p < .05$). Table 5.3 reports the results of the analysis for the significant predictor variables. Students' scores on the spring 1980 MAT accounted for 64% of the variation of 1981 MAT mathematics

TABLE 5.2.  Partial Correlations of Teacher Attitude and Classroom Process Variables and Student Mathematics MAT

| Description | $r$ | $p$ |
|---|---|---|
| Teacher sense of responsibility | −.21 | .51 |
| Rand Efficacy 1 | .78 | .003 |
| Rand Efficacy 2 | .006 | .98 |
| Teacher stress in teaching basic skills | −.03 | .92 |
| Teacher stress in teaching | −.18 | .57 |
| Efficacy Vignettes | −.27 | .39 |
| Webb Efficacy | .50 | .10 |
| Teacher negative affect | −.60 | .01 |
| Teacher positive affect | .10 | .70 |
| Pupil negative affect | −.52 | .03 |
| Pupil positive affect | .17 | .51 |
| Teacher strong control | −.66 | .004 |
| Teacher moderate control | −.20 | .43 |
| Pupil disorder | −.26 | .31 |
| Pupil follows routine | −.24 | .36 |
| Teacher central and directed | .03 | .91 |
| Differentiated activities | −.12 | .65 |
| Guided discovery | .44 | .08 |
| Narrow, one-answer interaction | −.13 | .62 |
| Guess or hypothesize | −.02 | .93 |
| Interest-attention | .32 | .21 |
| Engagement rate | .45 | .07 |

*Note.* Spring 1980 Metropolitan Achievement Test scores were held constant.

TABLE 5.3.  Multiple Regression Analysis of 1981 Mathematics Metropolitan Achievement Test

| Variable | $df$ | $F$ | Beta | $R$ | $R^2$ |
|---|---|---|---|---|---|
| 1980 Metropolitan Mathematics Test | 2/9 | 45.09* | .77 | .80 | .64 |
| Rand Efficacy 1 | | 18.33* | .49 | .94 | .88 |

* $p < .01$

scores, $F(2,9) = 45.09$, $p < .01$. Teachers' scores on Rand Efficacy 1 increased to 88%, the amount of variation accounted for, a sizable contribution, $F(2,9) = 18.33$, $p < .01$. None of the remaining variables (Rand Efficacy 2, Webb Efficacy, teachers' strong control, or pupils' negative affect) significantly improved the prediction of students' MAT mathematics scores. The beta-weights (standardized regression coefficients) indicate that a 1-point increase in students' pretest score would yield a .77-point increase in their posttest performance, and each 1-point increase in teachers' Rand Efficacy 1 scores would add a .49-point increase in students' achievement scores.

Partial correlations between teacher attitude, classroom process variables, and students' Metropolitan language test scores were computed holding spring 1980 scores constant. The results appear in Table 5.4. Significant relationships were obtained between Metropolitan language scores and Rand Efficacy 2 ($r = .83$, $p = .02$) and pupil classroom routine ($r = -.68$, $p = .03$), and a trend toward significance emerged for Rand Efficacy 1 ($r = .71$, $p = .07$) and Metropolitan language scores.

A stepwise multiple regression analysis was computed to examine the unique contributions of the Rand and the Webb Efficacy measures, teacher strong control, and pupil negative affect to students' Metropolitan language achievement. In the initial step, the students' 1981 Metropolitan language test scores were regressed on their previous year's test scores; the remaining variables then were entered in single steps determined by the respective contribution of each variable to reducing unexplained variance. Two steps in the multiple regression analysis were completed before the additional predictors were found to be insignificant ($p < .05$). Table 5.5 reports the results of the analysis for the significant predictor variables. Students' scores on the spring 1980 Metropolitan language test accounted for 36% of the variation in the 1981 MAT language scores, $F(2,5) = 23.10$, $p < .01$. Rand Efficacy 2 increased the amount of variance

TABLE 5.4. Partial Correlations of Teacher Attitude and Classroom Process Variables and Student Metropolitan Language Achievement

| Description | r | p |
|---|---|---|
| Teacher sense of responsibility | −.11 | .84 |
| Rand Efficacy 1 | .71 | .07 |
| Rand Efficacy 2 | .83 | .02 |
| Teacher stress in teaching basic skills | −.34 | .46 |
| Teacher stress in teaching | −.29 | .53 |
| Efficacy Vignettes | .44 | .32 |
| Webb Efficacy | .58 | .17 |
| Teacher negative affect | −.43 | .21 |
| Teacher positive affect | .41 | .24 |
| Pupil negative affect | −.29 | .41 |
| Pupil positive affect | −.41 | .23 |
| Teacher strong control | −.33 | .34 |
| Teacher moderate control | −.03 | .94 |
| Pupil disorder | −.39 | .26 |
| Pupil follows routine | −.68 | .03 |
| Teacher central and directed | .29 | .42 |
| Differentiated activities | −.03 | .93 |
| Guided discovery | .12 | .73 |
| Narrow, one-answer interaction | .14 | .71 |
| Guess or hypothesize | −.08 | .83 |
| Interest-attention | −.06 | .87 |
| Engagement rate | .11 | .76 |

*Note.* Spring 1980 MAT scores were held constant.

TABLE 5.5.  Multiple Regression Analysis of 1981 Metropolitan Langauge
Achievement Test

| Variable | df | F | Beta | R | $R^2$ |
|---|---|---|---|---|---|
| 1980 Metropolitan Language Test | 2/5 | 23.10* | 1.37 | .60 | .36 |
| Rand Efficacy 2 | | 13.13* | 1.03 | .91 | .82 |

\* $p < .01$

accounted for by 46% to 82%, $F(2,5) = 13.13$, $p < .01$. The remaining
variables did not increase significantly the amount of variance explained.
The beta-weights indicate that a 1-point increase in the students' 1980
achievement test scores would yield a 1.37-point increase in their 1981
scores, and a 1-point increase in teachers' perceived efficacy would yield a
1.03-point increase in Metropolitan language achievement scores.

Partial correlations calculated for teacher attitude, classroom process
variables, and Metropolitan reading test scores, controlling for spring 1980
test scores, are presented in Table 5.6. A significant negative relationship
was obtained between teachers' use of narrow one-answer questions and
students' reading scores ($r = -.69$, $p = .03$).

TABLE 5.6.  Partial Correlations of Teacher Attitude and Classroom Process
Variables and Student Metropolitan Reading Achievement

| Description | r | p |
|---|---|---|
| Teacher sense of responsibility for student achievement | .28 | .60 |
| Rand Efficacy 1 | −.14 | .76 |
| Rand Efficacy 2 | −.40 | .37 |
| Teacher stress in teaching basic skills | −.06 | .90 |
| Teacher stress in teaching | .09 | .85 |
| Efficacy Vignettes | −.33 | .46 |
| Webb Efficacy | −.29 | .53 |
| Teacher negative affect | −.02 | .97 |
| Teacher positive affect | −.12 | .74 |
| Pupil negative affect | .20 | .58 |
| Pupil positive affect | .29 | .41 |
| Teacher strong control | −.08 | .83 |
| Teacher moderate control | −.38 | .28 |
| Pupil disorder | .06 | .86 |
| Pupil follows routine | .10 | .78 |
| Teacher central and directed | −.34 | .33 |
| Differentiated activities | .21 | .56 |
| Guided discovery | .08 | .84 |
| Narrow, one-answer interaction | −.69 | .03 |
| Guess or hypothesize | .17 | .64 |
| Interest-attention | −.12 | .73 |
| Engagement rate | −.15 | .67 |

*Note.* Spring 1980 MAT scores were held constant.

## Teacher Attitude and Classroom Process Factors

The means and standard deviations of teacher attitude and classroom process variables are presented in Table 5.7. To examine the relationships between teachers' attitudes and the environment for learning paradigm factors, an intercorrelation matrix was computed (see Table 5.8). The number of relations of the attitude measures with classroom process was disappointingly small—no greater than expected by chance. The relations were in the expected direction, however. Teachers who felt greater responsibility for pupil achievement had less pupil negative affect (a high score on responsibility indicated a low sense of responsibility). Teachers who felt more stress in teaching basic skills used greater amounts of moderate control, $r = .33$, $p < .05$. Teachers who felt more stress in teaching in general used more varied activities, $r = .46$, $p < .01$. Teachers who felt more effective (Webb Efficacy) used less negative affect, $r = -.35$, $p < .05$, and less guided discovery, $r = -.36$, $p < .05$. Although not large enough to be significant given the small sample size, an interesting trend is evident between Rand Efficacy 1 and teachers' use of harsh modes of control ($r = -.26$, $p = .13$) and student disorder ($r = -.22$, $p = .20$). Also too small to reach statistical significance, a relationship may be indicated between Rand Efficacy 2 and teachers' positive emotional climate ($r = .23$, $p = .17$). There was an indication of a possible negative rela-

TABLE 5.7.  Means and Standard Deviations of Teacher Attitudes and Classroom Process Variables

| *Description* | N | M | SD |
|---|---|---|---|
| Teacher sense of responsibility | 34 | 1.97 | .80 |
| Rand Efficacy 1 | 36 | 3.25 | .97 |
| Rand Efficacy 2 | 36 | 3.33 | 1.17 |
| Stress in teaching basic skills | 36 | 2.64 | 1.25 |
| Stress in teaching | 36 | 2.47 | .74 |
| Efficacy Vignettes | 36 | 4.64 | .78 |
| Webb Efficacy | 36 | 1.48 | .16 |
| Teacher negative affect | 45 | 51.49 | 5.85 |
| Teacher positive affect | 45 | 49.90 | 4.52 |
| Pupil negative affect | 45 | 51.42 | 4.94 |
| Pupil positive affect | 45 | 50.17 | 4.22 |
| Teacher strong control | 45 | 50.84 | 3.14 |
| Teacher moderate control | 45 | 50.49 | 2.57 |
| Pupil disorder | 45 | 51.23 | 5.66 |
| Pupil follows routine | 45 | 50.79 | 5.85 |
| Teacher central and directed | 45 | 50.30 | 3.79 |
| Differentiated activities | 45 | 50.12 | 2.59 |
| Teacher guided discussion | 45 | 50.06 | 2.33 |
| Teacher narrow, one-answer | 45 | 50.96 | 5.01 |
| Teacher encourages guess, hypothesis | 45 | 49.76 | 2.89 |
| Interest-attention | 45 | 48.16 | 8.90 |

TABLE 5.8. Correlations between Teacher Attitudes and Behaviors Based on a Paradigm of the Classroom Atmosphere for Learning

| | 1 | 2 | 3 | 4 | 5 | 6 | 7 | 8 | 9 | 10 | 11 | 12 | 13 | 14 | 15 | 16 | 17 | 18 | 19 | 20 | 21 |
|---|---|---|---|---|---|---|---|---|---|---|---|---|---|---|---|---|---|---|---|---|---|
| Responsibility | 1 | — | | | | | | | | | | | | | | | | | | | | |
| Rand Efficacy 1 | 2 | -30 | — | | | | | | | | | | | | | | | | | | | |
| Rand Efficacy 2 | 3 | -37$^a$ | 33$^a$ | — | | | | | | | | | | | | | | | | | | |
| Stress in teaching basic skills | 4 | 02 | -33$^a$ | -27 | — | | | | | | | | | | | | | | | | | |
| Stress in teaching | 5 | 02 | -13 | -15 | 60$^b$ | — | | | | | | | | | | | | | | | | |
| Efficacy Vignettes | 6 | -33 | -10 | 36$^a$ | 01 | 01 | — | | | | | | | | | | | | | | | |
| Webb Efficacy | 7 | -29 | 35$^a$ | 17 | -24 | -21 | 19 | — | | | | | | | | | | | | | | |
| Student engagement rate | 8 | -04 | -04 | -04 | 14 | -07 | 14 | -09 | — | | | | | | | | | | | | | |
| **Emotional climate** | | | | | | | | | | | | | | | | | | | | | | |
| Teacher negative | 9 | 18 | -05 | -07 | -13 | -10 | -30 | -35$^a$ | -27 | — | | | | | | | | | | | | |
| Teacher positive | 10 | 01 | 06 | 23 | 08 | -05 | 19 | 06 | 01 | -22 | — | | | | | | | | | | | |
| Pupil negative | 11 | 35$^a$ | 02 | 09 | -15 | 13 | -10 | -08 | -57$^d$ | 68$^c$ | -03 | — | | | | | | | | | | |
| Pupil positive | 12 | 23 | -02 | -13 | -21 | -21 | -16 | -18 | -12 | -04 | 48$^c$ | 08 | — | | | | | | | | | |
| **Behavior** | | | | | | | | | | | | | | | | | | | | | | |
| Teacher strong control | 13 | 28 | -26 | 02 | 02 | -09 | -01 | -04 | -27 | 72$^d$ | -13 | 62 | -09 | — | | | | | | | | |
| Teacher gentle to moderate control | 14 | 20 | -17 | -21 | 33$^a$ | 26 | 02 | -06 | 07 | 23 | 32$^a$ | 18 | 11 | 27 | — | | | | | | | |
| Pupil disorder versus order | 15 | 19 | -22 | 04 | -12 | 28 | -14 | -12 | -64$^d$ | 31$^a$ | 16 | 62$^d$ | 31$^a$ | 18 | 14 | — | | | | | | |
| Pupil follow routine | 16 | -22 | -01 | 06 | 17 | 08 | -01 | 04 | -04 | -12 | 21 | -13 | -04 | -23 | -09 | -01 | — | | | | | |
| **Learning task** | | | | | | | | | | | | | | | | | | | | | | |
| Teaching central and directed | 17 | 28 | 00 | -08 | 07 | -03 | -04 | -14 | 33$^a$ | 23 | -01 | 13 | 02 | 36$^a$ | 40$^b$ | -16 | -57$^d$ | — | | | | |
| Differentiated activities | 18 | -34 | 07 | 03 | 18 | 46$^b$ | 14 | -11 | -32 | -28 | 24 | -10 | 16 | -31$^a$ | -16 | 32$^b$ | 26 | -60$^d$ | — | | | |
| **Thinking** | | | | | | | | | | | | | | | | | | | | | | |
| Teaching guided discovery | 19 | 06 | 15 | 07 | 02 | -10 | 12 | -36$^a$ | 08 | -31$^a$ | 29 | -30$^a$ | 28 | -37$^b$ | -07 | 05 | 06 | -09 | 28 | — | | |
| T narrow, one answer | 20 | 32 | -08 | 13 | -05 | -19 | 21 | -01 | 14 | 17 | 09 | 14 | 17 | 39$^b$ | 38$^b$ | -12 | -20 | 61$^d$ | -51$^d$ | 11 | — | |
| T encourages guess, hypothesis | 21 | -22 | 06 | -03 | 11 | 18 | -05 | -18 | -09 | -14 | 20 | -12 | 05 | -46$^b$ | -00 | 28 | 13 | -37$^a$ | 39$^b$ | 11 | -62$^d$ | — |
| Interest-attention | 22 | -02 | -17 | -09 | 27 | -05 | 21 | 15 | 76$^d$ | 25 | -07 | -48$^c$ | -20 | -19 | 16 | -70$^d$ | 11 | 11 | -36$^a$ | -11 | 19 | -18 |

*Note.* Decimals have been omitted.　　$^a$ $p < .05$.　　$^b$ $p < .01$.　　$^c$ $p < .001$.　　$^d$ $p < .0001$.

tionship between teachers' sense of efficacy measured by the vignettes and negative emotional climate ($r = -.30, p = .08$).

## An Empirical Search for Behavioral Correlates of Teachers' Sense of Efficacy

The failure to find significant relationships between teachers' sense of efficacy and the learning paradigm factors scores may be due to the restriction in variance in both the attitude and the behaviors of the basic skills teachers; however, the trends reflected in the correlations between the various efficacy measures and teacher behavior suggest that sense of efficacy is somewhat related to teachers' maintenance of a positive emotional climate and teachers' avoidance of harsh modes of behavior control.

Because all the process data obtained from the CCS and TPOR observations were not represented in the paradigm factor scores, correlations between all the process items and the two Rand Efficacy items were calculated, in order to search for potentially informative relationships. Caution must be exercised, however, in interpreting these relationships. A total of 766 correlations were obtained; a number of spurious relationships can be expected due to chance variation and the low reliability of individual observation items. Correlation of Rand Efficacy 1 and the

TABLE 5.9.  Correlations of Rand Efficacy 1 with Classroom Process Variables (significance level, $p \leq .10$)

| Classroom process variable | r | p |
|---|---|---|
| T makes P center of attention | −.41 | .01 |
| T makes some thing center of P's attention | −.45 | .007 |
| T involves P in uncertain situation | .33 | .05 |
| T has P make his own analysis of subject matter | −.29 | .09 |
| T withholds judgment on P's behavior or work | .33 | .05 |
| T gives, promises, reward | .28 | .10 |
| T praises, general, individual | .30 | .08 |
| T sounds defensive | .29 | .09 |
| T yells | −.29 | .09 |
| P teases | .29 | .09 |
| P agreeable, cooperative | −.31 | .07 |
| T states behavioral rule | −.29 | .09 |
| T directs with reason (follow-up) | .30 | .08 |
| T directs without reason | −.36 | .03 |
| T reminds, prods (follow-up) | −.34 | .04 |
| T scolds, punishes (follow-up) | −.29 | .09 |
| T nods, smiles, gives facial feedback | .41 | .02 |
| T uses body English, waits | −.37 | .03 |

classroom process variables with significance levels equal to or less than .10 are presented in Table 5.9.

Like the factor scores, consideration of the set of classroom process items having an association with Rand Efficacy 1 suggests that teachers' use of strong control techniques has a negative relationship to teachers' sense of efficacy—viz., correlations with teacher (T) yells, T states behavioral rule, T directs without reasons, T reminds, prods, T scolds, punishes. In addition, a number of the relationships suggest that the teacher with a high sense of teaching efficacy has a positive, supportive style (T gives, promises, rewards, T praises, general, individual, T directs with reason, T nods, smiles, gives facial feedback) that permits open communication with students—pupil (P) teases, P agreeable, cooperative—and involvement of students in decision making (T involves P in uncertain situation, T witholds judgment of P's behavior or work).

Teachers' instructional style was related to teachers' beliefs about the efficacy of teaching. *Teacher makes something the center of pupil's attention* was the category used for seatwork; *teacher makes pupil center of attention* was used to code activities in which the students led the class discussion Thus teachers with a strong belief in the efficacy of teaching were less likely than teachers with a weak sense of teaching efficacy to use seatwork and pupil-controlled activities. *Teacher has pupil make own analysis of subject matter* was used to code student-directed and student-initiated learning activities. *Teacher involves pupil in uncertain situation* was used for situations in which the teacher responded to the student's question with a question or refused to solve a problem for a student, and *teacher withholds judgment on pupil's behavior or work* was used for situations in which the teacher, when asked a question replied, "What do you think?" or "Try it and find out." Thus, teachers with strong beliefs in the efficacy of teaching were less likely than teachers with a low sense of teaching efficacy to use a great deal of seatwork or to turn activities over to the control of pupils. Further, teachers who believed in the efficacy of teaching tended to hold students responsible for performance by refusing to answer questions for them and by insisting that they attempt challenging questions and problems.

Correlations of Rand Efficacy 2 and the classroom process variables with significance levels equal to or less than .10 are presented in Table 5.10. Examination of this table provides further support for the conclusion that the teacher with a high sense of efficacy promotes development of a secure, accepting classroom atmosphere (negative correlations with P shows fear; P is left out; T scolds, punishes, and a positive correlation with T touches; pats P), supports student initiative (P seeks assurance; P shows apathy; P says, "No, I won't," etc.; P commands or demands; T complies with P request; T suggests, guides; T gives feedback, cites reason), and focuses on meeting the needs of all students (T attends P closely; P is left out; T gives individual attention; T asks for P status).

TABLE 5.10.   Correlations of Rand Efficacy 2 with Classroom Process Variables
(significance level, $p \leq .10$)

| Classroom process variable | r | p |
|---|---|---|
| Total group with T | −.32 | .06 |
| Small group with T | .29 | .09 |
| T attends P closely | .33 | .05 |
| T attends simultaneous activity | −.60 | .0002 |
| Seatwork without T | .29 | .09 |
| T gives reason, direction | −.36 | .03 |
| P seeks reassurance | .38 | .03 |
| P shows fear | −.32 | .06 |
| P shows apathy | −.44 | .007 |
| P says, "No, I won't," etc. | .28 | .10 |
| P commands or demands | .29 | .08 |
| P pushes or pulls, holds | −.33 | .05 |
| P is left out | −.40 | .01 |
| T gives individual attention | .32 | .06 |
| P praises another | −.30 | .08 |
| T complies with P request (T initiated) | .30 | .08 |
| T complies with P request (P initiated) | .32 | .06 |
| T asks for P status | .35 | .04 |
| T suggests, guides | −.36 | .03 |
| T gives feedback, cites reason | −.41 | .02 |
| T gives behavioral rule | .30 | .08 |
| T scolds, punishes | −.41 | .01 |
| T touches, pats P | .33 | .06 |

## DISCUSSION

### Student Achievement

Our findings strongly support the hypothesis that teachers' sense of efficacy is related to student achievement. Furthermore, the results support the assumption that teachers' efficacy attitudes are situation-specific. Students' mathematics achievement was significantly related to teachers' beliefs in the efficacy of teaching. When teachers' sense of teaching efficacy was added to the regression equation, the variance accounted for by the students' prior achievement was increased by 24%. Students' language achievement was significantly related to teachers' sense of personal efficacy. When teachers' sense of personal efficacy was added to the regression equation the variance accounted for increased by 46%. Students' reading achievement was not associated with any measure of teachers' sense of efficacy.

Although it is possible that these results are due to the limitations of the single-item measures of perceived efficacy, they are consistent with our conceptual analysis of teachers' sense of efficacy and merit further investigation. We postulated that teachers' sense of efficacy is a situation-specific variable, dependent on the particular characteristics of the ecological system in which each teacher works. Efficacy beliefs are not unidimensional and, consequently, can be expected to have different relationships to different subject matter, depending on teachers' beliefs about the subject being taught and the students in the class. For example, cultural beliefs about mathematical ability are likely to influence teachers' beliefs about the efficacy of teaching mathematics (Ernest, 1976). Many teachers doubt their own ability to learn mathematics and may generalize their belief to students. When working with low-achieving students in mathematics, such teachers may succumb to the low-efficacy belief that these students cannot learn math.

In contrast, teachers are less likely to hold low efficacy beliefs about the teaching of language skills. The results of the functional literacy test administered to high school students in the state of Florida each year may contribute to the differences in efficacy beliefs about mathematics and language skills. From 1978 when the literacy test was first administered, through 1985, the percentage of students passing the mathematics portion of the State Student Assessment Test (SSAT) increased from 74% to 84%, whereas the percentage passing the language portion moved from 88% to 97% (Cassil, 1985). Thus, teachers' beliefs about the efficacy of mathematics teaching may be the most salient efficacy belief in determining students' achievement behavior in mathematics. Language teachers may be more confident of the efficacy of language teaching so that their beliefs about their perceived competence become the stronger predictor of student achievement in the language class.

The failure to find a relationship between teachers' sense of efficacy and students' reading achievement is further evidence of the situation-sensitive nature of teachers' sense of efficacy. The basic skills language classes were intended to focus on specific language skills, not the teaching of reading.

The other relationships obtained between students' mathematics achievement test scores and the classroom interaction variables are consistent with previous findings from process–product research. Mathematics achievement was negatively related to negative affect between the teacher and students and to the teachers' use of strong control strategies. Thus, our data are consistent with other studies showing that a negative classroom climate is detrimental to learning.

Only two significant relationships were found between students' language achievement and reading achievement and the classroom process variables. Students following a routine was negatively associated with language achievement. This is probably an indication that classrooms having a minimum of teacher direction provided a less effective environment for learning. The significant negative correlation between teachers' use of narrow, one-answer interactions and reading achievement is not consistent with other process–product results, but because the basic skills classes were not intended to teach reading, this relationship may be spurious.

The lack of a significant relationship between engagement rate and student achievement was surprising in light of the results of other process–product studies that have found a significant relationship between these two variables. There was a trend toward significance between students' mathematics achievement and engagement rate, but no evidence of a relationship with language achievement. The prevailing use of workbooks in the classes may have made it more difficult for observers accurately to determine if students were actually engaged in the learning task.

## Teachers' Efficacy Attitudes

The correlations obtained among the attitude measures support our conception of teachers' sense of efficacy as a multidimensional, situation-specific construct. The correlation between teachers' sense of teaching efficacy and their sense of personal teaching efficacy was significant but moderate. We had based our decision to treat Rand Efficacy 1 and Rand Efficacy 2 as two independent dimensions on five prior samples of teachers in which the two measures were not related (Ashton et al., 1982). Our sample of basic skills high school teachers is the first sample in which we found a significant relationship between the two items. It seems reasonable to assume that the relationship between the two efficacy dimensions is stronger among the high school basic skills teachers because the experience of teaching low-achieving students increases the role that perceived teaching efficacy assumes in teachers' evaluations of their own compe-tence. In classrooms in which most students are perceived to be motivated and capable, the teachers' belief that some students cannot be taught is less relevant to their expectations of successful teaching than it is in classrooms where the students have been identified by standardized tests as likely to fail—an ideal setting for the triggering of expectation effects if teachers are prone to such biases (Cooper & Good, 1983).

The relationships obtained among the four efficacy measures—Rand 1, Rand 2, Webb Efficacy, and the Vignettes—offer further evidence of the validity of our conception of the two independent dimensions: teaching efficacy and personal teaching efficacy. Although the Webb Efficacy Questionnaire was developed before we were aware of the need to distingush between the two dimensions of teachers' sense of efficacy, five of the seven items on that instrument appear to measure teachers' sense of teaching efficacy. The Vignettes were written to measure teachers' per-ceived competence in teaching. The significant correlations obtained between Rand Efficacy 1 and the Webb Efficacy measure and between Rand Efficacy 2 and the Vignettes, and the lack of a relationship between

Rand Efficacy 1 and the Vignettes and between Rand Efficacy 2 and the Webb Efficacy measure, support our contention that sense of teaching efficacy and sense of personal teaching efficacy are distinct constructs.

The situation-specific influence of teachers' sense of efficacy also is reflected in the finding that teachers' scores on the Rand measures were related to stress in teaching basic skills but unrelated to teachers' general feelings of stress in teaching. Thus, not all the factors related to teachers' stress are related to teachers' sense of efficacy. Stress and efficacy are distinct psychological variables, though in the specific instance of basic skills classes, teachers' sense of efficacy became related to their feelings of stress. We suspect that the relationship between stress and teachers' feelings is reciprocal. Analytical methods that are sensitive to reciprocal effects should be used to shed further light on the relationship between teachers' stress level and their sense of efficacy.

Teachers who assumed more responsibility for their students' learning tended to have higher Rand efficacy scores. This finding suggests the need to explore further the dynamic relationships between feelings, thought, and behaviors, in order to better understand the process by which efficacy expectations influence behavior. The relationship between feelings of responsibility and efficacy may indicate that teachers' sense of responsibility mediates the relationship between teachers' sense of efficacy and their behavior. This is consistent with Weiner's (1980) attributional explanation of behavior. Weiner proposed that feeling, not thought, motivates achievement behavior. Thus, teachers who believe they can make a difference in students' performance accept responsibility for student failure and feel guilty when their students fail; the guilt then motivates the teachers' efforts to teach more effectively in the future. The addition of the dimension of responsibility and concomitant feelings of guilt to the model of teachers' sense of efficacy and student achievement may be helpful in understanding teachers' motivation. Self-efficacy refers to the teacher's judgment that "I can," whereas the teacher's sense of responsibility adds the necessary impetus for action—"I should."

## Teacher Attitudes and Classroom Processes

No strong relationships were found between teacher attitudes and their behaviors in the classroom. However, some trends indicate potentially fruitful directions for future research. Teachers who doubted the efficacy of teaching tended to use harsh methods in controlling students' behavior and were more likely to have disorderly classes than were teachers who believed in the efficacy of teaching. Teachers who believed in their ability to teach tended to have a warmer classroom climate than did less confident teachers. Once again, the causal direction of the relationships cannot be determined from our analysis; they are likely to be reciprocal, but research is needed to explore the magnitude and direction of the relationships.

## The Empirical Search for Relationships

Teachers with a strong belief in the efficacy of teaching tended to use praise and nonverbal signs of acceptance such as nodding, smiling, and other positive facial feedback. They tended to avoid behaviors that created a tense, negative climate such as yelling, reminding students of rules, giving directions without reasons, prodding students, punishing them, or using public displays of waiting to control student behavior. The similarity between the behaviors of teachers with a strong belief in the efficacy of teaching and the behaviors associated with positive teacher expectancy effects (Harris & Rosenthal, 1985) supports our contention that teachers' sense of teaching efficacy is an expectancy construct.

The teachers who were most confident of their teaching assigned seatwork to students and were more likely to instruct students in small groups. This finding differs from the support of whole-group instruction found in most process–product studies, but it may be due to the small size of the basic skills classes. Good (1983) suggested that whole-group instruction tends to be superior to small-group or individualized instruction because the teacher is better able to insure that students are engaged in appropriate tasks. In small classes, the typical advantages of whole-group instruction may be less powerful.

The strongest trends revealed in the relationships between teachers' perceived competence and the classroom process variables are those suggesting that confident teachers tended to give individual attention to all students. The behaviors that support this conclusion include attending students closely, giving students undivided attention (rather than trying to attend to a number of different student activities simultaneously), not leaving some students out of class activities, giving pupils individual attention, and checking on students' progress before moving on to a new topic.

The student behaviors associated with teachers' personal teaching efficacy suggest that confident teachers tended to accept students' feelings, because the students in their classes were likely to express their feelings by seeking reassurance from the teacher, refusing to perform some behavior requested by the teacher, and making demands on the teacher. Though these behaviors might be expected to arouse tension or anxiety in the class, we did not find that to be the case. Students were not likely to show fear or to engage in physical aggression. Other behaviors of confident teachers suggest that they fostered positive relations with their students by complying with students' requests and avoiding the use of scolding or punishing.

The management style of confident teachers appears to differ somewhat from the style of teachers who believe strongly in the efficacy of teaching. Confident teachers tended to give behaviorial rules without providing reasons, guidelines, or feedback to students regarding their behavior. Teachers with a high sense of teaching efficacy tended to give reasons for their directions.

A clearer picture of the relationships between the two efficacy dimensions and classroom process variables might have emerged, if we had separately analyzed the results of the mathematics and language classes. We decided to combine these groups because the relationships appeared similar across the subject-matter groups, and combining them increased the likelihood of finding significant relationships. This procedure, however, may have obscured relationships that are subject-matter specific. We are led to this possibility by the finding that teachers' beliefs in the efficacy of teaching were more salient in mathematics classes, whereas teachers' perceived competence was more predictive of student achievement in language classes. Future efficacy research should investigate subject-specific relationships.

The direction of the relationship between teachers' and students' behavior cannot be determined from our correlational analyses. We predict that the relationship is reciprocal, but studies of the way high and low sense-of-efficacy teachers establish their classroom climate at the beginning of the year would help us understand the magnitude and direction of the relationships between student and teacher behavior.

## CONCLUSION

The significant relationships obtained between the basic skills mathematics teachers' Rand Efficacy 1 scores and their students' Metropolitan mathematics test scores, and the communication skills teachers' Rand Efficacy 2 scores and their students' Metropolitan language test scores, suggest that teachers' sense of efficacy is an important variable to be considered in relation to student achievement. Inasmuch as teachers' sense of teaching efficacy was related to student achievement in mathematics and teachers' belief in their personal teaching efficacy was related to student achievement in communication, the relationship of teachers' sense of efficacy and student achievement may vary as a result of subject matter. The subject-specific nature of the sense of efficacy–student achievement relationship is further supported by the finding of no relationship between teachers' sense of efficacy and students' reading achievement. The basic skills communication classes were designed to teach basic langauge skills, not reading.

The profile of the teacher with a high sense of efficacy that emerges from the pattern of correlations between the Rand items and the classroom process items resembles the effective junior high teacher described by Evertson, Anderson, Anderson, and Brophy (1980):

Generally, the more successful teachers were rated as being more task oriented, affectionate, enthusiastic, oriented to students' personal needs, competent, confident, and academically effective. (p. 46)

The relationship of acceptance of student ideas to effective teaching of low ability students was noted in the Evertson et al. (1980) Junior High Study:

> In general, the teachers of lower ability classes who were more academically successful seemed to encourage their students to express themselves, even to the extent of tolerating relatively high rates of called-out questions and comments. These teachers also tended to be friendlier, accepting more social contacts from their students and being more tolerant of personal requests. (p. 58)

Given the small sample size and the unique characteristics of the compensatory education classes we studied, the conclusions that can be drawn from this study are limited and tentative. In spite of these limitations, the findings are consistent in the description they provide of the relationship of teachers' sense of efficacy to student achievement, and they support our conclusions from the earlier ethnographic study. Teachers with a strong sense of efficacy tended to have a classroom climate that is warm and supportive of student needs. Their students tended to feel secure and accepted and they scored higher on achievement tests than did the students of teachers with a lower sense of efficacy. Although the correlational nature of the study precludes any causal inferences regarding the effect of teachers' sense of efficacy on student achievement, and our theoretical model posits a reciprocal relationship, the strength of our findings warrants the design of experimental research to examine the impact of teachers' sense of efficacy on student achievement.

# 6

# Refining the Conceptual Framework: The Search for Intelligibility

## INTRODUCTION

In this chapter, we discuss how the results of our research can be used to refine the ecological framework presented in Chapter 1. We identify the ecological variables that our research suggests are related to teachers' sense of efficacy, and we describe how their contributions to teachers' sense of efficacy could be examined using structural causal modeling. We also consider how our research relates to research on other psychological variables. Finally, we examine the purpose of future research on teachers' sense of efficacy. The chapter will have greatest relevance to those interested in pursuing efficacy research. Others may wish to move on to Chapter 7.

## TEACHERS' SENSE OF EFFICACY AND STUDENT ACHIEVEMENT

Our findings support the conclusion of the two Rand Corporation studies (Armor et al., 1976; Berman et al., 1977) that there is a relationship between teachers' sense of efficacy and student achievement. From the relationships we found in our study of high school basic skills classrooms, we posit the model that appears in Figure 6.1. The solid black arrows indicate relationships found in our study. The broken arrows indicate relationships that are postulated in our theoretical framework but were not tested in the basic skills study. We include the illustration to suggest the process by which teachers' sense of efficacy becomes translated into student performance.

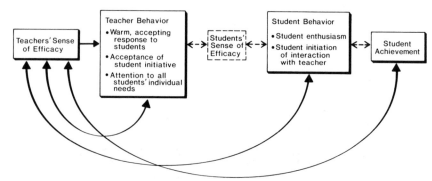

**Figure 6.1**    A Mediational Model of the Relationship between Teachers' Sense of Efficacy and Student Achievement

We caution, though, that a diagram cannot capture the dynamic interplay of human relationships involved in teachers' efficacy attitudes.

We found that the specific dimension of teachers' sense of efficacy relating to students' achievement depended on the subject matter being taught. This finding indicates that the relationship between teachers' sense of efficacy and student achievement is more complex and situation-specific than suggested in the Rand studies. It should be noted as well that pupils in both the Armor et al. (1976) study and in our basic skills study were predominantly minority students whose achievement was below their grade level mean on national norms. As we explained in Chapter 5, we chose to study basic skills classes in order to increase the likelihood of finding a relationship between teachers' sense of efficacy and student achievement. The relationships we found were strong, whereas those that may be found in studies of heterogeneously grouped classes may be less dramatic because teachers' sense of efficacy may be a less salient variable in such classes.

Although we did not examine students' perceived efficacy in our research, it is a crucial element in the model. Cooper and Good (1983) described three studies in which they examined the relationship between teacher expectations, teacher behavior, and students' self-efficacy beliefs. Their findings are consistent with our model. They found that students' self-efficacy was strongest in classrooms where teachers used criticism infrequently. In addition, they identified important considerations for the design of future studies of students' sense of efficacy. Such studies should include both teachers' and students' sense of efficacy, in order to determine how these two variables affect each other and are translated into achievement behavior.

The direction of the relationship between teachers' sense of efficacy and student achievement has yet to be examined. Bandura's (1977) model of reciprocal determinism posits a bidirectional relationship between perceived efficacy and human performance, but the correlational research that has been conducted on teachers' sense of efficacy provides no insight into the question of reciprocal causation. The framework presented in this chapter could be used to develop nonrecursive structural equation models (Cooley, 1978; Pedhazur, 1982) to refine our theoretical understanding of the variables that influence and are influenced by teachers' sense of efficacy.

Consideration of the results of our research in terms of the framework presented in Chapter 1 suggests certain variables that should be included in a structural model of the relationship between teachers' efficacy attitudes and student achievement. Our data indicate that classroom climate is the most important microsystem variable to include in such a structural model. Teachers with a strong sense of teaching efficacy were more accepting and supportive of their students than were teachers with a low sense of teaching efficacy, and they avoided harsh criticism and other behaviors that tend to discourage students. Teachers with a high sense of personal teaching efficacy tended to give close attention to all students and were careful not to ignore the low-achieving students in their classes.

The mesosystem variables identified by our middle school study as contributors to teachers' sense of efficacy are (1) team teaching, (2) teachers' participation in school decisions, and (3) multi-age grouping. We believe that these school organizational variables had an impact on those conditions of teaching that tend to diminish teachers' sense of efficacy. For example, team teaching can help reduce the teachers' sense of isolation. Teaming provides opportunities for teachers to develop relationships that can be sources of strength when teaching becomes stressful. Participation in policy decisions can help overcome the sense of powerlessness that stifles teachers' enthusiasm for teaching. Multi-age grouping places students with teachers for a 3-year period. The 3 years spanning middle school attendance are years of significant physical, intellectual, and emotional growth for students. Observing students' development over an extended period of time gives teachers more confidence that they are influencing students' growth.

These hypothesized relationships could be examined with structural causal modeling techniques. We expect that team teaching decreases teachers' sense of isolation; participation in school decisions decreases teachers' sense of powerlessness; and an extended assignment with the same students decreases teachers' sense of uncertainty about their effectiveness. Improvement in each of these conditions of teaching should increase teachers' sense of efficacy.

Two exosystem variables appeared to affect teachers' sense of efficacy: (1) the salaries teachers are paid, and (2) legislative and school board decisions that influence classroom instruction. Because teachers' salaries are lower than the wages of many blue-collar workers, some teachers experience a sense of status panic. They begin to question the value of work that is so poorly rewarded by society. Legislative decisions that restrict teachers' freedom to make decisions about appropriate classroom instruction contribute to their feelings of powerlessness. Some teachers believe that their effectiveness is limited by curriculum decisions made by state legislatures, the state department of education, and local school boards.

The macrosystem variables that appear to affect teachers' sense of efficacy are the cultural beliefs about the nature of intelligence and the influence of family background on student motivation and ability. These beliefs influence teaching efficacy expectations, which, in turn, affect teachers' judgments of their personal teaching efficacy.

In summary, the micro-, meso-, exo-, and macrosystem variables that we have identified interact to exert influence on two dimensions—(1) teachers' sense of efficacy and (2) student achievement. The subject matter being taught is another important variable. Structural causal modeling techniques can help us better understand the relationships among the variables in the ecology of school systems.

## The Measurement of Teachers' Sense of Efficacy

Our finding that the Rand item measuring teachers' sense of teaching efficacy correlated significantly with the Webb Efficacy scale (a measure of teachers' beliefs in the efficacy of teaching) but not with the Efficacy Vignettes (a measure of teachers' perceived competence) supports our contention that two independent dimensions exist within the construct of teachers' sense of efficacy. However, the Rand measures of efficacy are inadequate from a psychometric perspective. The negative skew and limited variability of teachers' scores on the Rand items reduce the likelihood of discovering statistically significant relationships, especially when sample size is small. The Webb Efficacy and Vignette measures also have psychometric limitations. The Webb Efficacy measure, a forced-choice scale, was developed to reduce the problem of social desirability bias by using a forced-choice format with choices matched for social desirability. However, more than 10% of our respondents refused to make a choice on at least one of the seven items. In addition, the internal consistency of the scale is inadequate. In three samples of teachers, the KR-20 reliability estimates ranged from .33 to .51 (Ashton et al., 1982). We developed the Efficacy Vignettes to measure teachers' perceived sense of efficacy across a wide range of teaching tasks. A 50-item questionnaire was constructed on the basis of teachers' responses to a Teaching Incidents Essay and a Role Perception item from our middle school study. We were hopeful that situational vignettes would elicit more teacher variability in that they provided a concrete referent that teachers have probably confronted in some form in their teaching experience, and they were difficult enough that teachers would not feel pressured to report that they could expertly handle each of the situations. Although the internal consistency of this measure was excellent, it did not correlate significantly with student achievement.

Gibson and Dembo (1984) reported on the construct validity of a Likert questionnaire designed to measure the two factors of teaching efficacy and personal efficacy. Results of their study give further support to the two-factor conception of teachers' sense of efficacy. Like the Rand measure, the 16-item instrument that resulted from Gibson and Dembo's validity study is a global measure of the two efficacy factors. Its length should make it a more sensitive measure than the Rand items. Gibson and Dembo demonstrated that their measure can be useful in process–product teacher effectiveness research. They compared four high and four low sense-of-efficacy teachers and the relationships they found between teachers' sense of efficacy and teachers' classroom behavior resembled the findings of our basic skills study. High sense-of-efficacy teachers were less likely to criticize students than were low sense-of-efficacy teachers, and also were more likely to stick with students who did not understand a problem or had not answered the teachers' question correctly. Low sense-of-efficacy teachers tended to move on to other students, accept an answer called out by another pupil, or provide the answer themselves.

Gibson and Dembo's results are consistent with the findings of other process–product studies (Dunkin & Biddle, 1974; Medley, 1978) and support the contention that teachers' sense of efficacy is a mediating cognitive process that contributes to the relationship between teacher behavior and student achievement. Research that includes investigation of meso-, exo-, and macrosystem variables as well as microsystem variables will be helpful in identifying factors that influence teachers' sense of efficacy and student achievement. However, a global measure of teachers' sense of efficacy is not consistent with Bandura's conception of perceived efficacy as a situation-specific cognitive mechanism, or with our observations of the situation-specific efficacy attitudes expressed by the teachers we interviewed. Refinement of our understanding of the efficacy construct requires a finer-grained analysis than traditional teacher effectiveness research is likely to yield.

Teaching is a multidimensional activity. Consequently, teachers will tend to vary in their effectiveness from one teaching task to another. For example, a teacher may be skilled in leading a class discussion but relatively ineffective as a lecturer. Teachers' perceptions of their effectiveness will reflect these differences. If we are to develop an understanding of how teachers come to judge their competence and how their self-appraisals affect their behavior, we need to study teachers' self-evaluations in relation to specific situations.

The microanalytic methodology Bandura developed to measure efficacy judgments in phobic behavior can be useful in the future study of teachers' sense of efficacy. The basic assumption underlying Bandura's microanalytic procedure is that sense of efficacy varies in magnitude, generality, and strength. *Magnitude* refers to the range of task difficulty for which the teacher feels competent. *Generality* refers to the range in the domain of behaviors for which a teacher feels efficacious. Does the teacher feel effective across a broad range of activities, or is the teacher's sense of efficacy limited to a small subset of teaching activities? *Strength* refers to the ease with which teachers' efficacy attitudes can be changed. Teachers with a weak sense of efficacy can be easily discouraged by an unsuccessful performance. A strong sense of efficacy will enable teachers to persevere in spite of difficulty.

To measure the magnitude of teachers' sense of efficacy requires the development of a hierarchy of teaching tasks ranging from simple to complex. One procedure for deriving the hierarchy would involve identifying teacher tasks and then asking teachers to rank the tasks in order of difficulty. Another procedure for developing a hierarchy of tasks would be to use existing taxonomies. For example, teachers might be asked to indicate their expectations regarding their efficacy in teaching children to think at each of the levels of Bloom's (Bloom, Engelhart, Furst, Hill, & Krathwohl, 1956) cognitive taxonomy. Then the order of tasks in the hierarchy could be validated by performance tests.

Measurement of teachers' perceived efficacy also should include the dimensions of generality and strength. The strategy that Bandura has used successfully to measure the dimensions of magnitude, generality, and strength requires individuals to indicate the tasks that they can perform and the strength of their perceived efficacy on a scale ranging in 10-unit intervals from a low point of 10 to a high point of 100. By focusing the efficacy judgment on the performance of a specific task in a specific situation, microanalytic measurement gives the strongest evidence possible of the relationship between perceived efficacy and performance (Bandura, 1981).

We recommend that Bandura's microanalytic procedure be used to investigate teachers' sense of teaching efficacy as well as their sense of personal teaching efficacy. The strength, magnitude, and generality of teachers' sense of teaching efficacy could be examined by developing a hierarchy of learning tasks based on three questions: (1) How difficult is it for students to learn (designate specific task)? (2) What types of students learn the task with ease? (3) What types of students learn the task with difficulty? The strength of the respondents' attitude could be assessed by asking teachers to indicate the degree of certainty with which each judgment was made. We are in need of ways of overcoming biases that hinder effective teaching. The measurement of teachers' situation-specific sense of teaching efficacy would enable us to identify the characteristics that contribute to a low sense of teaching efficacy and also enable us to assess the effectiveness of strategies designed to overcome a low sense of teaching efficacy.

Our theoretical understanding of the efficacy construct may be expanded by the development of small-scale experiments of the type that have been conducted to investigate students' self-efficacy (Schunk, 1984). Schunk identified four research topics that have yielded useful information about the development of students' self-efficacy: (1) the process by which individuals develop perceptions of their efficacy, (2) attribution feedback, (3) goal-setting, and (4) reward contingencies. Investigation of teachers' sense of efficacy in terms of these issues may be equally productive.

## Development of Efficacy Attitudes

Evaluation of efforts to improve teachers' performance is one useful way of studying the development of teachers' sense of efficacy. Changing teachers' sense of efficacy is likely to be a complex process. Guskey (1984) evaluated the effectiveness of an in-service workshop on mastery learning and found that teachers whose students improved on the learning tasks increased the extent of responsibility they assumed for both student success and failure and liked teaching more, but their confidence in their teaching ability decreased. Guskey speculated that teachers' perceived efficacy decreased in response to students' achievement gains because the participants were self-confident, veteran teachers who were surprised to learn that minor changes in their teaching practices would increase the effectiveness of their instruction and enable more of their students to succeed. He reasoned,

> To suddenly gain proof that you can do better could disrupt your confidence that you are as good as you can be. These teachers probably felt that the high degree of confidence in their teaching abilities they had expressed earlier was perhaps misgiven. (p. 254)

Implicit in Guskey's analysis is the hypothesis that the gains in their students' achievement increased the teachers' beliefs in the efficacy of teaching and led them to doubt their own competence. Thus, at least temporarily, gains in sense of teaching efficacy affected personal teaching efficacy adversely. Participation in the workshop and use of the new techniques had little effect on the efficacy attitudes of teachers whose students did not improve their performance. This finding supports Bandura's contention that successful performance is the most powerful source of efficacy information, although he did not anticipate that successful performance under some conditions could reduce feelings of self-efficacy. Longitudinal analyses of changes in teachers' sense of efficacy are needed to investigate the complex effects of experience on the development of the two dimensions of teachers' sense of efficacy.

## Attribution Feedback

The explanations teachers give for success or failure of their behavior affect their sense of efficacy. Weiner (1979) identified three attribution dimensions that affect efficacy expectations: (1) stability, (2) locus, and (3) control. *Stability* refers to whether the cause of success or failure is fixed or fluctuating; *locus* refers to whether the cause is external or internal to the individual; and *control* refers to whether the cause is controllable or uncontrollable. Weiner predicts that the attributions of *stable, internal,* and *controllable* are most likely to lead to positive efficacy expectations. For example, teachers are likely to have a strong sense of efficacy if they attribute student learning to their own consistent hard work (a stable, internal, and controllable attribution) and to their students' ability and motivation.

Ames (1983) concluded that teacher attributions depend on the situation, the information teachers have about their own and their students' performance, and the teachers' values. Ames pointed out that his analysis "is consistent with Heider's (1958, pp. 120–121) view that attributions are affected by 'what ought to be' (value belief) and 'what one would like to be' (self-worth belief), as well as by 'what is' (perception of situation)" (p. 109).

Investigation of teachers' attributions for their success and failure may be helpful in identifying strategies to increase their sense of efficacy. According to Ames's analysis, important variables that may affect teachers' attributions include the situation, the teachers' values, and specific characteristics of the teachers' and the students' performance. The ecological framework described in Chapter 1 suggests important situational variables that may influence teachers' attributions, for example, school climate, class size, and legislative and district mandates that prescribe specific curriucula and evaluation strategies.

## Goal Setting

Schunk (1984) reviewed a number of studies demonstrating that proximal goals have an important effect on children's perceived self-efficacy. When children set goals that were readily attained, they performed better and had a stronger sense of efficacy than when their goals were distant or nonexistent. As we demonstrated in Chapter 2, teachers' uncertainty about whether they are having an effect on student learning is a major threat to their sense of efficacy. Lortie (1975) pointed out that educational goals tend to be vague, ambiguous, and often conflicting. Teachers' sense of efficacy may benefit if teachers plan together and set readily attainable and observable goals for themselves and their students. Although teachers must exercise caution that their proximal goals are not trivial, identifying specific objectives and evaluating success in attaining such goals can give teachers a better sense of their own competence.

## Reward Contingencies

Using Deci's (1975) distinction between the informational and controlling functions of rewards, Schunk (1984) argued that rewards increase perceived efficacy when they convey information about the individual's competence; rewards may reduce sense of efficacy if an individual believes the rewards are used to manipulate or control him or her. For example, if teachers believe that their principal gives rewards, such as preferred classes and extra materials, to teachers who support the principal's position, the rewards may diminish the teacher's sense of perceived efficacy. Consequently, a teacher's perceptions of the intent of those who issue rewards will determine the effect of the rewards on a teacher's sense of efficacy.

A variety of incentive plans have been proposed to increase teacher motivation and satisfaction with the profession (e.g., Boyer, 1983; National Commission on Excellence in Education, 1983; Sizer, 1984). Many of the incentive plans are competitive. For example, Boyer recommended annual cash awards to outstanding teachers identified annually by districts and states and newspapers and businesses. The merit-pay plans being implemented in a number of states are similarly competitive. Competition has limited effectiveness as an incentive (Johnson & Johnson, 1974), because usually it motivates only that small percentage of individuals who believe they have a chance to succeed, and it often diminishes the motivation of those who believe they cannot compete with their more competent peers. Consequently, competitive financial incentive plans are unlikely to have a widespread positive impact on teachers' sense of efficacy or the quality of classroom instruction.

Of course, teachers' salaries need to be increased to reflect the value of teaching to the society and to reduce the status panic that discourages many teachers. However, Lortie (1975) concluded that teachers gain most of their job satisfaction from the experience of "reaching" their students, and Boyer (1983) pointed out that such psychic rewards of teaching have become "harder to come by" (p. 162). Those interested in enhancing teachers' motivation should seek ways to increase the emotional rewards that teachers find so satisfying yet so infrequent in today's classroom.

## Teacher Education: An Effective Context for the Microanalytic Study of Teachers' Sense of Efficacy

Study at the microanalytic level of the development of teachers' sense of efficacy could be most efficiently conducted as students progress through their professional learning. When students enter a teacher education program, the generality, magnitude, and strength of their sense of efficacy in teaching should be assessed and reassessed intermittently as they participate in experiences that are likely to affect their sense of efficacy.

We are most likely to increase our understanding of the origins and functions of teachers' sense of efficacy if we focus on the relationship between perceived efficacy and performance on individual tasks. If such analyses were conducted in the context of teacher education, they would serve two purposes: (1) they would inform us about the development and influence of teachers' sense of efficacy, and (2) they would provide information about the effectiveness of various strategies of teacher education. For example, Bandura (1977) identified four sources of efficacy information: (1) successful performance, (2) vicarious experience, (3) verbal persuasion, and (4) emotional arousal. The relative effectiveness of these four sources in increasing students' perceived efficacy could be examined by comparing instructional strategies that vary in terms of the sources of efficacy information. For instance, a study could examine the following four strategies: (1) the student is required to teach a social science concept to a student (successful performance), (2) the student observes an effective teacher teach the concept to a student (vicarious experience), (3) the student listens to a professor describe a strategy for teaching the concept (verbal persuasion), and (4) students' level of stress about performance is increased by emphasizing the importance of the grade they will receive on their performance (emotional arousal). The effect of each of these strategies on students' perceived efficacy and their performance could be assessed to determine its relative effectiveness. With such a study, the theoretical question of the relative effectiveness of various sources of efficacy would be examined as well as the practical question of which strategies are the most effective teacher education practices.

Given the situation-specific nature of teachers' sense of efficacy, it is likely that the development of perceived efficacy fluctuates with the specific educational experiences of teacher-education students. Perceived efficacy may be higher for certain tasks when students enter the teacher-education program, decrease as students recognize the difficulties involved in the task, increase as they have successful experience, and decrease again if additional complexity is added to the task. Careful documentation of the effects of teacher-education experiences on teachers' sense of efficacy would be useful in developing effective teacher-education experiences. Further, if microanalytic procedures were used to monitor teachers' sense of efficacy as they began their first year of teaching, it might be possible to identify the situations that threaten their sense of efficacy so that they could be helped to avoid the culture shock and resulting disillusion that so often accompany the first year of teaching (Evans, 1976).

## SENSE OF EFFICACY: AN INTEGRATIVE CONSTRUCT

A surge of renewed interest in motivation theory has generated a considerable volume of research in psychology and education. A number of theoretical perspectives have guided this research, including attribution theory (Weiner, 1979), personal causation (deCharms, 1968, 1976), expectancy theory (Dusek & Joseph, 1983), and intrinsic motivation (Deci, 1975). Though the constructs and processes examined through these perspectives are similar, a comprehensive theory incorporating these various perspectives has not been developed. The construct of perceived efficacy is relevant to each of these current motivational theories and, consequently, offers an organizing focus for the development of a comprehensive theory of motivation.

## Attribution Theory

Attribution has become one of the most popular and influential theories in educational research. Based on the assumption that humans are motivated to explain the causes of environmental events, attribution theory offers useful insights into achievement behavior. From the work of Weiner (1979), Dweck (1976), and others, we have learned that students' motivation is enhanced when they attribute their success to ability and/or effort, and their motivation is decreased when they attribute their failure to their level of ability. However, attribution theory is in need of an explanatory construct that accounts for the human compulsion to explain the causes of environmental events. Sense of efficacy provides that explanation. Humans are motivated to make attributions regarding behavioral outcomes in order to obtain information about their personal effectiveness. Individual survival ultimately depends on personal efficacy; consequently, we are motivated to increase our efficacy and to avoid situations that threaten that efficacy.

In discussing the results of our basic skills study, we suggested that teachers' sense of efficacy and sense of responsibility are implicated in the process by which attributions influence achievement. According to Weiner (1980), attributions arouse feelings that motivate future behavior. Those feelings are a response to the individual's self-efficacy appraisal. For example, when students fail to learn a concept a teacher has taught, and the teacher attributes the students' failure to his or her own inadequate preparation, that teacher will feel guilty and prepare more effectively for the next lesson. Thus, attributions and self-efficacy are intricately related and their relationship should be further investigated.

## Personal Causation

deCharms (1967, 1976) has argued that the basis of human motivation is personal causation—the experience of orginating one's actions and producing a change in the environment. He demonstrated the importance of personal causation in a 4-year longitudinal study of low-income black children from the fifth to eighth grades who received personal causation training. The training had a significant effect on students' achievement, and follow-up studies indicated that students who participated in the training had stronger feelings of personal causation and planned more for the future than did similar students who did not receive the training. The boys who participated in the training were more likely to graduate from high school than similar boys who did not receive the training.

Studies of teachers' classroom behavior have shown that teachers who promoted personal causation in students encouraged their students to influence classroom activities. Their classroom behavior resembles the classroom behavior of teachers in our basic skills study who possess a strong sense of perceived efficacy. This similarity suggests that teachers with a strong sense of personal teaching efficacy may foster personal causation in their students which, in turn, is likely to influence students' self-efficacy.

The advice deCharms (1984) gave to teachers to maximize motivation in the classroom conveys the message that teachers should have high teaching efficacy expectations:

> The first and most important thing that teachers must do is to believe that all pupils can be *origins*, and that teachers can influence pupils in that direction. (p. 306)

deCharms went on to write that teachers who encourage personal causation must have a strong sense of personal teaching efficacy:

> Teachers must believe that they themselves can be origins and can have desired effects on students. (p. 306)

## Expectancy Theory

A significant body of research has demonstrated the influence of teacher expectancies on student performance (Dusek, Hall, & Meyer, 1985). The process of how teacher expectations are translated into teacher behavior and student performance becomes clearer if the concept of perceived self-efficacy is included as a mediating variable. Because of beliefs about students' motivation and capability, teachers expect certain students to perform in specific ways (sense of teaching efficacy). These expectations influence the teachers' sense of personal teaching efficacy. The teachers' assessment of the likelihood of being able to influence students' performance then influences the teachers' choice of activities, the effort they expend, and their persistence. The teachers' behavior is interpreted by the students in terms of their sense of perceived efficacy and affects their performance through the mediating effect of the students' perceived competence. The students' performance affects the teachers' future expectations, and the cycle continues.

## Intrinsic Motivation

Deci's (1975) work on intrinsic motivation also can be subsumed under efficacy theory. Deci concluded that intrinsic motivation is undermined when individuals are denied choices and are pressured by external events.

Self-efficacy theory suggests that the individual's sense of personal efficacy is threatened by such external pressures, thus accounting for the decline in intrinsic motivation. The value of the addition of the efficacy construct to the intrinsic motivation model is evident in explaining the results of recent research on teaching styles by Deci and his colleagues. Deci, Schwartz, Sheinman, and Ryan (1981) found that teachers may demonstrate a teaching style that controls or supports student autonomy. Investigating conditions that contribute to teacher style, Deci, Spiegel, Ryan, Koestner, and Kauffman (1982) reported that when teachers were pressured by performance standards, they assumed a more controlling style. They talked more, were more critical of students, gave more commands, and allowed less choice and student initiative. These results can be attributed to the teacher's need to maintain a sense of efficacy. Teachers use a more controlling style in an attempt to counteract threats to personal efficacy. In classroom research on teachers' styles and student motivation, Deci et al. (1981) found that students of autonomy-oriented teachers were more intrinsically motivated and had higher self-esteem than the students of more controlling teachers. Self-efficacy theory suggests that the children's perceived self-efficacy was enhanced by their teachers' autonomy orienta-tion. Our own efficacy research supports this interpretation. In our study of basic skills teachers, we found that teachers with a high sense of efficacy behaved in ways that are similar to the description of the autonomy-oriented teachers in the study by Deci et al. Teachers with a high sense of efficacy were more open to student initiative and encouraged students to participate in classroom decision making. Although we did not measure students' sense of efficacy, our theoretical framework postulates that students' sense of efficacy mediates the relationship between teacher behavior and student achievement.

In summary, the construct of *sense of efficacy* is useful in explaining findings of classroom research that have been conducted from other perspectives. The possibility of combining those perspectives into a more comprehensive theory of motivation should be explored.

## THE PURPOSE OF FUTURE RESEARCH ON TEACHERS' SENSE OF EFFICACY

A crucial question that must be addressed in future research on teachers' sense of efficacy is the purpose of that research. Our emphasis on elaborating the theoretical framework carries with it the danger that we may lose sight of the purpose of this elaboration.

The purpose of psychological theory has been the subject of serious scrutiny in recent years. Sarason (1981) pointed out that the failure to consider the integral role of the social context in explaining human behavior is psychology's great mistake. He concluded that the future of the discipline depends on the emergence of a new psychology that recognizes the intrinsic role of the social context in individual behavior. Gergen (1982) criticized the traditional goals of psychology—the formulation of general laws for the purpose of prediction and control. Gergen argued that human development is "fundamentally indeterminant" (p. 163) and the dependence of human behavior on the specific social context precludes the development of theory that is transhistorical. Given these limitations and his basic assumption that social science is a "human construction," "a communal creation," Gergen called for a new role for theoretical development—a generative role—the "creation of intelligibility" (p. 165). By this, Gergen meant that theory should elucidate our understanding of human behavior by serving "as a lens for structuring momentarily what is fundamentally unstructured" (p. 167). Moreover, Gergen argued that theory used in this way

> may increase the adaptive potential of an individual or culture.... Not only should generative theory give one reason to pause and reconsider current modes of activity, but ideally should point to other forms of action and their potential results. (pp. 168–169)

Sarason's and Gergen's criticisms of traditional research and theory are particularly cogent to our research on teachers' sense of efficacy. Our research is grounded in the experiences of teachers in schools in the United States in the 1980s; therefore, our theory of teachers' sense of efficacy posits relationships that hold for the specific circumstances of this particular historical period. If all teachers came to have equally high efficacy attitudes, no relationship with student achievement would exist and the construct of teachers' sense of efficacy would merit no special interest. However, teachers do vary in their efficacy beliefs, and the particular sociocultural influences of this period contribute to those beliefs. Thus, we need to apply Gergen's notion of generative theory within this social context to develop a theory of teachers' sense of efficacy that has

> generative capacity, that is, the capacity to challenge the guiding assumptions of the culture, to raise fundamental questions regarding contemporary social life, to foster reconsideration of that which is "taken for granted," and thereby to generate fresh alternatives for social action. (p. 109)

In the next chapter, we describe an approach to research and theory development that we believe has the generative potential that Gergen recommends.

# 7

# Educational Reform through Ecological Research on Teachers' Sense of Efficacy

## A PROFESSION IN JEOPARDY

The research reported in this monograph supports the contention that teachers' sense of efficacy is an important contributor to teacher motivation. The extent to which teachers feel capable of affecting student achievement influences both the effort they exert in classroom instruction and their willingness to persist in working with their most difficult students. Our data indicate a significant relationship between teachers' sense of efficacy and student achievement in high school basic skills classrooms. However, our research also indicates that the psychosocial conditions in the schools—the isolation of teachers, their uncertainty, their lack of support and recognition, and their sense of powerlessness and alienation—make it difficult for teachers to maintain a high sense of efficacy. Current educational reform literature (Boyer, 1984; National Commission on Excellence, 1983) claims that schools are failing to develop students' academic ability. To that claim, our research adds an additional claim—that the educational system is failing to meet the motivational needs of teachers and, as a result, the teaching profession is in jeopardy.

## THE ECOLOGICAL APPROACH TO RESEARCH AND REFORM

### The Need for Transforming Experiments

Our discussion of social-psychological conditions of the school in Chapter 2 revealed that the problems that threaten teachers' sense of efficacy are grave, far-reaching, and structural. Minor technical changes, such as devising new curricula, establishing competency testing, introducing effective teaching strategies, lengthening the school day, erecting merit pay plans, or any other single-issue intrusion, will not ameliorate significantly the negative conditions of teaching. Major reforms are needed that address the systemic problems threatening teachers' sense of efficacy. Unfortunately, most schools lack structures for self-improvement and established processes for instituting and evaluating significant change. In his analysis of traditional educational research, Bronfenbrenner (1976) pointed out that "most of our scientific ventures into social reality perpetuate the *status quo.* . . . We are loath to experiment" (p. 14). Bronfenbrenner criticized the conservatism of conventional research practices in education and called for the design of "transforming" experiments. Such experiments would involve

> the innovative restructuring of prevailing ecological systems in ways that depart from existing institutional ideologies and structures by redefining goals, roles, and activities, and providing interconnections betweeen systems previously isolated from each other. (p. 14)

The goal of the transforming experiments is to radically restructure the educational environment in ways that allow individuals to fulfill their potential. The conditions of schooling described by the teachers we interviewed warrant drastic changes in the teaching profession. Transforming experiments offer a vehicle for developing more humane teaching conditions.

## The Limitations of Individualized Reform

We believe that Bronfenbrenner's (1976) ecological approach to educational reform is critical to the effort to improve schooling in the United States. Most reform efforts have failed. Of course, there are numerous reasons why reforms have not significantly improved the quality of education in the United States. However, we suspect that a major cause lies in what we call the individualization of reform and staff development efforts. *Individualization* refers to the propensity to trace the failings of schools to the shortcomings of individual teachers and/or administrators. When individual behavior is seen as the central cause of school failure, reform efforts focus on individuals and attempt to appropriately modify their attitudes and actions. Little attention is paid to the social context in which individuals must operate.

We can use our own efficacy research to illustrate the ease with which researchers can individualize reform proposals. On the basis of the positive relationships we found between teachers' efficacy scores, teacher behaviors, and student achievement, we might be encouraged to offer in-service programs designed to improve teachers' efficacy attitudes. After all, if we could change teachers' attitudes, we might also alter teachers' behavior, their students' behavior, and ultimately student achievement. However, our interviews with teachers and our observations in their classrooms convinced us that the logic of such a reform effort is flawed at its root. Teachers' efficacy attitudes are not simply mistaken ideas awaiting correction, and are not likely to be changed by preaching a gospel of positive thinking during in-service training sessions. Teachers' attitudes regarding their ability to teach and their students' abilities to learn are but a part of the multifaceted compromises teachers make with the social and organizational structure of school life. We have come to believe that low efficacy attitudes are caused by a whole complex of systems and events that ultimately alienate many teachers from their work. Thus, attempts to adjust the attitudes of low-efficacy teachers, without first (or simultaneously) altering the structural causes of alienation, are likely to fail. Sadly, but inevitably, the same logic that tempted us to individualize our reform effort, would, on the occasion of its failure, tempt us to blame our lack of success on the recalcitrance of individual teachers rather than on the futility of our plan.

## Ecological Reform

An alternative to the individualization of reform and the "hyperbureaucratization" it implies (see Callahan, 1962; Tesconi & Morris, 1972; Wise, 1979) is a program of ecological reform designed to democratize the workplace. The aim of ecological reform is not to bend individual behavior to conform to externally imposed notions of school improvement, but, rather, to transform schools so that they no longer alienate teachers, administrators, and students, and to free the intelligence of those who work in schools, so they might better analyze their problems, invent solutions, and improve the quality of education. Rather than "de-skilling" teachers (Apple, 1981) by lessening their autonomy and subjecting them to prepackaged, teacher-proof curriculum materials, the goal of ecological reform is to empower teachers and to increase their sense of efficacy, by helping them take greater control of, and responsibility for, their professional lives. As Dewey (1950) observed years ago, effective schools are those that provide opportunities for the "free and full play" of individual vigor. Such schools permit everyone, "from the first grade teacher to the principal of the high school some share in the exercise of educational power" (cited in Wirth, 1983, p. 97).

In his proposal for ecological research, Bronfenbrenner (1976, 1977, 1979) envisioned a research design that would simultaneously advance both scientific understanding and social policy. Traditionally, we have conducted research as though theory development and validation must precede practical application. Bronfenbrenner's proposal is significant in its recognition that educational reform need not always follow theory, but offers the opportunity to test, develop, and refine our theories of education and human development in the process of reform.

In keeping with Bronfenbrenner's conviction that theory development and social change can be mutually enriching, we believe that the ecological framework described in Chapter 1 can direct experiments in educational reform and refine our understanding of the efficacy isssue. Ecological reform experiments offer a way to improve the efficacy attitudes of teachers by improving the quality of teachers' work lives, expanding their repertoire of teaching skills, and enhancing the "ethos" of the school.

An ecological approach to the problem of low efficacy attitudes would begin by addressing the causes of teacher dissatisfaction and alienation. The research literature on the quality of work life offers specific suggestions for improving working conditions (Pratzner, 1984). Work is likely to be satisfying when we value what we do, when it challenges and extends us, when we do it well, and when we have ample evidence confirming our success. In order for our work to be fulfilling, significant others on the job and in the community must appreciate the importance of our efforts and acknowledge the quality of our performance. We must have the opportunity to take part in decisions that affect us and to help solve problems that face us. We must clearly understand how our efforts contribute to the mission of the institution for which we work (Herzberg, Mausner, Peterson, & Capwell, 1957; Maslach, 1976; Rawls, 1971; Ruch, Hershauer, & Wright, 1976).

Teachers become alienated because, at almost every level, they are deprived of the knowledge necessary to sustain job satisfaction and professional self-respect. Their pay is low, but the problem runs deeper than dollars. Teachers' accomplishments are difficult to assess, especially in classes of low-achieving students; they are isolated from colleagues and rarely receive the support and recognition they desire from their administrators, other teachers, or parents; many are overworked and believe they do not have the time they need to perform their duties well; they gain satisfaction from working with young people, but with increasing numbers of students they are finding it difficult to achieve and sustain friendly and responsible relationships.

The goal of ecological reform is not to tighten management controls over teachers but to find ways to liberate their problem-solving capabilities. Teachers must be helped to define their own problems, to design inquiry strategies, and to decide how to make use of their collaborative expertise, and they must be allowed to take action (Stenhouse, 1975). Outside consultants must become information resources who help clarify the choices open to teachers, not "experts" who tell teachers what to do.

In his book, *The Reflective Practitioner*, Schon (1983) outlined an integrated conception of theory and practice that can help teachers achieve greater fulfillment in their work. Schon suggested that teachers' loss of professional self-esteem is symptomatic of a larger crisis that is rooted in a growing skepticism about professional effectiveness in the larger sense, a skeptical reassessment of the professions' actual contribution to society's well-being through the delivery of competent services based on special knowledge. Professional knowledge is mismatched to the changing character of the situations of practice—the complexity, uncertainty, instability, uniqueness, and value conflicts which are increasingly perceived as central to the world of professional practice. (p. 14)

Schon's characterization of situations of practice matches the description of teaching that emerged in our interviews with teachers (see Chapter 2). Teachers' feelings of uncertainty about whether they can really make a difference in students' lives, the insecurity they experience when they realize that what worked in one situation does not work in another, the frustration they feel at having to cope with multiple publics—their administrators, colleagues, students, and parents—mirror the world of practice depicted by Schon.

According to Schon, the crisis of confidence in the teaching profession is attributable to the traditional relationship between theory and practice. The dominant epistemology of practice, based on logical positivism, consists of "instrumental problem solving made rigorous by the application of scientific theory and technique" (p. 21). Schon argued that this conception of practice is inappropriate:

When ends are fixed and clear, then the decision to act can present itself as an instrumental problem. But when ends are confused and conflicting, there is as yet no "problem" to solve. A conflict of ends cannot be resolved by the use of techniques derived from applied research. It is rather through the nontechnical process of framing the problematic situation that we may organize and clarify both the ends to be achieved and the possible means of achieving them. (p. 41)

Schon added that "the situations of practice are not problems to be solved but problematic situations characterized by uncertainty, disorder, and indeterminacy" (p. 15). To deal more appropriately with the situations of practice, Schon recommended a model of professional practice he calls *reflection-in-action*. Through reflection, the practitioner analyzes the situation of practice to discover new meanings in the situation of uncertainty. Each situation is treated as unique, and research "is triggered by features of the practice, undertaken on the spot, and immediately linked to action" (p. 308). Training in the process of reflection-in-action and opportunities to engage in reflection-in-practice offer teachers one approach for dealing with the negative conditions of teaching and increasing their sense of efficacy.

## A Structure for Ecological Reform

The aim of ecological reform is to allow individuals to find ways to integrate themselves into the work place. As Wirth (1983) pointed out while discussing the work of Freire (1973),

"To be more fully human" means to have a relationship of *integration* as opposed to *adaptation*. Integration results from the capacity to adapt oneself to reality *plus* the critical capacity to make choices and to transform that reality. When we lose our ability to make choices and are subjected to the choices of others, when decisions are no longer our own because they are imposed by external prescriptions, we are no longer integrated. We have "adjusted" or "adapted." We have become *objects* instead of integrated, active, human *subjects*. (p. 193)

Disempowered individuals become spectators of, rather than participants in, their own institutions. They are diminished by their work and saddened by a future that experience has rendered gray and unpromising. Such individuals are unable to derive even ironic satisfaction from the fact that the very institution that has detached them from their potential has, in small but human increments, diminished its own productive capacities.

Quality-of-work-life advocates operate on the premise that over time an institution works at maximum efficiency only when it fosters the development of its own membership. They agree with Dewey's contention that the moral measure and "final value of *all institutions* is their educational influence" (Dewey & Tufts, 1910, emphasis added). However, building institutions that are educative and human enhancing, rather than miseducative and human diminishing, is a difficult task. As Wiener (1954), the father of cybernetics pointed out, "It is easier to set in motion [institutions] in which human beings [use only] a minor part of their capacity ... than to create a world in which human beings fully develop" (p. 524).

Throughout our study of teacher efficacy attitudes we were struck by the fact that teachers are losing connection with their schools, students, and colleagues, and even with their profession. Like Sizer (1984), we found that

teachers are rarely consulted, much less given significant authority, over the rules and regulations governing the life of their school; these usually come from "downtown." Rarely do they have any influence over who their immediate colleagues will be; again, "downtown" decides.... Teaching often lacks a sense of ownership, a sense among the teachers working together that the school is theirs, and its future and their reputation are indistinguishable. Hired hands own nothing, are told what to do, and have little stake in their enterprises. Teachers are often treated like hired hands. Not surprisingly they often act like hired hands. (p. 184)

The goal of ecological reform within the school is to bring teachers into a new relationship with their work, students, and colleagues. Such relationships cannot be mandated by management fiat or engineered by visiting consultants; they can be fashioned only by teachers themselves. However, an uncertain and status-panicked profession will not move effortlessly from adaptation to integration. As we saw in Chapter 2, teachers presently have a stake in their own isolation, resignation, and conformity. They have adapted because they needed to in order to survive in the system. Many are able to endure the uncertainties of their profession only by finding a measure of protection and anonymity in the shadows of the bureaucratic status quo.

Fortunately, a rich and growing body of literature exists that details how ecological reforms can be accomplished (Carnoy & Shearer, 1980; Emery, 1969; Emery & Thorsrud, 1976; Emery & Trist, 1973; Herbst, 1974, 1976; Maccoby, 1979; Zwerdling, 1978). A promising plan for democratic reform in education has been set out in *The Structure of School Improvement* by Joyce, Hersh, and McKibbin (1983). There are a number of weaknesses in the book (Webb, 1984), but its great strength is that it presents a plan for ecological reform that gradually increases the involvement of teachers and improves the cooperative environment of the school. The book's three-stage reform program is designed to transform schools into self-monitoring, self-renewing, human-enhancing institutions run by competent and cooperative professionals.

The procedures that Joyce and his colleagues detail begin by bringing together a group of teachers, administrators, parents (what the authors refer to as *A Committee of Responsible Parties* [CRP]) to "scrutinize the health of [the] school and oversee its improvement" (p. 1). The goal of the CRP is at once modest and ambitious. It is modest because the committee begins by focusing on small and manageable problems that need improvement. It goes through a series of steps designed to solve the identified problem. However, while solving the problem, it accomplishes something more; it begins to fashion an environment that is conducive to self-assessment and change. Teachers are consulted, their ideas are taken seriously, and their worries are taken into account. Channels of communication are opened and barriers of isolation are lowered. Responsibilities are shared, and staff members begin to see, through their own experiences, that the quality of education can be elevated, and the conditions of teaching improved. The institution becomes less reified as teachers begin to see that they can make a useful contribution to the change effort.

With one success under their belt, the CRP identifies another problem and repeats the planning and innovation procedures used earlier. The cycle of improvement continues until a climate conducive to more ambitious innovation is well established. At this point, the second stage of the reform process begins. Larger problems within the school are identified and studied, and more ambitious, far-reaching solutions are devised. Consultants are brought in, when needed, to do specific tasks identified by teachers. As improvements are made, and the change process becomes well established, the third stage of the reform program begins. During this stage the responsible parties undertake an examination of the school's mission and its organizational structure.

By combining the process of reflection-in-action with a structure similar to that proposed by Joyce and his colleagues, teachers could begin to assume more power over school decisions. However, the process of ecological reform is difficult, and there is much to be learned about democratizing the workplace and improving the conditions of teaching. Consequently, researchers must be involved in the reform process. Careful documentation of the reform effort and its effects is essential. The value of such research in revealing the difficulties of educational reform has been demonstrated in a number of significant studies (Gross, Giacquinta, & Bernstein, 1971; Smith & Keith, 1971). However, if research is to contribute to sustaining efficacy attitudes, we must abandon the typical research strategy of treating research subjects as if they were objects (Bronfenbrenner, 1976). Researchers should become collaborators with educators in the improvement process. Very few examples of a collaborative relationship between researchers and practitioners exist despite frequent calls for collaboration in the educational literature (Krathwohl, 1977; Schubert, 1980; Slavin, 1978). Klausmeier's (1982) description of his efforts to improve student achievement on the basis of his research on cognitive learning provides one example of how collaborative research can be used to improve schools.

The prospects for ecological change are not encouraging because the winds of change in education are blowing in another direction—toward legislated learning (Wise, 1979), Tayloristic accountability (Wirth, 1983), and checklist measures of teacher effectiveness (e.g., Florida Performance Measurement System, Peterson, Micceri, & Smith, 1985). Ironically, while education is becoming more bureaucratized, some industries are modifying their hierarchical structures (Goodlad, 1983). The General Motors Corporation, for example, recently committed millions of dollars to the construction of new plants designed to increase worker participation and improve the quality of work life (Wirth, 1983). Wirth has documented similar activities in other industries in the United States and Europe. Their experience can be of immense value to educators interested in fashioning ecological reform programs.

Researchers should carefully study both the reform process and its attendant outcomes (Bronfenbrenner, 1977; Schaefer, 1967). As Wirth noted,

> It would be a salutary exercise in honesty and humility to admit we don't know many of the answers and to permit groups of teachers to design a variety of programs to which they are professionally committed, [and] then study them in collaboration with researchers to see what can be learned and reported. (p. 124)

## TEACHING CONDITIONS IN NEED OF REFORM: AN ECOLOGICAL ANALYSIS

Our research sheds some light on the problems that must be addressed if teachers and students are to develop and maintain positive efficacy attitudes within the context of the school. Using the process of reflection-in-action described by Schon (1983) and by the Committee of Responsible Parties outlined in Joyce et al. (1983), educators and researchers could undertake transforming experiments designed to improve the working conditions in schools and the efficacy attitudes of teachers and students. Such experiments have the potential for improving education by reducing faculty isolation and uncertainty, opening lines of communication, legitimating and supporting thoughtful inquiry and innovation, constructing systems to evaluate change efforts, and democratizing the school workplace. Transforming experiments may also yield valuable information about the quality of teachers' work lives and their efficacy attitudes, and further explain how these variables interact and affect the classroom performance of teachers and students. Teachers and researchers have a growing body of literature to guide them in designing transforming experiments. The literature on school and teacher effectiveness, together with the research on teacher efficacy attitudes, provide a useful yardstick against which Committees of Responsible Parties can judge where a school needs improvement and how that improvement best can be accomplished.

An ecological approach to school change suggests that although educational reform may start at the level of the microsystem (teachers and students working in the classroom), lasting changes must permeate throughout the meso-, exo-, and macrosystems of the educational environment. We will consider each of these systems separately, but it is important to keep in mind that the model of reform being suggested here is designed to reverberate across all levels of the system and transform the entire ecology of the school environment.

## Transforming the Microsystem

All teachers confront the problem of maintaining a sense of professional competence in an environment that continually threatens them with failure. Although competence threats exist for all teachers, the efficacy attitudes study described in Chapter 3 revealed that high sense-of-efficacy and low sense-of-efficacy teachers use different strategies to cope with the threat of failure. High sense-of-efficacy teachers maintained academic standards for their low-achieving students, were challenged by the opportunity to help such students, focused on academic work in their classes, and strived to establish friendly relations with their pupils. Low sense-of-efficacy teachers, in contrast, were frightened by the threat that low-achieving students presented to their sense of professional competence. They held low expectations for their students, demanded little from them academically, and were guarded and authoritarian in the classroom.

*Transforming teacher behavior.* Transforming experiments are needed to investigate ways of helping teachers cope with the efficacy threats posed by low-achieving students. A great deal is known about providing teachers with skills in classroom management and instruction, and in relating to students, and there is reason to believe that increasing teachers' skills in these areas will lessen their self-doubt and their on-going sense of vulnerability. A number of researchers (Anderson, Evertson, & Brophy, 1979; Good, Grouws, & Ebmeier, 1983; Stallings, Needels, & Stayrook, 1979) have developed experimental teacher in-service programs based on the results of studies that have found significant correlations between specific teacher behaviors and student achievement. These experimental studies have shown that student achievement can be significantly increased if teachers are taught effective teaching behaviors.

Our correlational study of high school basic skills teachers adds to the process–product research literature on which such experimental studies have been based. Teachers with a high sense of efficacy created a more positive classroom climate than their low-efficacy counterparts. They were less likely to punish or scold students, more likely to accept student ideas and feelings, and more likely to include all students in instruction and seatwork activities. The interactions that we observed between high-efficacy teachers and their students resemble the "origin" classroom climate that deCharms (1976) and Deci (1975) have shown fosters motivation and self-efficacy in students.

Maintaining positive relations with students may be especially important for motivating students in today's schools. In our study (Ashton, Webb, & Doda, 1983) as in others (Lortie, 1975; Raschke et al., 1985), disruptive students were identified as a major source of teachers' stress. Apparently, many teachers are having difficulty maintaining good relationships with their pupils. An ethnographic study conducted by Woods (1978) of over 200 pupils in a modern secondary school in Great Britain sheds some light on the nature of the difficulties between teachers and students. Woods concluded that many students no longer respond to the Protestant-ethic notion of work advocated by teachers:

> To these pupils at least, it is not the work that is important, and any intrinsic satisfaction to be had from it is dependent on the relationship with the teachers concerned. This squares with their general emphasis on social criteria in their outlook on school. (p. 173)

This description of British students resembles descriptions of secondary pupils in classrooms in the United States (Everhart, 1979).

Experimental programs designed to help teachers develop human relations skills and to enable them to create and maintain positive interactions with their students should bolster the self-efficacy of teachers. Teachers especially need to learn how to maintain positive attitudes when students become hostile. Brophy and Evertson (1981) observed that teachers tend to become angry when dealing with hostile students, thereby escalating classroom conflicts. Transforming experiments could identify effective ways to help teachers develop human relation skills that contribute to their sense of efficacy.

Although experimental programs that train teachers to use more effective behaviors in their classrooms may increase their sense of efficacy, the limitations of this approach must be recognized. Although correlating specific teaching behaviors with student achievement data can be useful, it is a conservative source of reform ideas. It will not produce the major changes in education that Goodlad (1984) has argued are needed to overcome common classroom problems. Only those behaviors that are already widely used in schools can be observed, recorded, and correlated with achievement variables. Therefore, the research can only validate some currently popular teaching practices. The paradigm, as currently implemented, does not allow for the identification and evaluation of innovative teaching practices. Such a conservative mode of research is inadequate for solving the motivational problems teachers and students face.

During our interviews, a number of teachers confided to us, with strained voices and teary eyes, that they felt unprepared to deal with the motivation problems of their most academically troubled students. Although strategies for improving teachers' management and instructional skills are available in the current literature, these methods appear inadequate to alleviate the professional self-doubt that teachers are experiencing. Brophy (1983) pointed out that not much research exists that can help teachers motivate their students to learn, because most motivation research has been conducted in settings that have litttle in common with the typical classroom. Bolder ventures are needed. The experimental model that has yielded such innovations as mastery learning (Bloom, 1981) and cooperative learning (Slavin, 1983) must now be applied to the problem of motivating "difficult" students.

The teacher training programs derived from the teacher effectiveness literature provide good examples of the individualization of reform. Their aim is to change the behavior of individual teachers. As we argued earlier in this chapter, individualized reform efforts fail to address the social-psychological conditions that foster low efficacy attitudes. For example, Coladarci and Gage (1984) described an unsuccessful attempt to increase student achievement through a short-term in-service teacher training program. They hypothesized that teacher resistance was the result of a lack of adequate contact between teachers and trainers and the failure of researchers to check on teachers to see if they were implementing the strategies they had been taught. An alternative explanation for the failure of these training programs to induce change in teachers' behavior emerges from our efficacy research—individualized reform ignores the social forces that contribute to faculty resistance to change.

The research on innovation and change has demonstrated that the success of any reform rests not simply on the quality of the reform proposal but on the process by which the reform is brought about. Reforms almost always fail when they do not involve school personnel from the start and do not create an environment conducive to change. Those reforms that attend to the ecology and ethos of the school are more likely to succeed (Joyce et al., 1983; Sarason, 1982). Teachers' sense of efficacy seems to be a crucial aspect of the school ethos and should be taken into account in school improvement projects (Berman et al., 1977).

*Summary.* It is not likely that dramatic changes in teacher attitudes or in the educational system will result from microsystem experiments designed to develop teachers' sense of efficacy by training them to behave like teachers with a high sense of efficacy. The description presented in Chapter 2 of the social-psychological milieu of teaching suggests that serious threats to teachers' sense of efficacy lurk in the social realities of most schools. The isolation, the lack of rewards and recognition, and feelings of powerlessness that many teachers experience threaten to estrange them from their work. Transforming experiments must influence the meso-, exo-, and macrosystems, if schools are to offer teachers and students the growth-promoting environment essential for development of efficacy.

### Transforming the Mesosystem

*School organization.* The teachers quoted in Chapter 3 reiterated Lortie's (1975) description of teaching as a socially isolated and ruggedly individualistic profession. A sense of lonely desperation pervades their accounts of inadequate materials, unmanageable students, and insensitive administrators. They spoke bitterly of being unappreciated, unsupported, and uncertain. The neglect and occasionally demeaning treatment teachers received from administrators contributed to their self-doubts and disillusionment with their profession.

In dramatic contrast, the middle school teachers we described in Chapter 4 spoke of sharing frustrations with team members and supporting one another in difficult times. The organizational structure of teaming and teachers' participation in school decision making appeared to contribute to the development of community in the middle school. Teachers described how they helped each other cope with student problems. The contrast between the isolation experienced at traditionally organized schools and the sense of community evident in the team-organized middle school suggests variables for transforming experiments to improve the efficacy attitudes of teachers and students. Teaming created the need for group planning, and the principal's structure for including teachers in decision making further encouraged teachers to develop collegial relationships with their colleagues. The sense of alienation that threatens to overwhelm teachers and estrange them from their work appears related to their feeling that they are are unable to influence important decisions affecting their professional lives. When curriculum, scheduling, and other important matters are imposed on teachers they feel a loss of control over a significant aspect of their work and are likely to lose enthusiasm for what they do. The sense of commitment and involvement that distinguished middle school teachers from the more resigned junior high teachers in our study seemed to be tied to the greater role middle school teachers played in decision making. Although the middle school teachers warned of the danger of being burdened with minor decisions that could be handled best by administrators, they stressed the need for involvement in important decisions.

Schneider (1984) offered guidelines that may be useful to principals in deciding when to involve teachers in decisions and when to make decisions on their own. Using the concept of zones of acceptance (Clear & Seager, 1971), Schneider concluded that when teachers are affected by a decision (high interest) and are informed on the issue (high expertise), they want to be involved in the process of decision making. From a random sample of 266 middle and junior high teachers in Wisconsin, Schneider identified a set of technical and managerial issues in which the teachers indicated high levels of interest and expertise. Teachers wanted a say in such areas as instructional objectives and materials, evaluation procedures, disciplinary policies, and instructional budgets. Schneider recommended that administrators should identify areas in which their teachers have interest and expertise and insure faculty participation in those areas of decision making.

The finding that more conflict occurred among the middle school teachers in our study than among junior high teachers shows that an organizational structure may have both negative and positive effects on teachers' sense of efficacy. Fuller et al. (1982) emphasized this point by distinguishing between *organizational efficacy* and *individual efficacy*. *Organizational efficacy* refers to the individual's expectancy that valued outcomes can be gained by influencing another person at a different level of the organization, and *individual* or *performance efficacy* refers to the teacher's perceived competence in accomplishing work tasks within the classroom, independent of other members of the school organization. Fuller et al. pointed out that organizational changes that benefit an individual's organizational efficacy may limit individual efficacy. For example, requiring teachers to plan instruction collectively can increase teachers' organizational efficacy but diminish their individual efficacy by reducing their autonomy to choose their own teaching strategies. Although organizational variables may influence organizational and performance efficacy in similar ways, fostering or diminishing both, these variables also may influence each of the two efficacy dimensions differently. Thus, careful investigation of the effects of organizational structure on the different dimensions of efficacy is needed to insure that one dimension does not benefit at the expense of another.

In the middle school we studied, the three-year relationship with students created by multi-age grouping appeared to have the most significant impact on teachers' sense of efficacy. The opportunity to see students develop over an extended period gave the teachers stronger evidence of their ability to influence students than did the typical one-year assignment of teachers and students.

We doubt, however, that team teaching, teachers' participation in school decisions, or the three-year assignment of the team to the same students is critical to the development of a sense of school community or a strong sense of efficacy. Other organizational arrangements that foster teacher collaboration and mutual support are likely to have similar positive effects. Klausmeier (1982) pointed out that the essential requirements for successful school improvement are arrangements that require teachers to plan together, allocate time during school hours for planning, and involve teachers in decisions. Little's (1982) research gives additional insight into the crucial components of community that should be explored in transforming experiments. She found that schools in which teachers discussed classroom practices, observed and criticized each other's performance, and collaborated on the design and preparation of curriculum were more successful than schools characterized by isolation. Little (1984, 1985) cautioned, however, that development of such environments is an arduous, context-specific process that takes on different characteristics as the experiment unfolds over time. The documentation of the processes involved in educational change is vitally important, particularly as they affect the participants' sense of efficacy.

In summary, our middle school study revealed three important areas for transforming experiments at the level of the mesosystem: Organizational arrangements that (1) encourage collaborative planning among teachers, (2) require teachers' participation in school decisions, and (3) give teachers extended periods of time to influence student growth are likely to have a positive effect on teachers' sense of efficacy.

*Home–school relations.* From the viewpoint of teachers with a low sense of efficacy, the lack of support students receive at home is the major mesosystem variable that impedes teachers' effectiveness. Teachers with a low sense of efficacy tend to believe that parents of low-achieving students are uncaring and do not understand the importance of education. Lightfoot (1978) and Entwisle and Hayduk (1978) have shown that these perceptions are inaccurate. Most parents believe that education is the best hope for improving their children's socioeconomic status, and they have high expectations for their children. The problem, as Lightfoot pointed out, is not in conflicting views over the value of education but, rather, in parents' and teachers' misperceptions of one another. When parents fail to respond to teachers' requests for support, teachers interpret the parents' behavior as disinterest, though it is more likely to be a self-protective reaction to the parents' belief that school is a hostile and ego-threatening environment.

Transforming experiments are needed to break through the alienating barriers that keep parents and teachers from forming the mutually supportive alliances needed to bolster self-efficacy.

## Transforming the Exosystem

Our interviews with teachers suggest that the exosystem has a powerful effect on teachers' efficacy attitudes. As discussed in Chapter 2, the inadequacies of teachers' salaries impose social-psychological as well as economic hardships on teachers. The realization that they are not re-warded at a level commensurate with other middle-class occupations induces a sense of status panic in many teachers that leads them to doubt the intrinsic value of their work. Experiments are needed that deal with salary disparities suggesting that society does not value teachers' work as highly as that of plumbers, truck drivers, garbage collectors, and other blue-collar workers. Nationwide, a number of economic plans are being developed that are intended to reward excellence in teaching. Our conversations with teachers suggest that unless the inadequacy of teachers' salaries relative to other professions is addressed, such incentive plans are only likely to add to teachers' frustration and dissatisfaction. In addition, incentive plans that teachers view as inequitable will further their dissatis-faction. Therefore, teachers must be involved in planning incentive programs, and careful consideration must be given to the potential impact of the plans on teachers' sense of efficacy.

The policies implemented by legislative mandate were especially salient influences on teachers' beliefs about their ability to influence student learning. They expressed concern that legislators and the state department of education were making decisions that had significant impact on their ability to teach effectively. Wise (1979) cautioned that such bureau-cratic intrusions into classrooms are a serious threat to teachers' sense of autonomy. Our study of the conditions of teaching, reported in Chapter 2, supports Wise's concern and suggests that teachers' sense of efficacy is at risk when states attempt to legislate learning.

## Transforming the Macrosystem

The cultural values that permeate our society contribute to the social-psychological milieu that affects teachers' sense of efficacy. The low status conferred on teachers in the United States adds to teachers' declining self-esteem. The widely held perception that "those who can, do, and those who can't, teach" makes it difficult for teachers to feel good about their work. If the profession is to attract qualified individuals who believe in the efficacy of teaching and keep the best teachers in the classroom, ways to overcome the public's negative perceptions of teaching must be identified.

As we pointed out in Chapter 1, in our review of the literature, social-psychological beliefs about the nature of intelligence and the role of the learner and the teacher are prominent in our culture. Our interviews with teachers were filled with evidence of these beliefs (see Chapter 3). Teachers with a low sense of efficacy often attributed students' learning problems to the students' lack of ability. These teachers did not share responsibility for the failures of low-ability students because they were convinced that there was nothing that any teacher could do to overcome the obstacles that low-ability students face. Consequently, teachers with a low sense of efficacy were threatened by the low-achieving students in their classes. Teachers with a high sense of efficacy, though recognizing the obstacles faced by low achievers, refused to use low ability as an excuse for not teaching the students who most needed firm, clear, and persistent instruction. The cultural beliefs about intelligence that contribute to teachers' sense of helplessness when they are working with low-achieving students must be overcome, if teachers are to sustain the motivation needed to make a difference with these students.

Research by Dweck and Bempechat (1983) indicates that beliefs about intelligence develop during childhood. They found that some children hold an *entity belief*. These children believe that intelligence is a stable, global trait. They believe that "they possess a specific, fixed amount of intelligence [and] that this intelligence is displayed throughout performance" (p. 243). Other children hold an *instrumental-incremental* belief that "intelligence consists of an ever-expanding repertoire of skills and knowledge [that can be] increased through one's own instrumental behavior" (p. 243–244).

The beliefs held by teachers with a low sense of efficacy reflect the entity theory of intelligence and those held by teachers with a high sense of efficacy reflect the instrumental-incremental theory. In an interview study of the beliefs of preservice teachers, Ginsberg and Newman (1985) found that the entity belief was the predominant belief among the preservice teachers. The danger of the entity theory is that it supports low-efficacy attitudes by contributing to the development of a sense of helplessness among teachers. Teachers who hold the entity theory of intelligence believe that there is nothing that they can do for students who lack the necessary intellectual ability. Identification of effective strategies for overcoming the implicit entity theory of intelligence is an important area in which to conduct transforming experiments.

Teachers' beliefs about the role of schooling can also foster low-efficacy beliefs. Ginsberg and Newman (1985) found that preservice teachers tend to believe that schooling offers individuals an opportunity to fulfill their potential and that when students fail it is because they lack the motivation needed to achieve their goals. The responses of teachers we interviewed support Ginsberg and Newman's conclusion. Only one of the teachers we interviewed expressed concern about the school's role in perpetuating social and racial inequities in the culture. The other teachers accepted the dominant cultural belief that our educational system offers equal opportunities for all students. Like Ginsberg and Newman, we believe that teacher education strategies are needed to develop teachers' awareness of and sensitivity to the obstacles that minorities and women continue to confront in our culture.

Minority groups that have been forced to assume a subordinate position in a culture develop differences in learning and behavior as compared to the dominant culture (Ogbu, 1982; Willis, 1977). The educational problems resulting from such cultural differences derive from structural inequalities in the culture and are not likely to respond to individualized reform efforts. With a more sophisticated understanding of the problems faced by minority groups, educators will be more likely to work to achieve the structural changes needed to increase their effectiveness with minority groups.

## FINAL THOUGHTS

The research we have reported in this volume supports the ecological approach to reform that we advocate in this chapter. The values that pervade the culture, the economic reward system, the legislative and judicial influences, the school organizational structures, and the relations among administrators, teachers, students, and parents interact to affect teachers' sense of efficacy. To be effective, transforming experiments must address the systemic problems that these ecological variables create. In discussing staff development, Goodlad (1983) pointed out that schools with more-satisfied teachers differed in the conditions of teaching from schools with less-satisfied teachers, especially in the collegial relationships among teachers and administrators. The schools did not differ in instructional strategies. Goodlad concluded that tackling the sensitive area of teacher autonomy, before addressing the more pressing problems of the conditions of teaching, would be an "unmitigated disaster" (p. 58). Our research on teachers' sense of efficacy supports Goodlad's conclusion and emphasizes the urgent need to address the deteriorating conditions of teaching, not by focusing on changing individual teachers, but rather by fostering efficacy attitudes through the democratization of the workplace. However, the effectiveness of reform must be evaluated at the level of the individual teacher and students in the classroom, because the ecology of schools is experienced in different ways by different teachers. More variation is seen in teachers' scores on efficacy measures within schools than between schools. Teachers with a high sense of efficacy may resist the low-efficacy norms that thrive in their school and maintain their commitment to make a difference with their low-achieving students. Similarly, teachers with a low sense of efficacy may maintain their fatalistic attitudes toward low-achieving students despite the high efficacy attitudes of the majority of their colleagues. We need to investigate the psychological and social dynamics that account for the individual differences in the ways teachers respond to the ecology of the school. Some teachers become demoralized by larger classes, heterogeneous grouping of students, the disdain of their principal, and the resistance or resentment of parents. Others seem unaffected by these conditions, and still others become energized by such challenges and intensify their efforts to exert an effect on their students' lives.

Variables that may contribute to these differences include teachers' beliefs systems (Tom, Cooper, & McGraw, 1984), their values (Ames, 1983), the support of their families and friends, their personal life histories and temperamental characteristics, and their teacher education programs (Denham & Michael, 1981). As we design studies to change the ecology of schools, we must carefully monitor the impact of the experiments on individual teachers and students. The worth of ecological reforms ultimately will be determined by the effects they have on the classroom behavior of individual teachers.

Teachers' sense of efficacy can be a sensitive measure of the effectiveness of reform as well as an indicator of the differing reactions of individual teachers to these reforms. The rich theoretical framework of ecological reform provides a wealth of ideas for designing transforming experiments. We realize that teachers may be effective even though they do not feel effective or, at the other extreme, that they may feel effective without being effective. However, the research on motivation suggests that the subjective perception of competence is more important for an individual's well-being than is the objective level of competence (Bandura, 1977). The goal of ecological reform is to transform schools into environments in which teachers and students can realize their full potential. If we are to make progress toward that goal, the promotion of a high sense of efficacy in teachers and students must become an educational aim as important as academic achievement.

# Middle School Teacher Questionnaire

Thank you for participating in this study. Without your help our work is impossible.

On the following pages, you will find a wide variety of questions. We have asked a number of questions regarding your feelings and beliefs about teaching. We've also asked about your actual teaching experiences, both good and bad. We've included other questions about your school setting and students to better understand the context of your teaching situation.

Please don't worry about the style and grammatical form of your responses. We understand that this is a long questionnaire and that you will have to work quickly. We're interested in your first reactions.

You needn't worry that you will ever be associated with your answers. Our first task will be to remove your name and assign a number to your questionnaire.

We will need your name, address, and social security number in order to send you the $10 stipend. Please complete the information below.

Thanks again for your participation.

_____

Name

_____

Address

_____

Social Security Number

1–10. Identification Numbers
11. Age? (circle one)
    1. 20 or below
    2. 21 to 25
    3. 25 to 30

                4. 31 to 35
                5. 36 to 40
                6. 41 to 50
                7. 51 or above

12. Sex? (circle one)        1. Male
                           2. Female

13. Degree certification (circle one)    1. Elementary
                           2. Secondary
                           3. Other _____
                                     (specify)

14. Subject taught: _____

Professional training beyond the bachelor's degree? (circle one)
1. No.
2. Yes. If yes, please describe degree and give date degrees(s) conferred.

      15. _____  16. _____
          Degree            Date
      17. _____  18. _____
          Degree            Date

19. Professional organizations to which you belong?
20. Subscriptions to educational literature you are presently receiving.
21. I would be willing to have an observer visit my classes once a week for five weeks—for which I would receive a stipend of $25.
Yes _____ No _____
22. I would be interested in participating in a summer workshop designed to discover ways to improve middle school teaching (for Teacher Center credit).
Yes _____ No _____
23. I would be interested in serving as a teacher consultant to your project from time to time.
Yes _____ No _____
24. When it comes right down to it, a teacher really can't do much because most of a student's motivation and performance depends on his or her home environment. (circle one)
1 Strongly agree  2 Agree    3 Neither agree    4 Disagree    5 Strongly
                                nor disagree                    disagree
25. If I really try hard, I can get through to even the most difficult or unmotivated students. (circle one)
1 Strongly agree    2 Agree    3 Neither agree    4 Disagree    5 Strongly
                                  nor disagree                    disagree
26. In general how stressful do you find being a middle school teacher?

| 1 | 2 | 3 | 4 | 5 |
|---|---|---|---|---|
| Not at all stressful | Mildly stressful | Moderately stressful | Very stressful | Extremely stressful |

27. I feel excessive stress as a teacher when _____
_____
28. People have a variety of approaches to dealing with stress. Describe what you do when you feel stress from teaching.
29. Which of these statements comes closest to describing your feelings about teaching.
    _____ 1. I am extremely satisfied with teaching as my occupation.

———— 2. I am very satisfied with teaching as my occupation.

———— 3. I am more satisfied than not with teaching as my occupation.

———— 4. I am equally satisfied and dissatisfied—I guess I'm in the middle.

———— 5. I am more dissatisfied than satisfied with teaching as my occupation.

———— 6. I am very dissatisfied with teaching as my occupation.

———— 7. I am extremely dissatisfied with teaching as my occupation.

30. Assume that a circle divided into eight sections represents your total life interests. How many of the eight sections would you say "belong" to your work as a teacher? ————

31. Some teachers seem to emphasize the importance of warmth and closeness to students while others seem to stress the importance of the teacher's getting students to work effectively. Which of the two do you consider more important? (circle one)
    1. Warmth and closeness
    2. Getting work done

32. If you could choose your students in the coming year, which of the following would you select? (circle one)
    1. A group of students whose emotional needs are a challenge to the teacher.
    2. A group of nice kids from average homes who are respectful and hard working.
    3. A group of creative and intellectually demanding students calling for special effort.
    4. A group of underprivileged children from difficult homes for whom school can be a major opportunity.
    5. Children of limited ability who need unusual patience and sympathy—sometimes they're called "slow learners."
    Which would be your second choice? ————————————————

33. Do you feel you work harder, about the same, or a little less than most teachers? (circle one)
    1 Harder            2 About the same            3 A little less

34. In your teaching situation, how much freedom do you feel you have to do what you think is best? (circle number)

    1          2          3          4          5          6          7
    Complete                                                    Almost
    freedom                                                     complete
                                                                freedom

35. When my students fail to learn a lesson that I have taught, their failure is probably due to ————————————————————————————————————.

All of us have certain things about our own role performance which we think are important. There are 10 numbered blanks on the page below. In the blanks, please write 10 verbs or short descriptive phrases, each referring to the simple statement, "*As a middle school teacher, I do the following things.*"

Answer as if you're giving the answers to yourself, not to somebody else. Write the answers in the order that they occur to you. We are interested in both positive and negative aspects. Don't worry about logic but try to be as clear as possible. Write each descriptive word or phrase as rapidly as possible. Your first impressions are good enough.

As a middle school teacher I do the following things:

_____

_____

_____

_____

_____

_____

_____

_____

_____

Many things are likely to affect one's effectiveness as a middle school teacher, and these things are likely to be different for different teachers. For yourself personally, think about what helps you to be an effective teacher and what makes it difficult to be effective as a teacher. List everything that you can think of that helps you to be effective in the classroom. Then list everything that you can think of that makes it difficult for you to be effective. Then indicate the importance of the effect of each of these influences on you by rating each of the influences you have identified on a scale of 0 to 9; let 0 indicate that the influence is not very powerful and 9 indicate that the influence has a strong and significant effect on you.

My effectiveness as a middle school teacher

| Is facilitated by | Is made difficult by |
|---|---|
| _____ | _____ |
| _____ | _____ |
| _____ | _____ |
| _____ | _____ |
| _____ | _____ |
| _____ | _____ |
| _____ | _____ |
| _____ | _____ |
| _____ | _____ |

36. When you are having a problem in teaching, whom do you talk with about it? Name them and their relationship to you.

37. How important is teaching to you?

    1 Extremely        2 Very          3 Not very        4 Not at all

      important           important          important        important

38. Some teachers think they can assess how their teaching is going. Others feel that it is very difficult. What do you think?

    _____ I believe that it is relatively easy to know when one is really teaching effectively.

    _____ I believe that it is possible to know one's own effectiveness at times.

    _____ I believe that it is relatively difficult to know when one is really teaching effectively.

39. If you had it to do all over again, would you choose to become a teacher?

    Yes _____   No _____

40. What percent of the students in this school do you expect to complete high school? (circle one)
    1. 90% or more
    2. 70% or more
    3. 50% or more
    4. 30% or more
    5. less than 30%
41. What percent of the students in this school do you think the principal expects to *complete* high school?
    1. 90% or more
    2. 70% or more
    3. 50% or more
    4. 30% or more
    5. less than 30%
42. What percent of the students in this *school* would you say want to complete high school?
    1. 90% or more
    2. 70% or more
    3. 50% or more
    4. 30% or more
    5. less than 30%
43. What percent of the students in your *class* would you say want to complete high school?
    1. 90% or more
    2. 70% or more
    3. 50% or more
    4. 30% or more
    5. less than 30%
44. On the average, what level of achievement can be expected of the students in this school?
    1. Much above the national norm
    2. Slightly above the national norm
    3. Approximately at the national norm
    4. Slightly below the national norm
    5. Much below the national norm
45. How many students in this *school* will seek extra work so that they can get better grades?
    1. Almost all of the students
    2. Most of the students
    3. About half of the students
    4. Some of the students
    5. Almost none of the students
46. How many students in your *class* will try hard to do better on tests than their classmates do?
    1. Almost all of the students
    2. Most of the students
    3. About half of the students
    4. Some of the students
    5. Almost none of the students

47. How many students in your *class* will seek extra work so that they can get better grades?
    1. Almost all of the students
    2. Most of the students
    3. About half of the students
    4. Some of the students
    5. Almost none of the students
48. How many students in your *class* try hard to improve on previous work?
    1. Almost all of the students
    2. Most of the students
    3. About half of the students
    4. Some of the students
    5. Almost none of the students
49. How many students in this *school* try hard to improve on previous work?
    1. Almost all of the students
    2. Most of the students
    3. About half of the students
    4. Some of the students
    5. Almost none of the students

How often, if at all, do students at this school have disagreements, arguments, or fights because of the following: (circle one)

| | Very often | Often | Sometimes | Not often | Not at all | Don't know |
|---|---|---|---|---|---|---|
| 50. Making jokes about someone's skin color | 6 | 5 | 4 | 3 | 2 | 1 |
| 51. Messing in someone's hair | 6 | 5 | 4 | 3 | 2 | 1 |
| 52. Joking about the way someone talks | 6 | 5 | 4 | 3 | 2 | 1 |
| 53. Being hassled for money | 6 | 5 | 4 | 3 | 2 | 1 |
| 54. Joking about someone's religion | 6 | 5 | 4 | 3 | 2 | 1 |
| 55. Being pushed around | 6 | 5 | 4 | 3 | 2 | 1 |
| 56. Being threatened | 6 | 5 | 4 | 3 | 2 | 1 |
| 57. Making jokes about someone's belongings | 6 | 5 | 4 | 3 | 2 | 1 |
| 58. Lying about things | 6 | 5 | 4 | 3 | 2 | 1 |
| 59. Making jokes about someone's family | 6 | 5 | 4 | 3 | 2 | 1 |
| 60. Name-calling | 6 | 5 | 4 | 3 | 2 | 1 |

61. Too many teachers in this school seem to be more concerned with their personal interests than with the overall welfare of the school. (circle number)
    1 Agree          2 No opinion          3 Disagree
62. Teachers in this school cooperate well. (circle one)
    1 Agree          2 No opinion          3 Disagree
63. There are cliques or groups among the teachers in this school that create an unfriendly atmosphere. (circle one)
    1 Agree          2 No opinion          3 Disagree

64. The poor work performance of some teachers on this school staff make it difficult for us to achieve adequate instructional goals.
65. A few of the teachers in this school think they run the place. (circle one)

   1 Agree                     2 No opinion                     3 Disagree
66. Teachers and other professional personnel in this school freely share ideas and materials. (circle one)

   1 Agree                     2 No opinion                     3 Disagree

# Middle School Teachers' Sense of Efficacy: Interview

Instructions: *I'd like to ask you a number of questions regarding the problems and rewards of teaching. Of course, your comments are confidential and will not be identified by your name, your school, or even the grade level you teach.*

1. Teachers are asked to pursue many goals and to accomplish many things. Of all the things that you do as a teacher, identify the one you think is most important. (Probe until you have a clear sense of what the teacher identifies as his or her primary objective.)
2. How can you tell if you are achieving the objective you have just identified? (Probe here until you get some specific indicators the teacher uses to define success.)
3. What kinds of things make it most difficult to achieve the objectives you have identified? (Probe here until the teacher identifies specific problems that impede progress.)
4. What kinds of students are most difficult to reach? That is, what type of students are least likely to meet your identified objective? (We are interested in student types, e.g., poverty kids, black kids, bright kids, rich kids, and so on. However, the teacher may find it easier to talk about specific students. That's fine, but stay with the questioning long enough so that you can go beyond specific personalities and get a sense of the "kinds of students" the teacher is talking about.)
5. In the first question I asked you to identify the objective you think is most important for you to accomplish. I'd like now to ask you what the second most important objective is. (Probe here until you get an objective that is clearly different from the first objective the teacher identified. For example, if the teacher's first objective was to teach math—an academic skill—we would want the teacher to identify an objective in another area. If a teacher said the second objective was to teach geometry, we would probe until she or he offered an objective that was less obviously academic.)

6. How can you tell if you are achieving the objective you have just identified? (Probe here until you get some specific indicators the teacher uses to define success.)
7. What kinds of things make it most difficult to achieve the objectives you have identified? (Probe here until the teacher identifies specific problems that impede progress.)
8. What kinds of students are most difficult to reach? That is, what type of students are least likely to meet your second most important objective? (We are interested in student types, e.g., poverty kids, black kids, rich kids, and so on. However, the teacher may find it easier to talk about specific students. That's fine, but stay with the questioning long enough so that you can go beyond specific personalities and get a sense of the "kinds of students" the teacher is talking about.)
9. Teachers often change their objectives as they gain experience in the classroom. I'd like you to compare your objectives with those you had as a beginning teacher. Are there any large differences? What are they? (Probe here until you get a clear sense of the different objectives *and* an understanding of why the teacher changed objectives.)
10. I have observed your _____ and _____ classes. (Identify classes by period.) Would you please identify your favorite student in that class. Tell me what there is about this student that appeals to you. (Probe until you have gained an understanding of what the teacher takes to be an ideal student. We want to know what kind of student catches her or his attention and tickles her or his fancy.)
11. Again limiting yourself to the classes which I have observed, who would you say is your worst student? (Probe until you know what kind of student most offends this teacher.)
12. What kind of support do you get from the administration?
13. What kind of help don't you get—but think you should get—from the administration?
14. Name one or two teachers in the school who are most like you. Identify why you believe they are like you.
15. Identify one or two teachers who are least like you and explain why you feel they are different from yourself.
16. Are there teacher cliques at school, and if so what are they like? (Probe here until you identify the factors that organize the cliques and the social results of clique behavior.)
17. Does the principal play favorites in this school? That is, are there in groups and out groups? If so, how do individuals get into the in group and stay out of the out group?
18. Most teachers would say there are students that they never reach. Are there students you have failed to reach this year? Who are they and what are they like? (Probe here until you know when the teacher will give up on a student. Try also to determine how many students fell into this category this year.)
19. What do you think the students you have just identified will be doing 5 years from now? Ten years from now? Twenty years from now?
20. Do you adopt different teaching strategies for different classrooms? Please describe those strategies and what you are trying to achieve by adopting those strategies.

21. What are your strong points as a teacher?
22. Where do you think you need to improve as a teacher?
23. Are there constraints on you that limit your effectiveness? If so, what are they? (Probe here to find out what the teacher would like to be doing but cannot do.)
24. Tell me what you think of the ability-grouping arrangements in this school.
25. How did your classes do this year?
    How can you tell?
    How did they do on the Metropolitan Achievement Tests?
    What do you think of these tests?
    What percentage of students do you feel did *not* make enough progress this year? Why?
26. (Note to the interviewer: This question demands some preparation. Identify a classroom situation that recently transpired. Turn the teacher's attention back to that situation. The instance you specify should be ambiguous enough that the teacher's explanation will give you some insight into his or her thinking. When you are sure that he or she remembers the situation you have specified, ask the following questions.) What were you trying to accomplish in that lesson (instance)? Did you accomplish what you set out to do? How can you tell? If you had to do it over again, what would you do differently?
27. (Note to the interviewer: Identify two or three students who appeared to be atypical and troublesome in the classroom. Ask the teacher the following questions.) Can you tell me something about _____? What has (his/her) year been like in your classroom? Why do you think (he/she) is not doing well here? (Our objective in these questions is to see what strategies the teacher might have used with the student in question, how early in the year the student was written off, and whether the teacher accepts any responsibility for the student's difficulties.)
28. How do you think the majority of your students would describe you if they were being candid? How do you think the majority of the faculty would describe you if they were being candid? How do you think the principal would describe you if she or he were being candid?
29. Compare this school with other schools with which you are familiar. Is it better or worse? Why? (Probe here until the teacher has identified what she or he takes to be the strong points and the weak points of the school.)
30. When you are having difficulty as a teacher, to whom do you go for help? (Probe for specific names.) What kinds of help do you get from that person? (Probe here until you understand whether the teacher gets specific suggestions or whether the relationship is more "therapeutic." That is, does the teacher commiserate with his or her helper, or analyze problems and try to solve them?)
31. What are the specific rules that you have in your classroom that you feel most of your students know and understand? What rules do you have that you find most difficult to enforce?
32. What do you find rewarding as a teacher? That is, what do you get from your students, peers, remuneration, and so on, that makes teaching worthwhile? Have you ever thought of leaving teaching? What kinds of things make you consider leaving the profession? If you had it to do over again, do you think you would choose teaching? Why?

33. If you could pursue only one objective as a teacher, what would that objective be? (Probe here until you get a sense of whether the teacher tends toward valuing basic skills or interpersonal relationships.)
34. What kinds of discipline problems have you had this year?
35. Do you have adequate materials? If not, what materials would you need in order to do your job well?
36. Describe a typical work day in your life. Begin with the time you get up and describe what you do until you go to bed at night.
37. We hear a good deal about teacher stress these days. What kinds of things have caused you stress this year?
38. How can you tell when you are under stress and what do you do about it?
39. Teachers sometimes claim that they change with experience. Think back to when you began teaching and consider how you have changed. Have your objectives changed? Have your teaching strategies changed? Have your relationships with students changed? Are you less idealistic? How so?
40. How do you feel about the competency test for new teachers? How would you feel about extending competency testing to teachers already in the field? What kinds of things would you think should be on a competency test if you were to write it?

# High School Basic Skills Teacher Questionnaire

1–10. Identification numbers

11. Number of years of teaching experience _____

12. Number of years of experience teaching low-socioeconomic students _____

13. Were you assigned to teach basic skills classes or did you volunteer for them?

_____ Assigned _____ Volunteered

14. Is the subject matter of the basic skills classes you teach in your major field of college preparation?

_____ Yes _____ No

15. How much freedom do you have in planning for your basic skills classes?

| 1 | 2 | 3 | 4 | 5 |
|---|---|---|---|---|
| Complete freedom | | | | Completely predetermined by others |

16. To what extent are your school's basic skills classes ability grouped?

_____ Not at all

_____ Somewhat

_____ A special effort is made to homogeneously group these classes.

17. Does the school administration have definite ideas about how instruction in basic skills classes should be provided to students?

_____ The school administration has a distinct point of view and promotes it.

_____ The school administration expresses some opinions but does not promote a point of view.

_____ The school administration generally allows teachers to develop their own programs.

18. How responsible do you feel for the academic achievement of students in your basic skills classes?

_____ Very responsible

_____ Responsible

_____ Somewhat responsible

_____ Not very responsible
_____ Not responsible at all

19. What kind of seating arrangements do you have in your classes?
    _____ Students always select their own seats
    _____ Generally students select their own seats
    _____ Some students select their seats; some are assigned
    _____ Generally teacher assigns seats
    _____ Teacher always assigns seats

20. To what extent is the school's basic skills instructional program coordinated schoolwide?
    _____ To a large extent, both in many aspects (content, sequence of objectives, materials) and throughout all grades
    _____ To some extent
    _____ Very little; each teacher generally plans the instructional program for his/her own class

21. How often do you work with your class *as a whole*?
    _____ Always
    _____ Often
    _____ Sometimes
    _____ Seldom
    _____ Never

22. How often are all your students working on the same lesson?
    _____ Always
    _____ Often
    _____ Sometimes
    _____ Seldom
    _____ Never

23. How would you characterize your teaching objectives in your basic skills classes?
    _____ They are the same for all students
    _____ They are the same for most of the students
    _____ They are the same for some students
    _____ They are different for most students
    _____ They are different for each student

24. Would you choose to teach these classes again, if you were given the opportunity to choose?
    _____ Definitely no
    _____ Probably no
    _____ Probably yes
    _____ Definitely yes

*Please indicate your degree of agreement or disagreement with each of the following statements.*

25. When it comes right down to it, a teacher really can't do much because most of a student's motivation and performance depends on his or her home environment. (circle number)

| 1 | 2 | 3 | 4 | 5 |
|---|---|---|---|---|
| Strongly agree | Agree | Neither agree nor disagree | Disagree | Strongly disagree |

26. If I really try hard, I can get through to even the most difficult or unmotivated students. (circle number)

| 1 | 2 | 3 | 4 | 5 |
|---|---|---|---|---|
| Strongly agree | Agree | Neither agree nor disagree | Disagree | Strongly disagree |

*Read each situation carefully. Consider similar situations from your own teaching experiences. Indicate how effective you would be in handling each situation by circling the appropriate number.*

| 1 | 2 | 3 | 4 | 5 | 6 | 7 |
|---|---|---|---|---|---|---|
| Extremely ineffective | | | Moderately effective | | | Extremely effective |

27. One of your students misbehaves frequently in your class and often is disruptive and hostile. Today in class he began roughhousing with a friend in the back of the class. You tell him firmly to take his seat and quiet down. He turns away from you, says something in a belligerent tone that you can't hear, and swaggers to his seat. The class laughs and then looks to see what you are going to do. How effective would you be in responding to this student in a way that would win the respect of the class?

| 1 | 2 | 3 | 4 | 5 | 6 | 7 |
|---|---|---|---|---|---|---|
| Extremely ineffective | | | Moderately effective | | | Extremely effective |

28. Maria, an educable mentally retarded student in your class, has been working diligently but still performs below grade level in all subjects. At a conference the mother says that she doesn't expect much of the girl, because Maria is "dumb" just like herself. How effective would you be in talking to Maria's mother about her feelings and about the effect that parents' expectations can have on their child's school achievement?

| 1 | 2 | 3 | 4 | 5 | 6 | 7 |
|---|---|---|---|---|---|---|
| Extremely ineffective | | | Moderately effective | | | Extremely effective |

29. Your county has mandated that all teachers must restructure their course requirements to insure adequate development of students' basic skills by including these elements in each lesson plan. How effective would you be in incorporating achievement of basic skills objectives into your lesson plans?

| 1 | 2 | 3 | 4 | 5 | 6 | 7 |
|---|---|---|---|---|---|---|
| Extremely ineffective | | | Moderately effective | | | Extremely effective |

30. Half a dozen low-achieving female students are not getting much from your class. Lately they have begun to "hang around together" and to advertise that they don't like you or your class. They have begun to fool around, disrupt your lessons, and occasionally "talk back." When you attempt to involve them in class work they either make jokes or sit sullenly. How effective would you be in eliminating their disruptive behavior?

| 1 | 2 | 3 | 4 | 5 | 6 | 7 |
|---|---|---|---|---|---|---|
| Extremely ineffective | | | Moderately effective | | | Extremely effective |

31. This year your principal has assigned you to teach a class of low-ability students in your subject matter area. The teacher who taught this class last year tells you

that it was the worst experience of her 20-year teaching career. How effective would you be in increasing the academic achievement of the students in this class?

| 1 | 2 | 3 | 4 | 5 | 6 | 7 |
|---|---|---|---|---|---|---|
| Extremely ineffective | | | Moderately effective | | | Extremely effective |

32. You have a student who never hands in assignments on time, seldom gets to class before the bell rings, and inevitably forgets to bring books or pencil to class. You have discussed this matter with his parents, but they don't seem to understand the importance of school achievement. How effective would you be in motivating this student to get to work?

| 1 | 2 | 3 | 4 | 5 | 6 | 7 |
|---|---|---|---|---|---|---|
| Extremely ineffective | | | Moderately effective | | | Extremely effective |

33. A new student has been assigned to your class. Her records indicate that she never does her homework and does not seem to care about her education. Her IQ score is 83, and her achievement scores have been below the 30th percentile. How effective would you be in increasing her achievement test scores?

| 1 | 2 | 3 | 4 | 5 | 6 | 7 |
|---|---|---|---|---|---|---|
| Extremely ineffective | | | Moderately effective | | | Extremely effective |

34. The student–teacher ratio in your class of compensatory education students is 20 to 1. You must plan your lessons to meet the individual needs of the students. How effective would you be in designing activities to match the individual interests and abilities of the students in your class?

| 1 | 2 | 3 | 4 | 5 | 6 | 7 |
|---|---|---|---|---|---|---|
| Extremely ineffective | | | Moderately effective | | | Extremely effective |

35. Because of repeated failure, one of your students confides to you that she has given up and will attend school only until she can find a way to drop out. How effective would you be in persuading her that she can be successful in school?

| 1 | 2 | 3 | 4 | 5 | 6 | 7 |
|---|---|---|---|---|---|---|
| Extremely ineffective | | | Moderately effective | | | Extremely effective |

36. A number of your students have been sleeping in class. They do poorly on in-class assignments and seldom turn in homework. You learn that they are taking drugs. How effective would you be in helping the students with their drug problem?

| 1 | 2 | 3 | 4 | 5 | 6 | 7 |
|---|---|---|---|---|---|---|
| Extremely ineffective | | | Moderately effective | | | Extremely effective |

37. A learning disabled student has been mainstreamed into your classroom. He has been described by his previous teachers as being extremely hyperactive and having severe reading problems. How effective would you be in teaching this student?

| 1 | 2 | 3 | 4 | 5 | 6 | 7 |
|---|---|---|---|---|---|---|
| Extremely ineffective | | | Moderately effective | | | Extremely effective |

Instructions: *Read each of the following paired statements and determine if you*
1. Agree most strongly with the first statement
2. Agree most strongly with the second statement

*Indicate your answer by circling the appropriate number.*

38. A. A teacher should not be expected to reach every child; some students are not going to make academic progress.
    B. Every child is reachable. It is a teacher's obligation to see to it that every child makes academic progress.
    Circle one:
    1. I agree most strongly with A.
    2. I agree most strongly with B.
39. A. Heterogeneously grouped classes provide the best environment for learning.
    B. Homogeneously grouped classes provide the best environment for learning.
    Circle one:
    1. I agree most strongly with A.
    2. I agree most strongly with B.
40. A. My skills are best suited for dealing with students who have low motivation and who have a history of misbehavior in school.
    B. My skills are best suited for dealing with students who are academically motivated and generally well behaved.
    Circle one:
    1. I agree most strongly with A.
    2. I agree most strongly with B.
41. A. Low-ability students should be encouraged to develop their vocational skills when they enter high school.
    B. Low-ability students should be encouraged to develop their academic skills when they enter high school.
    Circle one:
    1. I agree most strongly with A.
    2. I agree most strongly with B.
42. A. Students who are not interested in education and who continually misbehave should be expelled from school until their attitudes improve.
    B. Students who are not interested in education and who continually misbehave should be kept in school so that trained teachers can help such students to improve their attitudes.
    Circle one:
    1. I agree most strongly with A.
    2. I agree most strongly with B.
43. A. Most of my low-ability, poorly motivated students will eventually graduate from high school.
    B. Most of my low-ability, poorly motivated students will not graduate from high school.
    Circle one:
    1. I agree most strongly with A.
    2. I agree most strongly with B.
44. A. When I let myself think about it, I experience anxiety because I can't really know for certain that I am making a difference in the lives of students.

B. When I evaluate my teaching, I have a feeling of professional confidence because I know rather certainly that I am making a difference in the lives of my students.

Circle one:

1. I agree most strongly with **A**.
2. I agree most strongly with **B**.

45. How stressful do you find teaching basic skills classes?

| 1 | 2 | 3 | 4 | 5 |
|---|---|---|---|---|
| Not at all stressful | Mildly stressful | Moderately stressful | Very stressful | Extremely stressful |

46. In general, how stressful do you find teaching?

| 1 | 2 | 3 | 4 | 5 |
|---|---|---|---|---|
| Not at all stressful | Mildly stressful | Moderately stressful | Very stressful | Extremely stressful |

*Please complete the following statements:*

47. When my students fail to learn a lesson that I have taught, their failure is probably due to

_____

48. When my students learn a lesson that I have taught, their success is probably due to

_____

49. Suppose you could go back to your college days and *start over again*: In view of your present knowledge, would you become a teacher?

_____ *certainly would* become a teacher
_____ *probably would* become a teacher
_____ *chances about even* for and against
_____ *probably would not* become a teacher
_____ *certainly would not* become a teacher

Thank you very much for completing our questionnaire.

# High School Basic Skills
## Teacher Interview

**LONG FORM**

Instructions: *I'd like to ask you a number of questions regarding the problems and rewards of teaching. Of course, your comments are confidential, and we will not identify your opinions by name, school, or even grade level.*

1. Teachers are asked to pursue many goals and to accomplish many things. Of all the things you do as a teacher, identify the one you think is most important. (Probe until you have a clear sense of what the teacher identifies as her or his primary objective.)
2. Is this your primary objective in your basic skills classes? (Probe until you have a clear sense of what the teacher identifies as his or her primary objective in basic skills classrooms.)
3. How can you tell if you are achieving your primary basic skills objective? (Probe until you have some specific indicators the teacher uses to define success.)
4. What kinds of things make it most difficult for you to achieve the general objective you identified in Question 1? (Probe until the teacher identifies specific problems which impede progress in basic skills classes.)
5. What kinds of students are most difficult to reach? (We are interested in student types, e.g., poverty children, black kids, bright students, rich kids, and so on.)
6. (If applicable, ask the following question): Within your basic skills classes what types of students are least likely to meet the objectives you have set for these classes? (Probe until the teacher identifies specific student types.)
7. What do you think these kinds of students will be doing 5 years from now? Fifteen years from now?
8. Of all the students you teach, would you please identify one or two of your favorite pupils. Tell me what there is about these students that appeals to you.

(Probe until you have gained an understanding of what type of student the teacher sees as ideal.)

9. Of all the students you teach, identify one or two of your worst students. What is there about these students that makes them difficult? (Probe until you know what kind of student offends this teacher.)

10. What kind of support does a basic skills teacher need from the school administration in order to do his or her job well? Are you getting that support here? Why or why not?

11. Do you have adequate materials for your basic skills classroom? If not, what kinds of materials would you need in order to do your job well? Why aren't you getting the materials you need?

12. Are there other constraints on you that limit your effectiveness as a basic skills teacher? If so, what are they? (Probe to find out whether the teacher blames him or herself or external conditions.) If the teacher identifies problems of only one kind (it's all my fault) ask why he or she does not identify other kinds of problems.

13. Do you adopt different teaching strategies for your basic skills classroom and your regular classes? Please describe those strategies.

14. Tell me what you think of the ability-grouping arrangements in this school.

15. How do you think the majority of your students would describe you if they were being candid? How do you think the majority of the faculty would describe you if they were being candid? How do you think the principal would describe you if he or she was being candid?

16. If you wanted to improve your classroom teaching, what kind of person would you want to observe in your class and to offer suggestions? (Probe for specific characteristics of that person and the *kinds of help* that person could offer.) Who in this area fits the description you just gave and would be able to offer you the help you want? (If the teacher identifies a specific person, ask if he or she has sought help from that person and if not, why not?)

17. What do you find rewarding as a teacher? That is, what do you get from your students, peers, social status, salary, etc., that makes teaching worthwhile? (Allow the teacher to answer this question but probe to see if he or she gets satisfaction from teaching in the basic skills area.)

18. Teachers sometimes claim they change with experience. Think back to when you began teaching and consider how you might have changed. Is teaching as satisfying for you as you hoped it would be? Why or why not? Have your relationships with students changed? Are you less idealistic now? How so?

19. Do you think teaching has changed over the past 5 to 10 years? How so? Why?

# High School Basic Skills
# Teacher Interview

**SHORT FORM**

Instructions: *I would like to ask you a number of questions regarding the problems and rewards of teaching. Of course, your comments will be considered confidential and we will not identify your opinions by name, school, or even grade level.*

1. How many basic skills classes do you teach during the day?
2. Is that too few, too many, or about the right number? Why do you say that?
3. On what basis were you chosen to teach basic skills classes? Did this make sense to you or would you prefer that other criteria be used for selecting basic skills teachers?
4. What would you think of being assigned to teach only basic skills classes? Please explain.
5. What do you think of the idea of testing students for competency in basic skills in the 3rd, 5th, 8th and 11th grades?
6. Do you think a passing score on the basic skills test should be a requirement for graduation from high school?
7. Do you assign homework in your regular classes? Why or why not?
8. Do you assign homework in your basic skills classes? Why or why not?
9. How do you decide what to teach in your basic skills classes?
10. Some teachers feel that the basic skills objectives are so specific that little or no lesson planning is required. Do you agree or disagree with that idea?
11. Do you generally employ whole-group instruction or do you teach small groups and individual lessons most of the time? Why?
12. Do you feel well prepared to teach basic skills classes? If so, what prepared you for this job? If not, why not?
13. How did your basic skills classes do this year? How can you tell? What percentage of your students passed their test? What percentage of students

who did not have to take state tests do you feel made enough progress during the year? How could you tell?

14. County data indicate that some schools in this area are doing better than others on basic skills tests. How is your school doing in comparison with others? What accounts for this?

15. What is the best thing about teaching basic skills students?

16. What is your biggest complaint or major concern about teaching basic skills classes?

17. What was the best class you ever taught? What was the worst class you ever taught? What was it about your good class that made it special? What was it about your worst class that made it difficult? Would just about any teacher have had the same difficulties that you had with your worst class? Would just about any teacher have had the same success with your best class? Are there any poor teachers at this school? We're not asking for their names. We're just asking if you are aware of any poor teachers. How do you know they're poor teachers? How do you know who the good teachers are? Are you a good teacher? How do you know? Do teachers make judgments about the abilities of their fellow teachers? On what basis do they make such judgments?

# APPENDIX E

# Climate and Control System

### Robert S. Soar and Ruth M. Soar

Teacher _____ Sch. _____ Gr. _____ Subj. _____ Obs. _____ Date _____ Time _____

| | | | CONTEXT | | | | |
|---|---|---|---|---|---|---|---|
| | | T. Initiates<br>P. Responds | Followup | | P. Initiates<br>T. Responds | | |
| | | Dis-<br>obey | Other | Inappro-<br>priate | Other | Inappro-<br>priate | Deviant<br>act | Other |
| Teacher Control | 01 | 02 | 03 | 04 | 05 | 06 | 07 |
| 10. Acknowledges, agrees, complies | | | | | | | |
| 11. Praises | | | | | | | |
| 12. Asks for status | | | | | | | |
| 13. Suggests, guides | | | | | | | |
| 14. Feedback, cites reason | | | | | | | |
| 15. Corrects without criticism | | | | | | | |
| 16. Questions for control | | | | | | | |
| 17. Questions, states behavioral rule | | | | | | | |
| 18. Directs with reason | | | | | | | |
| 19. Directs without reason | | | | | | | |
| 20. Uses time pressure | | | | | | | |
| 21. Reminds prods | | | | | | | |
| 22. Interrupts, cuts off | | | | | | | |
| 23. Supervises pupil closely, immobilizes | | | | | | | |
| 24. Criticizes, warns | | | | | | | |
| 25. Orders, commands | | | | | | | |
| 26. Scolds, punishes | | | | | | | |
| 27. Nods, smiles, facial feedback | | | | | | | |
| 28. Uses "body English," waits | | | | | | | |
| 29. Gestures | | | | | | | |
| 30. Touches, pats | | | | | | | |
| 31. Shakes head, eye contact | | | | | | | |
| 32. Takes equipment, book | | | | | | | |
| 33. Signals, raps | | | | | | | |
| 34. Glares, frowns | | | | | | | |
| 35. Holds, pushes, spanks | | | | | | | |
| 36. Ignores, abandons | | | | | | | |
| 37. Involvement | | | | | | | |

*Note.* This coding sheet displays the student and teacher behaviors we observed. A copy of the Climate and Control System (CCS) manual for training observers can be obtained from Robert Soar, Foundations of Education, University of Florida, Gainesville, Florida 32611.

## Groupings

41. T. not available
42. Pupil as individual
43. Total group with teacher
44. Small group with teacher
45. Individual with teacher
46. Structured group without T
47. Free groups

## Teacher

48. Teacher central
49. Moves freely among pupils
50. Teacher orients
51. Uses surrogate blackboard/AV
52. Attends pupil briefly
53. Attends pupil closely
54. Attends pupils in succession
55. Attends simultaneous activity

## Rewards

56. Gives, promises, rewards
57. Praises behavior—specific
58. Praises work—specific
59. Praises, general, individual
60. Praises, general, group

## Pupil Work

61. Pupil central
62. Pupil—no choice
63. Pupil—limited choice
64. Pupil—free choice
65. Seat work without teacher
66. Seat work with teacher
67. Works with much supervision
68. Works with little supervision
69. Work with socialization
70. Cooperative work
71. Collaborative work
72. Competitive work

## Pupil Behaviors

73. Task related movement
74. Follows routine without reminders
75. Aimless wandering
76. Asks permission
77. Reports rule another
78. Tattles
79. Shows bravado
80. Gives reason, direction
81. Speaks aloud without permission
82. Seeks reassurance, support
83. Shows pride
84. Shows fear, shame, humiliation
85. Shows apathy
86. Almost never
87. Occasionally
88. Frequently

## Pupil Interest-Attention to Task

89. Rank 1 low to 5 high

## POSITIVE AFFECT

*Teacher Verbal*

A41  Says, "Thank you," etc.

A42  Agrees with child

A43  Supports child

A44  Gives individual attention

A45  Warm, congenial

A46  Praises child

A47  Develops "we feeling"

A48  Is enthusiastic

A49  Other

A50  Code Involvement

*Pupil Verbal*

A51  Says "Thank you," etc.

A52  Sounds friendly

A53  Agrees, peer support

A54  Initiates contact

A55  Offers to share, cooperate

A56  Banters

A57  Is enthusiastic

A58  Praises another

A59  Helps another

A60  Other

A61  Code Involvement

*Teacher Nonverbal*

A62  Accepts favor for self

A63  Waits for child

A64  Gives individual attention

A65  Warm, congenial

A66  Listens carefully to child

A67  Smiles, laughs, nods

A68  Pats, hugs, etc.

A69  Sympathetic

A70  Other

*Pupil Nonverbal*

A71  Helpful, shares

A72  Leans close to another

A73  Chooses another

A74  Smiles, laughs with another

A75  Pats, hugs another

A76  Agreeable, cooperative

A77  Enthusiastic

A78  Horseplay

A79  Other

*Code Involvement:*
0. None involved  2. Up to one-half
                      the class
1. Few involved  3. More than half

# NEGATIVE AFFECT

| *Teacher Verbal* | *Teacher Nonverbal* |
|---|---|
| A 1  Says "stop it," etc. | A22  Waits for child |
| A 2  Uses sharp tone | A23  Frowns |
| A 3  Rejects child | A24  Points, shakes finger |
| A 4  Criticizes, blames, warns | A25  Pushes or pulls, holds |
| A 5  Sounds defensive | A26  Shows disgust |
| A 6  Yells | A27  Takes material |
| A 7  Scolds, humiliates | A28  Refuses to respond to child |
| A 8  Other | A29  Other |
| A 9  Code Involvement | |
| | *Pupil Nonverbal* |
| *Pupil Verbal* | A30  Makes face, frowns |
| A10  Says "No," "I won't," etc. | A31  Pouts, withdraws |
| A11  Teases | A32  Uncooperative, resistant |
| A12  Laughs | A33  Stamps, throws, slams |
| A13  Tattles | A34  Interferes, threatens |
| A14  Commands or demands | A35  Takes, damages property |
| A15  Makes disparaging remark | A36  Picks at child |
| A16  Demands attention | A37  Pushes or pulls, holds |
| A17  Sounds defensive | A38  Hits, hurts |
| A18  Finds fault | A39  Is left out |
| A19  Threatens | A40  Other |
| A20  Other | |
| A21  Code Involvement | |

# References

Abramson, L. Y., Seligman, M. E. P., & Teasdale, J. D. (1978). Learned helplessness in humans: Critique and reformulation. *Journal of Abnormal Psychology, 87,* 49–74.

Adler, M. (1982). *The Paideia Proposal. An educational manifesto.* New York: Macmillan.

Alexander, W., & George, P. (1981). *The exemplary middle school.* New York: Holt, Rinehart and Winston.

Algina, J. (1978). Comment on Bartko's "On various intraclass correlation reliability coefficients." *Psychological Bulletin, 85,* 135–138.

Ames, R. (1983). Teachers' attributions for their own teaching. In J. Levine & M. Wang (Eds.) *Teacher and student perceptions: Implications for learning* (pp. 105–124). Hillsdale, NJ: Erlbaum.

Anderson, J. (1968). *Bureaucracy in education.* Baltimore: Johns Hopkins University Press.

Anderson, L. M., Evertson, C. M., & Brophy, J. E. (1979). First-grade reading study. *Elementary School Journal, 79,* 193–233.

Apple, M. (1981). Curriculum form and the logic of technical control. *Economic and Industrial Democracy, 2*(3), 293–319.

Armor, D., Conry-Oseguera, P., Cox, M., King, N., McDonnell, L., Pascal, A., Pauly, E., & Zellman, G. (1976). *Analysis of the School Preferred Reading Program in selected Los Angeles minority schools.* (Report No. R-2007-LAUSD). Santa Monica, CA: The Rand Corporation. (ERIC Document Reproduction Service No. ED 130 243)

Ashton, P., Olejnik, S., Crocker, L., & McAuliffe, M. (1982, March). *Measurement problems in the study of teachers' sense of efficacy.* Paper presented at the meeting of the American Educational Research Association, New York.

Ashton, P., Webb, R., & Doda, N. (1983). *A study of teachers' sense of efficacy.*

(Final Report. National Institute of Education Contract No. 400–79–0075). Gainesville, FL: University of Florida. (ERIC Document Reproduction Service No. ED 231 834)

Bandura, A. (1977). Self-efficacy: Toward a unifying theory of behavioral change. *Psychological Review, 84,* 191–215.

Bandura, A. (1978). The self system in reciprocal determinism. *American Psychologist, 33,* 344–358.

Bandura, A. (1981). Self-referent thought: A developmental analysis of self-efficacy. In J. Flavell & L. Ross (Eds.), *Social cognitive development. Frontiers and possible future* (pp. 200–239). Cambridge: Cambridge University Press.

Bandura, A. (1982). Self-efficacy mechanism in human agency. *American Psychologist, 37*(2), 122–147.

Bartko, J. J. (1967). On various intraclass correlation reliability coefficients. *Psychological Bulletin, 83,* 762–765.

Becker, H., Geer, B., & Hughes, E. (1968). *Making the grade.* New York: Wiley.

Berman, P., McLaughlin, M., Bass, G., Pauly, E., & Zellman, G. (1977). *Federal programs supporting educational change.* Vol. 7: *Factors affecting implementation and continuation.* Santa Monica, CA: The Rand Corporation. (ERIC Document Reproduction Service No. ED 140 432)

Bernier, N. (1981). Beyond instructional context identification: Some thoughts for extending the analysis of deliberate education. In J. L. Green & C. Wallat (Eds.), *Ethnography and language in educational settings* (pp. 291–302). Norwood, NJ: Ablex.

Bidwell, C. (1973). The social psychology of teaching. In R. Travers (Ed.), *Second handbook of research on teaching* (pp. 413–449). Chicago: Rand McNally.

Bidwell, C., & Kasarda, J. (1975). School district organization and student achievement. *American Sociological Review, 40,* 55–70.

Blauner, R. (1964). *Alienation and freedom.* Chicago: University of Chicago Press.

Bloom, B., Engelhart, G., Furst, W., Hill, W., & Krathwohl, D. (1956). *Taxonomy of educational objectives: Handbook I. The cognitive domain.* New York: McKay.

Bloom, B. (1978). New views of the learner: Implications for instruction and curriculum. *Educational Leadership, 35,* 563–576.

Bloom, B. (1981). *All our children learning. A primer for parents, teachers, and other educators.* New York: McGraw-Hill.

Blumberg, P. (1980). *Inequality in an age of decline.* New York: Oxford University Press.

Bossert, S. T. (1979). *Tasks and social relationships in classrooms: A study of instructional organization and its consequences.* New York: Cambridge University Press.

Bowles, S., & Gintis, H. (1976). *Schooling in capitalist America: Educational reform and the contradictions of economic life.* New York: Basic Books.

Boyer, E. (1982, January). *Teaching in America.* First Annual President's Lecture. New Haven, CT: Yale University.

Boyer, E. (1983). *High school: A report on secondary education in America.* New York: Harper & Row.

Brim, O. G. (1975). Macro-structural influences on child development and the need for childhood social indicators. *American Journal of Orthopsychiatry, 45,* 516–524.

Bronfenbrenner, U. (1976). The experimental ecology of education. *Educational Researcher, 5*, 5–15.

Bronfenbrenner, U. (1977). Toward an experimental ecology of human development. *American Psychologist, 32*, 513–531.

Bronfenbrenner, U. (1979). *The ecology of human development.* Cambridge, MA: Harvard University Press.

Bronowski, J. (1956). *Science and human values.* New York: Harper & Row.

Bronowski, J. (1978). *The origins of knowledge and imagination.* New Haven, CT: Yale University Press.

Brookover, W. B., Beady, C., Flood, P., Schweitzer, J., & Wisenbaker, J. (1979). *School social systems and student achievement: Schools can make a difference.* New York: Praeger.

Brookover, W., & Erickson, E. (1969). *Society, schools, and learning.* Boston: Allyn & Bacon.

Brookover, W. B., Gigliotti, R., Henderson, R., & Schneider, J. (1973). *Elementary school environment and achievement.* East Lansing, MI: Michigan State University, College of Urban Development.

Brookover, W. B., & Lezotte, L. W. (1977). *Changes in school characteristics coincident with changes in student achievement* (Executive summary). East Lansing, MI: Michigan State University, College of Urban Development.

Brookover, W. B., Schweitzer, J. H., Schneider, J. M., Beady, C. H., Flood, P., & Wisenbaker, J. M. (1978). Elementary school social climate and school achievement. *American Educational Research Journal, 15*, 301–318.

Brophy, J. (1981). Teacher praise: A functional analysis. *Review of Educational Research, 51*, 5–32.

Brophy, J. (1983). Conceptualizing student motivation. *Educational Psychologist, 18*(3), 200–215.

Brophy, J. E., & Evertson, C. M. (1981). *Student characteristics and teaching.* White Plains, NY: Longman.

Brophy, J. E., & Good, T. L. (1974). *Teacher-student relationships: Causes and consequences.* New York: Holt, Rinehart and Winston.

Brown, B. B. (1968). *The experimental mind in education.* New York: Harper & Row.

Cahen, L., Filby, N., McCutcheon, G., & Kyle, D. (1983). *Class size and instruction.* White Plains, NY: Longman.

Callahan, R. E. (1962). *Education and the cult of efficiency.* Chicago: The University of Chicago Press.

Campbell, D., & Fiske, D. (1959). Convergent and discriminant validation by the multitrait-multimethod matrix. *Psychological Bulletin, 56*, 81–105.

Carew, J. V., & Lightfoot, S. L. (1979). *Beyond bias: Perspectives on classrooms.* Cambridge, MA: Harvard University Press.

Carnoy, M., & Shearer, D. (1980). *Economic democracy: The challenge of the 1980s.* White Plains, NY: M. E. Sharpe.

Cassil, A. (1985, May 26). Hawthorne students score high. *Gainesville Sun*, p. 1.

Chapman, D. W., & Hutcheson, S. M. (1982). Attrition from teacher careers: A discriminant analysis. *American Educational Research Journal, 19*, 93–106.

Chapman, D., & Lowther, M. (1982). Teachers' satisfaction with teaching. *Journal of Educational Research, 75*, 241–247.

Cichon, D., & Koff, R. H. (1978, March). *The teaching events stress inventory.*

Paper presented at the meeting of the American Educational Research Association, Toronto, Canada. (ERIC Document Reproduction Service No. Ed 160 662)

Clear, D. K., & Seager, R. C. (1971). Legitimacy of administrative influence as perceived by selected groups. *Educational Administration Quarterly, 7*, 46–63.

Cohen, E. G. (1972). Sociology and the classroom: Setting the conditions for teacher–student interaction. *Review of Educational Research, 42*, 441–452.

Cohen, E. G. (1979, September). *The desegregated school: Problems in status, power and interracial climate.* Paper presented at the meeting of the American Psychological Association, New York.

Cohen, M. W. (1981). Effective schools: What the research says. *Today's Education, 70*(2), 58–61.

Coladarci, T., & Gage, N. (1984). Effects of a minimal intervention on teacher behavior and student achievement. *American Educational Research Journal, 21*(3), 539–556.

Coleman, J., Campbell, E., Hobson, C., McPartland, J., Mood, A., Weinfeld, F., & York, R. (1966). *Equality of educational opportunity.* Washington, DC: U.S. Government Printing Office.

Coleman, R. P., & Rainwater, L. (1978) *Social standing in America.* New York: Basic Books.

Cooley, W. (1978). Explanatory observational studies. *Educational Researcher, 7*(9), 9–15.

Cooper, H. M., Burger, J. M., & Seymour, G. E. (1979). Classroom context and student ability influences on teacher perceptions of classroom control. *American Educational Research Journal, 16*, 189–196.

Cooper, H., & Good, T. (1983). *Pygmalion grows up. Studies in the expectation communication process.* White Plains, NY: Longman.

Covington, M. V., & Omelich, C. L. (1981). As failures mount: Affective and cognitive consequences of ability demotion in the classroom. *Journal of Educational Psychology, 73*, 796–808.

Dearman, N., & Plisko, V. (Eds.). (1982). *The condition of education.* Washington, DC: U.S. Government Printing Office.

deCharms, R. (1968). *Personal causation.* New York: Academic Press.

deCharms, R. (1976). *Enhancing motivation: Change in the classroom.* New York: Irvington.

deCharms, R. (1984). Motivation enhancement in educational settings. In C. Ames, & R. Ames (Eds.), *Research on motivation in education. Vol. 1* (pp. 275–310). New York: Academic Press.

Deci, E. (1975). *Intrinsic motivation.* New York: Plenum.

Deci, E. L., Schwartz, A. J., Sheinman, L., & Ryan, R. M. (1981). An instrument to assess adults' orientations toward control versus autonomy with children: Reflections on intrinsic motivation and perceived competence. *Journal of Educational Psychology, 73*, 642–650.

Deci, E. L., Spiegel, N. H., Ryan, R., Koestner, R., & Kauffman, M. (1982). Effects of performance standards on teaching styles: Behavior of controlling teachers. *Journal of Educational Psychology, 74*(6), 852–859.

Denemark, G., & Nutter, N. (1984). The case for extended programs of initial teacher preparation. In L. Katz & J. Raths (Eds.), *Advances in teacher education. Vol. 1* (pp. 203–246). Norwood, NJ: Ablex.

Denham, C., & Michael, J. (1981). Teacher sense of efficacy: A definition of the construct and a model for further research. *Educational Research Quarterly, 5,* 39–63.

Dewey, J. (1939). *Intelligence in the modern world.* New York: Random House (Modern Library).

Dewey, J. (1950). *Reconstruction in philosophy.* New York: The American Library.

Dewey, J., & Tufts, J. (1910). *Ethics.* New York: Holt.

Dreeben, R. (1970). *The nature of teaching. Schools and the work of teachers.* Glenview, IL: Scott, Foresman.

Dreeben, R. (1973). The school as a workplace. In R. Travers (Ed.), *Second handbook of research on teaching* (pp. 450–473). Chicago: Rand McNally.

Duke, D., Showers, B., & Imber, M. (1980). Teachers and shared decision making: The costs and benefits of involvement. *Educational Administration Quarterly, 16*(1), 93–106.

Dunkin, M. J., & Biddle, B. J. (1974). *The study of teaching.* New York: Holt, Rinehart and Winston.

Durkheim, E. (1966). *The rules of sociological method.* New York: Free Press.

Dusek, J., Hall, V. Jr., & Meyer, W. (Eds.). (1985). *Teacher expectancies.* Hillsdale, NJ: Erlbaum.

Dusek, J., & Joseph, G. (1983). The bases of teacher expectancies. *Journal of Educational Psychology, 75*(3), 327–346.

Dweck, C. (1976). Children's interpretation of evaluative feedback: The effect of social cues on learned helplessness. *Merrill-Palmer Quarterly, 22,* 105–110.

Dweck, C., & Bempechat, J. (1983). Children's theories of intelligence: Consequences for learning. In S. Paris, G. Olson, & H. Stevenson (Eds.), *Learning and motivation in the classroom* (pp. 239–256). Hillsdale, NJ: Erlbaum.

Dweck, C. S., Davidson, W., Nelson, S., & Enna, B. (1978). Sex differences in learned helplessness: II. The contingencies of evaluative feedback in the classroom; III. An experimental analysis. *Developmental Psychology, 14,* 268–276.

Ellett, C. D., & Masters, J. A. (1977). *The structure of teacher attitude toward dimensions of their working environment: A factor analysis of the School Survey and its implications for instrument validity.* Paper presented at the meeting of the Georgia Educational Research Association, Atlanta.

Ellett, C., & Masters, J. A. (1978, August). *Learning environment perceptions: Teacher and student relations.* Invited paper presented at the annual meeting of the American Psychological Association, Toronto, Canada.

Ellett, C. D., & Walberg, H. J. (1979). Principals' competency, environment, and outcomes. In H. S. Walberg (Ed.), *Educational environments and effects* (pp. 140–164). Berkeley, CA: McCutcheon.

Emery, F. (1969). *Form and content in industrial democracy.* London: Tavistock.

Emery, F., & Thorsrud, E. (1976). *Democracy at work.* Leiden: Martinus Nijhoff, Social Sciences Division.

Emery, R., & Trist, E. (1973). *Towards a social ecology.* New York: Plenum/ Rosetta.

Entwisle, D., & Hayduk, L. (1978). *Too great expectations: The academic outlook of young children.* Baltimore, MD: Johns Hopkins University Press.

Ernest, J. (1976). Mathematics and sex. *American Mathematical Monthly, 83,* 595–614.

Etzioni, A. (1969). *The semi-professions and their organization.* New York: Free Press.

Evans, E. (1976). *Transition to teaching.* New York: Holt, Rinehart and Winston.

Everhart, R. B. (1979). The fabric of meaning in a junior high school. *Theory into Practice, 18*(3), 152–157.

Evertson, C. M., Anderson, C. W., Anderson, L. M., & Brophy, J. E. (1980). Relationships between classroom behaviors and student outcomes in junior high mathematics and English classes. *American Educational Research Journal, 17,* 43–60.

Feagin, J. (1975). *Subordinating the poor.* Englewood Cliffs, NJ: Prentice-Hall.

Fenstermacher, G. D. (1979). A philosophical consideration of recent research on teacher effectiveness. In L. S. Shulman (Ed.) *Review of Research in Education* (Vol. 6, pp. 157–185). Itasca, IL.: F. E. Peacock.

Fox, R. S., Jung, C., Schmuck, R., Van Egmond, E., & Ritvo, M. (1970). *Diagnosing the professional climate of your school.* Portland, OR: Northwest Regional Educational Laboratory. (ERIC Document Reproduction Service No. ED 042 708).

Freire, P. (1973). *Education for critical consciousness.* New York: Seabury Press.

Frieze, I., Fisher, J., Hanusa, B., McHugh, M., & Valle, V. (1979). Attributions of the causes of success and failure as internal and external barriers to achievement in women. In J. Sherman & F. Denmark (Eds.), *Psychology of women: Future directions of research* (pp. 124–162). New York: Psychological Dimensions.

Fromm, E. (1963). *Escape from freedom.* New York: Holt, Rinehart and Winston.

Fuller, B., Wood, K., Rapoport, T., & Dornbusch, S. (1982). The organizational context of individual efficacy. *Review of Educational Research, 52*(1), 7–30.

Gallup, A. (1985). The Gallup Poll of teacher attitudes toward the public schools. *Phi Delta Kappan, 66*(5), 323–330.

Gallup, G. (1980). The 12th annual Gallup Poll of the public's attitudes toward the public schools. *Phi Delta Kappan, 62*(1), 33–48.

Gallup, G. (1984). The 16th annual Gallup Poll of the public's attitudes toward the public schools. *Phi Delta Kappan, 66*(1), 23–38.

Garrett, G. (1977). *The effect of sex as a variable in teacher perception.* (Eric Document Reproduction Service No. ED 225 943)

Gehlen, A. (1980). *Man in an age of technology.* New York: Columbia University Press.

Gehrke, N. (1981). A grounded theory study of beginning teachers' role personalization through reference group relations. *Journal of Teacher Education, 32*(6), 34–38.

Gergen, K. (1982). *Toward transformation in social knowledge.* New York: Springer-Verlag.

Getzels, J. W., & Jackson, P. W. (1963). The teacher's personality and characteristics. In N. L. Gage (Ed.), *Handbook of research on teaching* (pp. 506–582). Chicago: Rand McNally.

Gibson, S., & Dembo, M. (1984). Teacher efficacy: A construct validation. *Journal of Educational Psychology, 76*(4), 569–582.

Ginsburg, M., & Newman, K. (1985). Social inequities, schooling, and teacher education. *Journal of Teacher Education, 34*(2), 49–54.

Glass, G., & Smith, M. (1979). Meta-analysis of research on class size and achievement. *Educational Evaluation and Policy Analysis, 1*(1), 2–16.

Good, T. (1983). Classroom research: A decade of progress. *Educational Psychologist, 18*(3), 127–144.

Good, T. L., & Grouws, S. A. (1979). The Missouri Mathematics Effectiveness Project. An experimental study in fourth-grade classrooms. *Journal of Educational Psychology, 71*, 355–362.

Good, T., Grouws, D., & Ebmeier, H. (1983). *Active mathematics teaching.* White Plains, NY: Longman.

Goodlad, J. I. (1975). *The dynamics of educational change: Toward responsive schools.* New York: McGraw-Hill.

Goodlad, J. I. (1984). *A place called school.* New York: McGraw-Hill.

Goodlad, J. (1983). The school as workplace. In G. Griffin (Ed.), *Staff development. The eighty-second yearbook of the National Society for the Study of Education. Part II* (pp. 36–62). Chicago: The University of Chicago Press.

Gross, N., Giacquinta, J., & Bernstein, M. (1971). *Implementing organizational innovations: A sociological analysis of planned educational change.* New York: Basic Books.

Gross, N., & Herriott, R. E. (1965). *Staff leadership in public schools.* New York: Wiley.

Guskey, T. (1984). The influence of change in instructional effectiveness upon the affective characteristics of teachers. *American Educational Research Journal, 21*(2), 245–259.

Hargreaves, D. H. (1972). Staffroom relationships. *New Society, 32*, 434–437.

Harris, M., & Rosenthal, R. (1985). Mediation of interpersonal expectancy effects: 31 meta-analyses. *Psychological Bulletin, 97*(3), 363–386.

Heider, F. (1985). *The psychology of interpersonal relations.* New York: Wiley.

Herbst, P. (1974). *Socio-technical design.* London: Tavistock.

Herbst, P. (1976). *Alternatives to hierarchies.* Leiden: Martinus Nijhoff, Social Sciences Division.

Herzberg, F., Mausner, B., Peterson, R., & Capwell, D. (1957). *Job attitudes: Review of research and opinion.* Pittsburgh: Psychological Service.

Holland, J. (1973). *Making vocational choices: A theory of careers.* Englewood Cliffs, NJ: Prentice-Hall.

Hornstein, H. A., Callahan, D. M., Fisch, E., & Benedict, B. A. (1968). Influence and satisfaction in organizations: A replication. *Sociology of Education, 41*(4), 380–389.

Huitt, W. C., & Rim, E. (1980, April). *A basic skills instructional improvement program: Utilizing research to improve classroom practice.* Paper presented at the meeting of the American Educational Research Association, Boston.

Huitt, W., Traver, P., & Caldwell, J. (1980). *Improving instruction by monitoring time-on-task.* Philadelphia: Research for Better Schools.

Jackson, P. W. (1968). *Life in classrooms.* New York: Holt, Rinehart and Winston.

Jencks, C., Smith, M., Acland, H., Bane, M., Cohen, D. K., Gintis, H., Heyns, B., & Michelson, S. (1972). *Inequality: A reassessment of the effect of family and schooling in America.* New York: Basic Books.

Johnson, D. W., & Johnson, R. T. (1974). Instructional goal structure: Cooperative, competitive or individualistic. *Review of Educational Research, 44*, 213–240.

Joyce, B., Hersh, R., & McKibbin, M. (1983). *The structure of school improvement.* White Plains, NY: Longman.

Kalis, M. C. (1980). Teaching experience: Its effect on school climate, teacher morale. *NASSP Bulletin, 64,* 89–102.

Klausmeier, H. (1982). A research strategy for educational improvement. *Educational Researcher, 11*(2), 8–13.

Krathwohl, D. (1977). Improving educational research and development. *Educational Researcher, 6*(4), 8–14.

Kyriacou, C., & Sutcliffe, J. (1977). Teacher stress: A review. *Educational Review, 29*(4), 299–306.

Laosa, L. M. (1982). School, occupation, culture, and family: The impact of parental schooling on the parent–child relationship. *Journal of Educational Psychology, 74*(6), 791–827.

Larkin, R. W. (1973). Contextual influences on teacher leadership styles. *Sociology of Education, 46,* 471–479.

Leacock, E. (1969). *Teaching and learning in city schools: A comparative study.* New York: Basic Books.

Leithwood, K. A., & Montgomery, D. J. (1982). The role of the elementary school principal in program improvement. *Review of Educational Research, 52*(3), 309–339.

Lerner, M. (1967). *America as a civilization* (Vols. 1–2). New York: Touchstone Books.

Levin, M. (1960). *The alienated voter.* New York: Holt, Rinehart and Winston.

Lewis, M. (1978). *The culture of inequality.* New York: New American Library.

Lightfoot, S. (1973). Politics and reasoning: Through the eyes of teachers and children. *Harvard Educational Review, 43*(2), 197–224.

Lightfoot, S. L. (1978). *Worlds apart: Relationships between families and schools.* New York: Basic Books.

Lipsky, M. (1980). *Street-level bureaucracy.* New York: Russell Sage.

Little, J. W. (1982). Norms of collegiality and experimentation: Workplace conditions of school success. *American Educational Research Journal, 19,* 325–340.

Little, J. (1984, April). *Designs, contexts, and consequences in the real world of staff development.* Paper presented at the meeting of the American Educational Research Association, New Orleans.

Little, J. (1985, April). *Schools' contributions to teaching as a profession: What we know about what we need to know.* Paper presented at the meeting of the American Educational Research Association, Chicago.

Lortie, D. C. (1975). *Schoolteacher: A sociological study.* Chicago: University of Chicago Press.

Maccoby, E. E., & Jacklin, C. N. (1974). *The psychology of sex differences.* Stanford, CA: Stanford University Press.

Maccoby, M. (1979). *What is productivity?* Cambridge: Harvard Project on Technology, Work and Character.

McDermott, R. P. (1977). Social relations as contexts for learning in school. *Harvard Educational Review, 47,* 202–215.

McDonald, F., & Elias, P. (1976). *Beginning teacher evaluation study. Phase II. 1973–74.* Princeton, NJ: Educational Testing Service.

McPherson, G. H. (1972). *Small-town teacher.* Cambridge, MA: Harvard University Press.

Maslach, C. (1976). Burned-out. *Human Behavior, 5,* 16–22.

Mayeske, G. W., Wister, C. E., Beaton, A. E., Weinfeld, F. D., Cohen, W. M., Okada, T., Proshek, J. M., & Tabler, K. A. (1972). *A study of our nation's schools* (DHEW Publication No. (OE) 72–142). Washington, DC: U.S. Department of Health, Education, and Welfare.

Medley, D.M. (1978). Alternative assessment strategies. *Journal of Teacher Education, 29,* 38–42.

Medley, D. M., Coker, H., & Soar, R. (1984). *Measurement-based evaluation of teacher performance: An empirical approach.* White Plains, NY: Longman.

Metz, M. H. (1978). *Classrooms and corridors. The crisis of authority in desegregated secondary schools.* Berkeley, CA: University of California Press.

Meyer, J., & Cohen, E. (1971). *The impact of the open-space school upon teacher influence and autonomy: The effects of an organizational innovation.* Stanford, CA: Stanford University. (ERIC Document Reproduction Service No. ED 062 291)

Mills, C. W. (1951). *White collar: The American middle class.* New York: Oxford University Press.

Mitchell, D. E. (1983, April). *Teacher incentive systems: Links to lesson structures and classroom performance.* Paper presented at the meeting of the American Educational Research Association, Montreal.

Mosenthal, P. (1984). The effect of classroom ideology on children's production of narrative text. *American Educational Research Journal, 21*(3), 679–689.

National Commission on Excellence in Education (1983). *A nation at risk: The imperative for educational reform.* Washington, DC: U.S. Government Printing Office.

National Education Association (1982). *Status of the American public school teacher: 1980–81.* Washington, DC: National Education Association Research Division.

Ogbu, J. (1982). Cultural discontinuites and schooling. *Anthropology and Education Quarterly, 13*(4), 290–307.

Pedhazur, E. J. (1982). *Multiple regression in behavioral research.* New York: Holt, Rinehart and Winston.

Persell, C. (1977). *Education and inequality.* New York: Free Press.

Peterson, D., Micceri, T., & Smith, B. (1985). Measurement of teacher performance: A study in instrument development. *Teaching and Teacher Education, 1*(1), 63–77.

Plisko, V. (1984). *The condition of teaching.* Washington, DC: National Center for Education Statistics,

Pratzner, F. C. (1984). Quality of school life: Foundations for improvement. *Educational Researcher, 13*(3), 20–25.

Raschke, D., Dedrick, C., Strathe, M., & Hawkes, R. (1985). Teacher stress: The elementary teacher's perspective. *Elementary School Journal, 85*(4), 559–564.

Rawls, J, (1971). *A theory of justice.* Cambridge, MA: Harvard University Press.

Rist, R. (1978). *The invisible children. School integration in American society.* Cambridge, MA: Harvard University Press.

Rohrkemper, M., & Brophy, J. (1979). *Influence of teacher role definition on strategies for coping with problem students.* East Lansing, MI: The Institute for Research on Teaching, Michigan State University.

Rosenholtz, S., & Simpson, C. (1984). The formation of ability conceptions: Developmental trend or social construction? *Review of Educational Research, 54*(1), 31–63.

Rosenholtz, S. J., & Wilson, B. (1980). The effect of classroom structure on shared perceptions of ability. *American Educational Research Journal, 17*, 75–82.

Rotter, J. B. (1966). Generalized expectancies for internal versus external control of reinforcement. *Psychological Monographs, 80*, 1–28.

Rowley, G. L. (1976). Reliability of observational measures. *American Educational Research Journal, 13*, 51–59.

Ruble, D. N. (1980). A developmental perspective on theories of achievement motivation. In L. Fyans, Jr., (Ed.), *Achievement motivation: Recent trends in theory and research* (pp. 225–245). New York: Plenum.

Ruch, W., Hershauer, J., & Wright, R. (1976). Toward solving the productivity puzzle: Worker correlates to performance. *Human Resource Management, 15*, 2–6.

Rutter, M., Maughan, B., Mortimore, P., Ouston, J., with Smith, A. (1979). *Fifteen thousand hours: Secondary schools and their effects on children.* Cambridge, MA: Harvard University Press.

Ryan, W. (1976). *Blaming the victim.* New York: Random House (Vintage Books).

Sarason, S. (1981). *Psychology misdirected.* New York: Free Press.

Sarason, S. (1982). *Problems of change and the culture of the school.* New York: Allyn & Bacon.

Schaefer, R. (1967). *The school as a center of inquiry.* New York: Harper & Row.

Schneider, G. (1984). Teacher involvement in decision making: Zones of acceptance, decision conditions, and job satisfaction. *Journal of Research and Development in Education, 18*(1), 25–32.

Schon, D. (1983). *The reflective practitioner: How professionals think in action.* New York: Basic Books.

Schubert, W. (1980). Recalibrating educational research: Toward a focus on practice. *Educational Researcher, 9*(1), 17–24.

Schunk, D. (1984). Self-efficacy perspective on achievement behavior. *Educational Psychologist, 19*(1), 48–58.

Shepard, J. M. (1971). *Automation and alienation: A study of office and factory workers.* Cambridge, MA: MIT Press.

Shulman, L. S., & Lanier, J. E. (1977). The Institute for Research on Teaching: An overview. *Journal of Teacher Education, 28*, 44–49.

Sieber, S., & Wilder, D. E. (1967). Teaching styles: Parental preferences and role definitions. *Sociology of Education, 40*(4), 302–315.

Sizer, T. (1984). *Horace's compromise: The dilemma of the American high school.* Boston: Houghton Mifflin.

Slavin, R. (1978). Basic vs. applied research: A response. *Educational Researcher, 7*(2), 15–17.

Slavin, R. (1983). *Cooperative learning.* White Plains, NY: Longman.

Smith, L. (1979). An evolving logic of participant observation, educational ethnography, and other case studies. In L. S. Shulman (Ed.), *Review of research in education* (Vol. 6, pp. 316–377). Itasca, IL.: F. E. Peacock.

Smith, L., & Keith, P. (1971). *Anatomy of an educational innovation: An organizational analysis of an elementary school.* New York: Wiley.

Soar, R. S., & Soar R. M. (1978). *Setting variables, classroom interaction, and multiple pupil outcomes.* (Final Report. National Institute of Education Grant No. NIE-G-76-0100). Gainesville, FL: University of Florida.

Soar, R. S., & Soar, R. M. (1980). *Climate and control system.* Unpublished manuscript, University of Florida, Gainesville, FL.

Soar, R. S., & Soar, R. M. (1982). Measurement of classroom process. In B. Spodek (Ed.) *Handbook of research in early childhood education* (pp. 592–617). New York: Free Press.

Soar, R. S., Soar, R. M., & Ragosta, M. (1971). *Florida climate and control system.* Institute for Development of Human Resources, University of Florida, Gainesville, FL.

Sparks, D. C. (1979). A biased look at teacher job satisfaction. *Clearing House, 52,* 447–449.

Spradley, J. (1980). *The ethnographic interview.* New York: Holt, Rinehart and Winston.

Squires, D. A., Huitt, W. G., & Segars, J. (1983). *Effective schools and classrooms: A research-based perspective.* Alexandria, VA: Association for Supervision and Curriculum Development.

Stallings, J. A., & Kaskowitz, D. (1974). *Follow-through classroom observation evaluation, 1972–73.* Menlo Park, CA: Stanford Research Institute.

Stallings, J., Needels, M., & Stayrooks, N. (1979). *How to change the process of teaching basic reading skills in secondary schools.* Menlo Park, CA: SRI International.

Stenhouse, L. A. (1975). *An introduction to curriculum research and development.* London: Heinemann Educational Books.

Super, D. E. (1970). *Work values inventory.* Boston: Houghton Mifflin.

Sykes, G. (1984). The deal. *The Wilson Quarterly, 7*(1), 59–77.

Tesconi, C., Jr., & Morris, V. (1972). *The anti-man culture. Bureautechnocracy and the schools.* Urbana, IL: University of Illinois.

Tom, D., Cooper, H., & McGraw, M. (1984). Influences of student background and teacher authoritarianism on teacher expectations. *Journal of Educational Psychology, 76*(2), 259–265.

Vanfossen, B. (1979). *The structure of inequality.* Boston: Little, Brown.

Vroom, V. (1964). *Work and motivation.* New York: Wiley.

Webb, R. B. (1981). *Schooling and society.* New York: Macmillan.

Webb, R. (1984). [Review of *The structure of school improvement*]. *Educational Studies, 15*(2), 178–180.

Webb, R. B., Damico, S., & Bell-Nathaniel, A. (1978). *Poverty and education: Investigating the ideology of stratification* (Technical Report, HEW Grant No. G-007701691). Washington, DC: Office of Education.

Weber, M. (1958). *Essays in sociology.* (H. Gerth & C. W. Mills, Trans.). New York: Oxford University Press.

Weiner, B. (1979). A theory of motivation for some classroom experiences. *Journal of Educational Psychology, 71,* 3–25.

Weiner, B (1980). The role of affect in rational (attributional) approaches to human motivation. *Educational Researcher, 9,* 4–11.

Wellisch, J. B., MacQueen, A. H., Carriere, R. A., & Duck, G. A. (1978). School management and organization in successful schools. *Sociology of Education, 51,* 211–226.

Wiener, N. (1954). *The human use of human beings.* New York: Doubleday.

Willis, P. (1977). *Learning to labour: How working class kids get working class jobs.* Farnborough: Saxon House.

Wirth, A. G. (1983). *Productive work—in industry and schools: Becoming persons again.* New York: University Press of America.

Wise, A. (1979). *Legislated learning. The bureaucratization of the American classroom.* Berkeley: University of California Press.

Woods, P. (1978). Relating to schoolwork: Some pupil perceptions. *Educational Review, 80,* 167–175.

Zwerdling, D. (1978). *Democracy at work.* Washington, DC: Association for Management.

# Author Index

# Subject Index